S0-AVS-052

FALL

2012

HOLLYWOOD
SCREENWRITING
DIRECTORY

media

BURBANK, CALIFORNIA

Copyright © 2012 by F+W Media, Inc.

All rights reserved.

No part of this publication may be reproduced in any form or by any electronic or mechanical means including information storage and retrieval systems without written permission from the publisher.

Printed and bound in the United States of America.

Published by F+W Media, Inc.
3510 West Magnolia Boulevard
Burbank, California 91505
www.fwmedia.com

Disclaimer

Every reasonable effort has been made to ensure the accuracy of the information contained in the Hollywood Screenwriting Directory. F+W Media, Inc. cannot be held responsible for any inaccuracies, or the misrepresentation of those listed in the Hollywood Screenwriting Directory.

Updates/Change Listing

Please submit corrections and updates to *corrections@screenwritingdirectory.com*.
Print ISBN 13: 978-1-4403-2916-6
Print ISBN 10: 1-4403-2916-8
ePub ISBN 13: 978-1-4403-2918-0
ePub ISBN 10: 1-4403-2918-4
PDF ISBN 13: 978-1-4403-2917-3
PDF ISBN 10: 1-4403-2917-6

Contents

How to Use the Hollywood Screenwriting Directory

A specialized directory created by The Writers Store based on our extensive experience serving the screenwriting community since 1982, the *Hollywood Screenwriting Directory* contains a range of Industry insiders, from ambitious upstarts to established studio shingles, along with management companies who package production deals and independent financiers/distributors with a production wing. For each listing, you'll find the kind of useable information you need: Street and email addresses, whether they accept unsolicited material, and how they prefer to receive the work.

While having access to this data is crucial, just as essential is an understanding of the right way to use it. Interns, Assistants, Story Editors, Creative Executives, and Heads of Productions are flooded with submissions daily. Any indication of incorrect format or other amateur flubs in the first few pages will quickly send your script to the trash.

It can't be emphasized enough how important it is that your submission be polished and professional before you send it out for consideration. Screenwriting software makes producing an Industry-standard screenplay simple and straightforward. Programs like *Final Draft* and *Movie Magic Screenwriter* put your words into proper format as you type, letting you focus on a well-told story rather than the chore of margins and spacing. We've also included a guide to proper screenplay format, along with sample title and first pages to help you send out a professional script every time.

Besides a properly packaged submission, it's also wise to know your audience before you send out any materials. If your script is an action thriller with a strong female lead, don't send it to Philip Seymour Hoffman's production company. Actors establish their own companies so that they're not reliant on studios for roles. Pad an actor's vanity (and his pipeline) by submitting materials catered specifically to him.

You may find that a good number of companies do not want unsolicited submissions. It's not that they're not open to new ideas; they're not open to liability. A script is property, and with it, come ramifications if not handled properly. If you choose to disregard the "no unsolicited submissions," sending your script with a submission release form gives it a better chance of getting read. Consult with an entertainment attorney to draft an appropriate form, or consult a guide like *Clearance and Copyright by Michael C. Donaldson*, which has submission release form templates. It's also prudent to protect your work. We recommend registering your script with the *WGA (Writers Guild of America, West)* or the *ProtectRite registration service.*

A benefit of the digital age is that the same companies that are not open to receiving unsolicited submissions will gladly accept a query letter by email. Take advantage of this opportunity. Craft a well-written and dynamic query letter email that sells you and your script. We have included a sample query, and some tips and guidelines on how to write great query letters.

While Hollywood is a creative town it is, above all, professional. Do a service to yourself and the potential buyer by being courteous. If you choose to follow up by phone, don't be demanding and frustrated. These people are overworked and do not owe you anything. It's okay to follow up, but be sure to do so with respect. And if you pique a buyer's interest and she asks for a treatment, you must be ready to send off this vital selling tool at once! That's why we've also included a handy guide to writing treatments in this volume.

While it may oftentimes feel like the opposite, The Entertainment Industry is looking for new writers and fresh material. BUT (and this is important) they're also looking for those aspiring scribes to take the time to workshop their scripts with an experienced professional and get them to a marketable level. The Writers Store can help you get ready for the big leagues through our slate of *screenwriting courses, personalized coaching* and *Development Notes service*, which works in a format that mirrors the same process occurring in the studio ranks.

Hollywood is the pinnacle of competition and ambition. But that's not to say that dreams can't happen—they can, and they do. By keeping to these professional guidelines and working on your craft daily, you can find the kind of screenwriting success you seek.

Good luck!
Jesse Douma
Editor

What is a Screenplay?

In the most basic terms, a screenplay is a 90–120 page document written in Courier 12pt font on 8 ½" × 11" bright white three-hole punched paper. Wondering why Courier font is used? It's a timing issue. One formatted script page in Courier font equals roughly one minute of screen time. That's why the average page count of a screenplay should come in between 90 and 120 pages. Comedies tend to be on the shorter side (90 pages, or 1 ½ hours) while Dramas run longer (120 pages, or 2 hours).

A screenplay can be an original piece, or based on a true story or previously written piece, like a novel, stage play or newspaper article. At its heart, a screenplay is a blueprint for the film it will one day become. Professionals on the set including the producer, director, set designer and actors all translate the screenwriter's vision using their individual talents. Since the creation of a film is ultimately a collaborative art, the screenwriter must be aware of each person's role and as such, the script should reflect the writer's knowledge.

For example, it's crucial to remember that film is primarily a visual medium. As a screenwriter, you must show what's happening in a story, rather than tell. A 2-page inner monologue may work well for a novel, but is the kiss of death in a script. The very nature of screenwriting is based on how to show a story on a screen, and pivotal moments can be conveyed through something as simple as a look on an actor's face. Let's take a look at what a screenplay's structure looks like.

THE FIRST PAGE OF A SCREENPLAY

Screenwriting software makes producing an Industry-standard script simple and straightforward. While screenplay formatting software such as *Final Draft*, *Movie Magic Screenwriter*, *Movie Outline*, *Montage* and *Scriptly* for the iPad frees you from having to learn the nitty-gritty of margins and indents, it's good to have a grasp of the general spacing standards.

The top, bottom and right margins of a screenplay are 1". The left margin is 1.5". The extra half-inch of white space to the left of a script page allows for binding with brads, yet still imparts a feeling of vertical balance of the text on the page. The entire document should be single-spaced.

SCREENPLAY ELEMENTS

Following is a list of items that make up the screenplay format, along with indenting information. Again, screenplay software will automatically format all these elements, but a screenwriter must have a working knowledge of the definitions to know when to use each one.

(A) The very first item on the first page should be the words FADE IN:.

(B) The first page is never numbered. Subsequent page numbers appear in the upper right hand corner, 0.5" from the top of the page, flush right to the margin.

(C) MORES AND CONTINUEDS
Use mores and continueds between pages to indicate the same character is still speaking.

(D) SCENE HEADING
Indent: Left: 0.0" Right: 0.0" Width: 6.0"
A scene heading is a one-line description of the location and time of day of a scene, also known as a "slugline." It should always be in, CAPS. Example: EXT. WRITERS STORE - DAY reveals that the action takes place outside The Writers Store during the daytime.

(E) SUBHEADER
Indent: Left: 0.0" Right: 0.0" Width: 6.0"
When a new scene heading is not necessary, but some distinction needs to be made in the action, you can use a subheader. But be sure to use these sparingly, as a script full of subheaders is generally frowned upon. A good example is when there are a series of quick cuts between two locations, you would use the term INTERCUT and the scene locations.

(F) ACTION
Indent: Left: 0.0" Right: 0.0" Width: 6.0"
The narrative description of the events of a scene, written in the present tense. Also less commonly known as direction, visual exposition, blackstuff, description or scene direction. Remember—only things that can be seen and heard should be included in the action.

CHARACTER
Indent: Left: 2.0" Right: 0.0" Width: 4.0"

(G) When a character is introduced, his name should be capitalized within the action. For example: The door opens and in walks LIAM, a thirty-something hipster with attitude to spare.

SAMPLE SCREENPLAY PAGE

(A) FADE IN:

(D) EXT. WRITERS STORE - DAY

(F) In the heart of West Los Angeles, a boutique shop's large OPEN sign glows like a beacon.

(M)   DISSOLVE TO:

INT. WRITERS STORE - SALES FLOOR - DAY

Writers browse the many scripts in the screenplay section.

(G) ANTHONY, Canadian-Italian Story Specialist extraordinaire, 30s and not getting any younger, ambles over.

(H)   ANTHONY
(I)   Hey, how's everyone doin' here?

A WRITING ENTHUSIAST, 45, reads the first page of "The Aviator" by John Logan.

                    WRITING ENTHUSIAST
          Can John Logan write a killer
          first page or what?

                    ANTHONY
          You, sir, are a gentleman of
          refined taste. John Logan is my
          non-Canadian idol.

The phone RINGS. Anthony goes to--

(E) THE SALES COUNTER

And answers the phone.

                    ANTHONY (CONT'D)
          Writers Store, Anthony speaking.

                    VOICE
(J)   (over phone)
          Do you have a "Chinatown" in
          stock?

I/E LUXURIOUS MALIBU MANSION - DAY

A FIGURE roams his estate, cell phone pressed to his ear.

                    ANTHONY (O.S.)
          'Course we have "Chinatown"!
          Robert Towne's masterpiece is
          arguably the Great American
          Screenplay...
                    (MORE) **(C)**

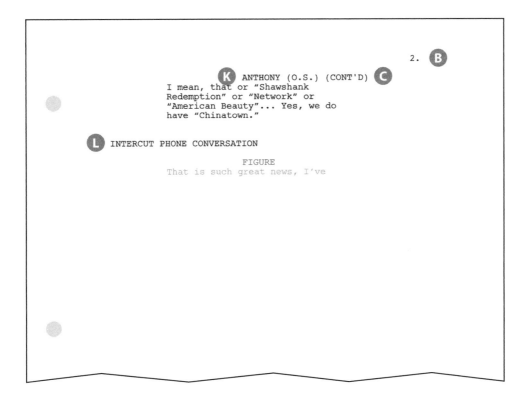

2. **B**

K ANTHONY (O.S.) (CONT'D) **C**
I mean, that or "Shawshank
Redemption" or "Network" or
"American Beauty"... Yes, we do
have "Chinatown."

L INTERCUT PHONE CONVERSATION

FIGURE
That is such great news, I've

H A character's name is CAPPED and always listed above his lines of dialogue. Minor characters may be listed without names, for example "TAXI DRIVER" or "CUSTOMER."

I *DIALOGUE*

Indent: Left: 1.0" Right: 1.5" Width: 3.5"

Lines of speech for each character. Dialogue format is used anytime a character is heard speaking, even for off-screen and voice-overs.

J *PARENTHETICAL*

Indent: Left: 1.5" Right: 2.0" Width: 2.5"

A parenthetical is direction for the character, that is either attitude or action-oriented. Parentheticals are used very rarely, and only if absolutely necessary. Why? First, if you need to use a parenthetical to convey what's going on with your dialogue, then it probably needs a good re-write. Second, it's the director's job to instruct an actor, and everyone knows not to encroach on the director's turf!

Ⓚ *EXTENSION*

Placed after the character's name, in parentheses

An abbreviated technical note placed after the character's name to indicate how the voice will be heard onscreen, for example, if the character is speaking as a voice-over, it would appear as LIAM (V.O.).

Ⓛ *INTERCUT*

Intercuts are instructions for a series of quick cuts between two scene locations.

Ⓜ *TRANSITION*

Indent: Left: 4.0" Right: 0.0" Width: 2.0"

Transitions are film editing instructions, and generally only appear in a shooting script. Transition verbiage includes:

CUT TO:

DISSOLVE TO:

SMASH CUT:

QUICK CUT:

FADE TO:

As a spec script writer, you should avoid using a transition unless there is no other way to indicate a story element. For example, you might need to use DISSOLVE TO: to indicate that a large amount of time has passed.

SHOT

Indent: Left: 0.0" Right: 0.0" Width: 6.0"

A shot tells the reader the focal point within a scene has changed. Like a transition, there's rarely a time when a spec screenwriter should insert shot directions.

Examples of Shots:

ANGLE ON --

EXTREME CLOSE UP --

LIAM'S POV --

SPEC SCRIPT VS. SHOOTING SCRIPT

A "spec script" literally means that you are writing a screenplay on speculation. That is, no one is paying you to write the script. You are penning it in hopes of selling the script to a buyer. Spec scripts should stick stringently to established screenwriting rules.

Once a script is purchased, it becomes a shooting script, also called a production script. This is a version of the screenplay created for film production. It will include technical instructions, like film editing notes, shots, cuts and the like. All the scenes are numbered, and revisions are marked with a color-coded system. This is done so that the production assistants and director can then arrange the order in which the scenes will be shot for the most efficient use of stage, cast, and location resources.

A spec script should *never* contain the elements of shooting script. The biggest mistake any new screenwriter can make is to submit a script full of production language, including camera angles and editing transitions.

It can be very difficult to resist putting this type of language in your script. After all, it's your story and you see it in a very specific way. However, facts are facts. If you want to direct your script, then try to go the independent filmmaker route. But if you want to sell your script, then stick to the accepted spec screenplay format.

SCRIPT PRESENTATION AND BINDING

Just like the format of a script, there are very specific rules for binding and presenting your script. The first page is the title page, which should also be written in Courier 12pt font. No graphics, no fancy pictures, only the title of your script, with "written by" and your name in the center of the page. In the lower left-hand or right-hand corner, enter your contact information.

In the lower left-hand or right-hand corner you can put Registered, WGA or a copyright notification, though this is generally not a requirement.

SAMPLE SCREENPLAY TITLE PAGE

Title
The name of your script, in 12pt Courier font.

RENDEZVOUS AT WRITERS STORE

By

John & Jane Smith

By-Line
The name of the author(s).

Contact Information
Your or your agent's. Include address, phone number, and email.

The Writers Store
3510 West Magnolia Blvd.
Burbank, CA 91505
310-441-5151
Myemail@writersstore.com

Query Letters

A query is a one-page, single-spaced letter that quickly tells who you are, what the work is, and why the work is appropriate for the market in question. Just as queries are used as the first means of contact for pitching magazine articles and novels, they work just the same for scripts.

A well-written query is broken down into three parts.

PART I: YOUR REASON FOR CONTACTING/SCRIPT DETAILS

Before even looking at the few sentences describing your story, a producer wants to see two other things:

1. **What is it?** State the title, genre, and whether it's a full-length script or a shorter one.
2. **Why are you contacting this market/person in particular?** There are thousands of individuals who receive scripts. Why have you chosen this person to review the material? Is it because you met them in person and they requested to see your work? Have they represented writers similar to yourself? Did you read that they were actively looking for zombie comedies? Spelling out your reason upfront shows that you've done your research, and that you're a professional.

PART II: THE ELEVATOR PITCH

If you wrote the first paragraph correctly, you've got their attention, so pitch away. Explain what your story is in about 3-6 sentences. The point here is to intrigue and pique only. Don't get into nitty-gritty details of any kind. Hesitate using a whole lot of character names or backstory. Don't say how it ends or who dies during the climax or that the hero's father betrays him in Act II. Introduce us to the main character and his situation, then get to the key part of the pitch: the conflict.

Try to include tidbits here and there that make your story unique. If it's about a cop nearing retirement, that's nothing new. But if the story is about a retiring cop considering a sex

SAMPLE QUERY LETTER

A **John. Q. Writer**
123 Main St.
Writerville, USA
(212)555-1234
johnqwriter@email.com

Agent
JQA & Associates
678 Hollywood St.
Hollywood, CA 90210

B Dear Mr./Ms (Last Name):

C My name is John Q. Writer and we crossed paths at the Screenwriters World Conference in Los Angeles in October 2012. After hearing the pitch for my feature-length thriller, October Surprise, you requested that I submit a query, synopsis and the first 10 pages of the script. All requested materials are enclosed. This is an exclusive submission, as you requested.

D U.S. Senator Michael Hargrove is breaking ranks with his own political party to endorse another candidate for President of the United States. At the National Convention, he's treated like a rock star V.I.P. -- that is, until, he's abducted by a fringe political group and given a grim ultimatum: Use your speech on live TV to sabotage and derail the presidential campaign you're now supporting, or your family back home will not live though the night.

E The script was co-written with my scriptwriting partner, Joe Aloysius. I am a produced playwright and award-winning journalist. Thank you for considering October Surprise. I will be happy to sign any release forms that you request. May I send the rest of the screenplay?

Best,
John Q. Writer

change operation in his bid to completely start over, while the police union is threatening to take away his pension should he do this, then you've got something different that readers may want to see.

PART III: THE WRAP-UP

Your pitch is complete. The last paragraph is where you get to talk about yourself and your accomplishments. If the script has won any awards or been a finalist in a prominent competition, this is the place to say so. Mention your writing credentials and experience. Obviously, any paid screenwriting experience is most valuable, but feel free to include other tidbits such as if you're a magazine freelancer or a published novelist.

Sometimes, there won't be much to say at the end of a query letter because the writer has no credits, no contacts and nothing to brag about. As your mother would tell you: If you don't have anything nice to say, don't say anything at all. Keep the last section brief if you must, rather than going on and on about being an "active blogger" or having one poem published in your college literary magazine.

Following some information about yourself, it's time to wrap up the query and propose sending more material. A simple way to do this is by saying "The script is complete. May I send you the treatment and full screenplay?"

Here are the elements of a query letter in the example on the facing page:

(A) Include all of your contact information—including phone and e-mail—as centered information at the top.

(B) Use proper greetings and last names.

(C) Include a reason for contacting the reader.

(D) Try and keep the pitch to one paragraph.

(E) Regarding your credentials, be concise and honest.

Treatments and Log Lines

INTRODUCTION TO THE TREATMENT

Nobody reads a full script in Hollywood anymore. Execs don't want to put in the time to read a 90-page comedy script, much less a 180-page epic. They want to know if the goods are there before they invest their precious time, and this is where the treatment comes in. Think of it as reading the back cover of a book before you invest in buying it. You'd never just pay for a book without knowing what type of story to expect. So it is with the movie industry. The treatment is the essential selling tool that can make or break your script.

WHAT IS A TREATMENT?

A treatment is a short document written in prose form and in the present tense that emphasizes, with vivid description, the major elements of a screenplay.

That's a very broad definition, to be sure. And while the main purpose of a treatment is as a selling tool, there are variations of the definition to consider.

1. A treatment could be your first attempt toward selling your screenplay to a producer, your first try at getting someone to pay you to write the script.
2. A treatment could be a sales tool for a script that you've already written—a shorter, prose version of the screenplay's story for producers to read, to pique their interest in your project and entice them to read your screenplay.
3. A treatment could describe how you intend to attack a rewrite, either of your own script or of another writer's script. Often when a producer hires a writer to do a rewrite, they'll ask for a treatment first.
4. A treatment could be the first step toward writing your screenplay—it could be one of the first steps toward getting your story down on paper. Maybe you don't have time to write the screenplay yet—a treatment can help cement the story in your mind (and on paper) so that you can work on it later.

WHY WRITE A TREATMENT?

Ultimately, the best reason to write a treatment is that the process of writing your treatment can help you write a better script. It can be easier to find and solve structural challenges, plot incongruities, lapses in logic, etc. in the prose treatment format than it is to find and solve those challenges in the screenplay format.

Writing a screenplay is a step-by-step process, and some steps are more involved than others. Writing a treatment is a very achievable step in the screenwriting process, and taking that step from beginning to end can be a rewarding boost for your writing ego.

Writing a treatment helps give tangible shape to your story, and makes sharing your story with others simpler and more precise. If you can share your story with others, you can get feedback, which may open up more channels in your brain and help your story to grow. The treatment format is much easier to read and comprehend for people who aren't familiar with the screenplay format.

You might not be ready to write your complete screenplay yet—you might not have time, you might not be fully committed to the idea. Writing a treatment is a good stopgap measure, so that an idea doesn't just exist as an idea—it may exist as something you can sell, share with a collaborator, or simply file away for a rainy day.

WHEN IS A TREATMENT USED?

A treatment is usually used when you begin the process of selling your script. When you pitch your script to a producer and he shows interest in your script, he will most likely ask you to send over the treatment. This way, he can review the story and see if he is interested in reading the full script.

Think of the treatment as your business card—the thing you leave behind after you've pitched your story.

You may have heard of writers who sell a script based only a treatment. Yes, this happens, but this happens only for established writers with a track record of produced scripts. They have proven to Hollywood that they can write a blockbuster script, so buyers know that if they like the treatment, they will most likely love the script.

The treatment can also be used as an outline for the writer before he begins his script. It's smart to either outline or summarize a script before you begin writing. If you can complete the story in a smaller form, you know that you'll be able to sustain it in the longer script format. Architects don't erect a building without first designing a blueprint and then creating a model of the structure. The outline is your blueprint and the treatment is your model.

TREATMENT VS. SYNOPSIS, COVERAGE, BEAT SHEET AND OUTLINE

The term treatment is thrown around loosely in Hollywood, and you can be sure that you'll hear a different definition each time you ask. Some buyers will request a treatment when they really want a synopsis, an outline or a beat sheet. So what are the definitions of the other items?

SYNOPSIS

A Synopsis is a brief description of a story's plot or a straightforward presentation of the scenes and events in a story. It is not a selling tool, but rather a summation of the story, and is typically no more than 2 pages long. It's generally used by professional script readers when writing coverage on a script.

COVERAGE

Coverage is the name of the document generated by the buyer's in house script readers. The main purpose of this document is to assess the commercial viability of the script. The reader supplies the buyer with the basic identifying information of the script, a synopsis, their comments on the script and a rating chart on all of the elements of the script, including characters, dialogue, action, setting, and commercial appeal. The reader then rates the script "pass" (no, thanks. Don't call us, cause we're certainly not gonna call you) "consider" (maybe someone we know can rewrite this puppy into something marketable) or "recommend" (this is the script that will move me from script reader hell to producing heaven!).

BEAT SHEET

A Beat Sheet lists the sequence of major events that takes place in a script. It shows what will happen to the main character, and the order in which the events will occur. It can be anywhere from a short paragraph to three pages. Each beat is described in only 1-2 sentences. Here is an extremely short example from "Die Hard."

1. New York Detective John McClane flies to Los Angeles to reconcile with his wife Holly at her company Christmas party.
2. When he arrives at Holly's high-rise office building, they argue and Holly leaves McClane alone in her executive bathroom.
3. From the bathroom, McClane hears terrorists, lead by Hans Gruber, break in and take over the building.
4. McClane witnesses the murder of Takagi, the CEO of the company, by Gruber and decides to take action.
5. McClane kills the brother of the lead henchman, Karl, and many other terrorists. He greatly angers Hans and Karl in the process.
6. McClane battles the terrorists with the help of a lone police officer.
7. The other police are against McClane and he feels alone in his fight. The police approach fails, so McClane is totally alone.
8. McClane fights Karl, kills him and prepares to go save Holly from Gruber.
9. Seemingly outnumbered, McClane appears to give up.
10. Using his New York wits, McClane kills Gruber and saves Holly.

OUTLINE

An outline is a list of the scenes that make up a screenplay, from FADE IN to FADE OUT. Every writer has a different method of outlining—some are very detailed, while some list only a sentence or even just a word for each scene.

A good way to start a screenplay is to write a beat sheet, an outline and then a treatment. If you work out the story problems with these three tools, you will find that writing the actual script is a breeze.

WHY DO I NEED A TREATMENT?

Besides being an important selling tool, a treatment allows you to see if your idea can sustain a feature-length film. Many writers take an idea straight to screenplay form, and then find 30 pages in that there is not enough story to continue the script. In this short summary form, you will also be able to identify any weaknesses in your plot, theme and characters. It is much easier to find and solve these challenges in the prose treatment form than it is to locate them in the screenplay format.

HOW LONG SHOULD IT BE?

Sadly, there is no cut and dry length for a treatment. Generally, treatments vary in length from 1–25 pages.

A general rule—the more power the executive holds, the shorter the treatment you should send them. It is recommended to have a few different versions of your treatment. Besides a lengthy summary of the story, have a quick one pager on hand.

WHAT IS THE FORMAT?

Your treatment should be written in prose form, and in 12 point Courier font. In essence, the treatment looks like a short story. There should be one line of space between each paragraph, and no indenting.

DON'T insert dialogue, slug lines, or anything else in screenplay format.

DO use standard punctuation for dialogue.

However, be careful not to rely on much dialogue in your treatment in order to effectively tell the story in 10 pages or less. A few carefully chosen thematic lines will suffice. For instance, the treatment for "Forrest Gump" would likely use the line, "Life is like a box of chocolates. You never know what you're gonna get," because it is used throughout the script as a thematic tag line.

WHAT SHOULD I ASPIRE TO DO WITH THE TREATMENT?

The treatment should not look, sound or read like an outline, a beat sheet or a screenplay. The essence of the story and the characters should be evoked through exhilarating language and imagery. It should sound like an excited moviegoer recanting the details of a film he just saw that was thought provoking, exhilarating and made him feel like he just had to share all the details with his friends. The prose you use in a treatment should be different than the narrative lines of a screenplay.

The beginning of the treatment has to grab the reader and not let go until the very end. Your reader should be able to see the script play out on the silver screen in front of his or her very eyes. After reading the treatment, the reader should be on fire to get this script to her boss, pronto!

THE LOG LINE

A Log Line is a one sentence description of your film. It's really that simple. You've seen log lines, even if you're not aware of it. In essence, TV Guide descriptions of films are log lines.

A log line may describe the following elements:

- Genre—comedy, drama, thriller, love story, etc.
- Setting—time and place, locale, other pertinent information
- Plot—the main narrative thrust of the story
- Character—the lead character or group of characters
- Theme—the main subject of the movie

A log line need not contain the following elements:

- Character names (unless the characters are historical figures)
- Back story
- Qualitative judgments—"A hilarious story…" "A fascinating tale…"
- Comparisons to other films—"It's 'Jaws' meets 'Mary Poppins'…"

Here are a few examples of log lines for well-known films. See if you can guess the film being described (the answers are right below, so don't cheat!):

1. A throwback to the serial adventure films of the 1930s, this film is the story of a heroic archeologist who races against the Nazis to find a powerful artifact that can change the course of history.
2. Set at a small American college in the early 1960s, this broad comedy follows a fraternity full of misfits through a year of parties, mishaps and food fights.
3. An illiterate boy looks to become a contestant on the Hindi version of "Who Wants to be A Millionaire" in order to re-establish contact with the girl he loves, who is an ardent fan of the show.
4. A man decides to change his life by saying 'yes' to everything that comes his way. On his journey, he wins $45,000, meets a hypnotic dog, obtains a nursing degree, travels the globe, and finds romance.
5. A behind-the-scenes view of the 2000 presidential election and the scandal that ensued in the weeks following.

Get the idea? The log line is designed to describe and to tease, like a line of advertising copy for your film. It has to be accurate, it can't be misleading. It's the first sentence a producer or executive is going to read, and you've got to make sure it isn't the last. Make it count.

By the way, the log lines above are for:

1. "Raiders of the Lost Ark"
2. "Animal House"
3. "Slumdog Millionaire"
4. "Yes Man"
5. "Recount"

WHY IS THE LOG LINE IMPORTANT IN A TREATMENT?

The log line is the first sentence an executive will ever read from your hand. It's also the shorthand that executives will use to discuss your project with each other. If a junior executive reads your treatment and likes it, she'll need to tell her boss about the project in order to move it to the next step (probably a meeting between you and the boss).

The boss will ask the junior executive "What's it about?" The junior executive will respond with your log line, if you've written it well and accurately. You are helping to provide the junior executive with the tools she needs to help move your project forward. If you don't provide a log line at the beginning of your treatment, you rely on the junior executive's ability to digest your treatment and come up with a good log line of her own. Even in a collaborative art form like filmmaking, it's never a good idea to leave a job undone for someone else to do if you are more capable of doing it yourself. And who knows your story better than you do? Write a great log line for your treatment, and you'll know that your treatment is being discussed in your own words.

WHO IS THE LOG LINE FOR?

The log line is for the buyer: the executive, the producer, the agent. By writing a log line for your treatment, you are helping them to process your material more efficiently. Getting a movie made is a sales process, a constant, revolving door sales process. You sell your work to an agent, who then sells your work to a producer, who then sells it to a director, who then sells it to actors and key crew members.

Once the movie is made, the sales process starts all over again, as the producer has to sell the movie to distributors and marketing executives, who have to sell the film to theater owners who have to sell the film to audiences. A good log line can ride the film all the way from start to finish, helping to sell it at each step.

SHOULD THE LOG LINE REFER TO OTHER MOVIES?

No. It used to be popular to write log lines that were entirely film references. This practice became so prevalent that it became a cliché, and should be avoided if at all possible. Nothing says "schlock" as quickly as a "Die Hard" reference—the classic action movie reference that every movie strived for in the early 1990s. "Speed" was called "Die Hard" on a bus. "Passenger 57" was called "Die Hard" on a plane. Descriptive as these log lines may be, they read as lazy writing, and if your writing isn't even original in the log line, who will be interested in reading your treatment or your script? Avoid hucksterism, overselling and hype. It's a turnoff.

HOW LONG SHOULD THE LOG LINE BE?

Your log line should be one sentence long. Pare it down to its essence, and don't let your sentence become a run-on. Try it out loud, see if it works. You don't have to follow every twist and turn of the plot in your log line, you only have to convey the flavor of the script. One sentence will do it.

WHAT IS THE DIFFERENCE BETWEEN THE LOG LINE AND THE THEME?

Your log line is a sales tool that is a teaser and an invitation to read your script. The theme may be contained in the log line, but not necessarily. Theme is the real answer to "What is your script about?" and Theme need not be confined to a one sentence answer. Theme is often related to the discovery that your main character makes during the course of the film. For instance, in "Raiders of the Lost Ark," Indiana Jones discovers that people are actually more important to him than historical artifacts. In "Animal House," the Deltas discover that the camaraderie that they've discovered in their fraternity is the real lasting value of their college experience, not their class work or their social status on campus.

IN CLOSING

You've spent months or years (or even decades) on your script, and so it may be frustrating to jump through the hoops of the submission process—but it's important. Don't give readers an excuse to ignore your work. You must craft a killer query, treatment and log line before the script gets its big shot. Compose them well, and you're on your way to selling that screenplay.

The Directory

@RADICAL MEDIA—NEW YORK BRANCH

435 Hudson Street, 6th Floor
New York, NY 10014

Phone: 212-462-1500
Fax: 212-462-1600
Email: *info@radicalmedia.com*

Submission Policy: Does not accept any unsolicited material

James Spindler
Title: Chief Creative Officer
Email: *spindler@radicalmedia.com*

@RADICAL MEDIA—SANTA MONICA BRANCH

1630 12th Street
Santa Monica, CA 90404

Phone: 310-664-4500
Fax: 310-664-4600

Submission Policy: Accepts Query Letter from produced or represented writers

Adam Neuhaus
Title: Senior Director—Development
Email: *neuhaus@radicalmedia.com*

100% ENTERTAINMENT

201 North Irving Boulevard
Los Angeles, CA 90004

Phone: 323-461-6360
Fax: 323-871-8203
Email: *sisaacs100@mac.com*

Submission Policy: Accepts Query Letter from unproduced, unrepresented writers via email
Genre: Memoir & True Stories, Science Fiction, TV Drama
Year Established: 1998

100% TERRYCLOTH

421 Waterview Street
Los Angeles, CA 90293

Phone: 323-515-3787
Fax: 424-354-4041
Email: *tm@terencemichael.com*

Submission Policy: Accepts Query Letter from unproduced, unrepresented writers via email

Terence Michael
Title: Producer

1019 ENTERTAINMENT

1680 North Vine Street, Suite 600
Hollywood, CA 90028

Phone: 323-645-6840
Fax: 323-645-6841
Email: *info@1019ent.com*

Submission Policy: Accepts Query Letter from unproduced, unrepresented writers via email
Genre: Memoir & True Stories, TV Drama, TV Sitcom

Terry Botwick
Title: Principal
Phone: 323-645-6840
IMDB: *www.imdb.com/company/co0263748*

10X10 ENTERTAINMENT

1640 South Sepulveda Boulevard, Suite 450
Los Angeles, CA 90025

Phone: 310-575-1235

Submission Policy: Accepts Query Letter from unproduced, unrepresented writers
Genre: Memoir & True Stories, TV Drama, TV Sitcom
Company Focus: TV

Ken Mok
Title: Producer/Founder
IMDB: *www.imdb.com/name/nm0596298*

Ross Greenberg
Title: Director of Development
Phone: 310-575-1235
IMDB: *www.imdb.com/name/nm1875727*

1821 PICTURES

10900 Wilshire Boulevard, Suite 1400
Los Angeles, CA 90024

Phone: 310-443-5399
Email: *asst@1821pictures.com*

Submission Policy: Accepts Query Letter from

unproduced, unrepresented writers via email
Genre: Memoir & True Stories, TV Drama, TV Sitcom, Animation
Year Established: 2005

Paris Kasidokostas-Latsis
Title: Owner
Phone: 310-443-5399
IMDB: *www.imdb.com/company/co0237259*

19 ENTERTAINMENT, LTD.

8560 West Sunset Boulevard, 9th Floor
West Hollywood, CA 90069

Phone: 310-777-1940

Submission Policy: Does not accept any unsolicited material
Genre: TV Drama, TV Sitcom, Animation

Mike Ferrel
Title: CEO
Phone: 310-777-1940

2-WAY TRAFFIC—A SONY PICTURES ENTERTAINMENT COMPANY

Middenweg 1
HS Hilversum 1217, The Netherlands

Phone: 31-35-750-8000
Email: *info@2waytraffic.com*

Submission Policy: Accepts Query Letter from unproduced, unrepresented writers
Company Focus: Feature Films, TV
Year Established: 2004

Jeff Lerner
Title: Senior Vice President, Scripted Development
Email: *jeff_lerner@spe.sony.com*
IMDB: *www.imdb.com/company/co0215148*

Kees Abrahams
Title: CEO
Phone: 31-35-750-8000
Email: *kees.abrahams@2waytraffic.com*

21 LAPS ENTERTAINMENT

c/o Twentieth Century Fox
10201 West Pico Boulevard
Building 41, Suite 400
Los Angeles, CA 90064

Phone: 310-369-7170
Fax: 310-969-0443

Submission Policy: Does not accept any unsolicited material
Genre: Action, Comedy, Drama
Company Focus: Feature Films, TV

Dan Levine
Title: President of Production
IMDB: *www.imdb.com/name/nm0505782*

Shawn Levy
Title: Principal
Phone: 310-369-4466
IMDB: *www.imdb.com/name/nm0506613*

Billy Rosenberg
Title: Vice-President of Development
Phone: 310-369-7170
IMDB: *www.imdb.com/name/nm1192785*

25/7 PRODUCTIONS

10999 Riverside Drive, Suite 100
North Hollywood, CA 91602

Phone: 818-432-2800
Fax: 818-432-2810

Submission Policy: Accepts Query Letter from unproduced, unrepresented writers
Genre: Memoir & True Stories, TV Drama, TV Sitcom, Animation
Year Established: 2003

David Broome
Title: President
Phone: 818-432-2800
IMDB: *www.imdb.com/company/co0200336*

26 FILMS

8748 Holloway Drive
Los Angeles, CA, 90069

Phone: 310-205-9922
Fax: 310-206-9926
Email: *asst@26films.com*

Submission Policy: Accepts Query Letter from unproduced, unrepresented writers via email

Nathalie Marciano
Title: Producer/CEO
IMDB: *www.imdb.com/name/nm0545695*

2929 PRODUCTIONS

1437 Seventh Street, Suite 250
Santa Monica, CA 90401

Phone: 310-309-5200
Fax: 310-309-5716

Submission Policy: Accepts Query Letter from unproduced, unrepresented writers
Genre: Action, Memoir & True Stories, Drama, Socio-cultural

Todd Wagner
Title: Principal
Phone: 310-309-5200
IMDB: *www.imdb.com/company/co0005596*

2S FILMS

1437 Seventh Street, Suite 250
Los Angeles, CA 90025

Phone: 310-789-5450
Fax: 310-789-3060

Submission Policy: Does not accept any unsolicited material
Genre: Comedy, Romance
Company Focus: Feature Films
Year Established: 2007

Molly Smith
Title: Partner/Producer
Phone: 310-789-5450
IMDB: *www.imdb.com/company/co0238996*

3 ARTS ENTERTAINMENT, INC.

9460 Wilshire Boulevard 7th Floor
Beverly Hills, CA 90212

Phone: 310-888-3200
Fax: 310-888-3210

Submission Policy: Accepts Query Letter from unproduced, unrepresented writers
Genre: TV Drama, TV Sitcom, Drama
Company Focus: Feature Films
Year Established: 1992

Erwin Stoff
Title: Partner/Talent Manager
Phone: 310-888-3200
IMDB: *www.imdb.com/name/nm0831098*

Howard Klein
Title: Partner/Talent Manager
Phone: 310-888-3200
Email: *hklein@3arts.com*
IMDB: *www.imdb.com/name/nm2232433*

3 BALL PRODUCTIONS

3650 Redondo Beach Avenue
Redondo Beach, CA 90278

Phone: 424-236-7500
Fax: 424-236-7501
Email: *3ball.reception@eyeworks.tv*

Submission Policy: Accepts Query Letter from unproduced, unrepresented writers via email
Genre: TV Drama

JD Roth
Title: CEO
Phone: 424-236-7500
IMDB: *www.imdb.com/company/co0100000*

Brandt Pinvidic
Title: Executive Vice-President, Development
Phone: 424-236-7500
IMDB: *www.imdb.com/name/nm1803480*

3 RING CIRCUS FILMS

1040 North Sycamore Avenue
Los Angeles, CA 90038

Phone: 323-466-5300
Fax: 323-466-5310
Email: *info@3ringcircus.tv*

Submission Policy: Accepts Query Letter from unproduced, unrepresented writers via email
Genre: Detective, Memoir & True Stories

John Sideropoulos
Title: CEO
Email: *john@3ringcircus.tv*
IMDB: *www.imdb.com/company/co0022780*

34TH ST. FILMS (TYLER PERRY'S SHINGLE)

8200 Wilshire Boulevard, Suite 300
Beverly Hills, CA 90211

Phone: 323-315-5743
Fax: 323-315-7117

Submission Policy: Accepts Query Letter from
unproduced, unrepresented writers
Genre: Action, Comedy, Family, Socio-cultural
Company Focus: Feature Films

Matt Moore
Title: Executive Vice-President Production and
Development
IMDB: *www.imdb.com/name/nm0601597*

Poppy Hanks
Title: Vice-President Production
Phone: 323-315-7963
IMDB: *www.imdb.com/name/nm2248393*

Amber Rasberry
Title: Creative Executive
Phone: 323-315-7963
IMDB: *www.imdb.com/name/nm2248393*

360 PICTURES

301 North Canon Drive, Suite 207
Beverly Hills, CA 90210

Phone: 310-205-9900
Fax: 310-205-9909

Submission Policy: Does not accept any
unsolicited material
Genre: Comedy, Science Fiction, Thriller

Frank Mancuso, Jr.
Title: Producer/President
Phone: 310-205-9900
IMDB: *www.imdb.com/company/co0157610*

40 ACRES & A MULE FILMWORKS, INC.

75 South Elliot Place
Brooklyn, NY 11217

Phone: 718-624-3703

Submission Policy: Does not accept any
unsolicited material
Genre: Action, Comedy, Memoir & True
Stories, TV Drama, Drama

Spike Lee
Title: Chairman
Phone: 718-624-3703
IMDB: *www.imdb.com/company/co0029134*

44 BLUE PRODUCTIONS, INC.

4040 Vineland Avenue, Suite 105
Studio City, CA 11217

Phone: 818-760-4442
Fax: 818-760-1509
Email: *reception@44blue.com*

Submission Policy: Accepts Query Letter from
unproduced, unrepresented writers via email
Genre: Memoir & True Stories, TV Drama, TV
Sitcom

Rasha Drachkovitch
Title: Co-Owner/President
Phone: 818-760-4442
IMDB: *www.imdb.com/company/co0012712*

495 PRODUCTIONS

4222 Burbank Boulevard
2nd Floor
Burbank, CA 91505

Phone: 818-840-2750
Fax: 818-840-7083
Email: *info@495productions.com*

Submission Policy: Does not accept any
unsolicited material
Genre: TV Drama, TV Sitcom
Company Focus: TV, Reality Programming
(Reality TV, Documentaries, Special Events,
Sporting Events)

SallyAnn Salsano
Title: Executive Producer/President
IMDB: *www.imdb.com/company/co0192481*

Stephanie Lydecker
Title: Head of Development
Phone: 818-840-2750
IMDB: *www.imdb.com/name/nm1738248*

4TH ROW FILMS

27 West 20th Street, Suite 1006
New York, NY 10011

Phone: 212-974-0082
Fax: 212-627-3090

Submission Policy: Does not accept any
unsolicited material
Genre: Memoir & True Stories, TV Drama, TV
Sitcom

Douglas Tirola
Title: President/Producer
Phone: 212-974-0082
IMDB: *www.imdb.com/company/co0192481*

51 MINDS

6565 Sunset Boulevard, Suite 301
Los Angeles, CA 90028

Phone: 323-466-9200
Fax: 323-466-9202
Email: *info@51minds.com*

Submission Policy: Accepts Query Letter from
unproduced, unrepresented writers via email
Genre: Comedy, TV Drama, Drama

Mark Cronin
Title: Executive Producer
Phone: 323-466-9200
Email: *info@51minds.com*
IMDB: *www.imdb.com/company/co0133414*

5IVE SMOOTH STONES PRODUCTIONS

8500 Wilshire Boulevard, Suite #527
Beverly Hills, CA 90211

Submission Policy: Accepts Query Letter from
unproduced, unrepresented writers via email
Genre: Comedy, Family
Company Focus: Feature Films

Terry Crews
Title: Actor/CEO
IMDB: *www.imdb.com/name/nm0187719*

Robert Wise
Title: President Scripted Development

72 PRODUCTIONS

8332 Melrose Avenue, 2nd Floor
West Hollywood, CA 90069

Phone: 323-651-1511
Fax: 323-651-1555

Submission Policy: Accepts Query Letter from
unproduced, unrepresented writers
Genre: Science Fiction, Thriller

Jen Chaiken
Title: Principal
Phone: 323-651-1511
IMDB: *www.imdb.com/company/co0196483*

72ND STREET PRODUCTIONS

1041 North Formosa Avenue
West Hollywood, CA 90046

Phone: 323-850-3139
Fax: 323-850-3179
Email: *contact@72ndstreetproductions.com*

Submission Policy: Accepts Query Letter from
unproduced, unrepresented writers via email
Genre: Drama
Company Focus: Feature Films, TV, Media
(Commercials/Branding/Marketing)

Steven Krieger
Title: Executive/Legal Counsel
Email: *skrieger@72ndstreetproductions.com*
IMDB: *www.imdb.com/name/nm2544844*

Tim Harms
Title: Producer
Email: *tharms@72ndstreetproductions.com*
IMDB: *www.imdb.com/name/nm0363608*

Lee Toland Krieger
Title: Director/Writer/Producer
Email: *lkrieger@72ndstreetproductions.com*
IMDB: *www.imdb.com/name/nm1767218*

777 GROUP

1015 Gayley Avenue, Suite 1128
Los Angeles, CA 90024

Phone: 312-834-7770
Email: *info@the777group.com*

Submission Policy: Accepts Query Letter from unproduced, unrepresented writers via email
Genre: Memoir & True Stories, TV Drama, TV Sitcom, Animation

Marcello Robinson
Title: CEO/President
Phone: 312-834-7770
Email: *info@the777group.com*
IMDB: *www.imdb.com/company/co0133127*

7ATE9 ENERTAINMENT

740 North La Brea Avenue
Los Angeles, CA 90038

Phone: 323-936-6789
Fax: 323-937-6713
Email: *info@7ate9.com*

Submission Policy: Accepts Query Letter from produced or represented writers
Genre: TV Drama, TV Sitcom, Animation
Company Focus: TV, Media (Commercials/Branding/Marketing)

Artur Spiegel
Title: Creative Director/Executive Producer
Phone: 323-936-6789
Email: *info@7ate9.com*
IMDB: *www.imdb.com/company/co0171281*

8:38 PRODUCTIONS

10390 Santa Monica Boulevard, Suite 200
Los Angeles, CA 90064

Phone: 310-789-3056
Fax: 310-789-3077

Submission Policy: Does not accept any unsolicited material
Genre: Romance, Family

Kira Davis
Title: Producer
Phone: 310-789-3056
IMDB: *www.imdb.com/company/co0252672*

81 PICTURES

141 West 28th Street, Suite 301
New York, NY 10001

Phone: 212-244-2865
Fax: 212-244-2874

Submission Policy: Accepts Query Letter from unproduced, unrepresented writers
Genre: Action, Memoir & True Stories, TV Drama, TV Sitcom, Drama

Adam Kassen
Title: Partner/Writer/Director
Phone: 212-244-2865

8790 PICTURES, INC.

11400 West Olympic Boulevard, Suite 590
Los Angeles, CA 90064

Phone: 310-471-9983
Fax: 310-471-6366
Email: *8790pictures@gmail.com*

Submission Policy: Accepts Query Letter from unproduced, unrepresented writers via email
Genre: Action, Comedy, Romance, TV Drama, Animation
Company Focus: Feature Films, TV

Joan Singleton
Title: Writer/Producer
Email: *8790pictures@gmail.com*
IMDB: *www.imdb.com/name/nm0802306*

Ralph S. Singleton
Title: Writer/Producer
Email: *8790pictures@gmail.com*
IMDB: *www.imdb.com/name/nm0802326*

8TH WONDER ENTERTAINMENT

7961 West 3rd Street
Los Angeles, CA 90048

Phone: 323-549-3456
Fax: 323-549-9475
Email: *info@8thwonderent.com*

Submission Policy: Accepts Query Letter from unproduced, unrepresented writers via email

Michael McQuarn
Title: CEO/President
Phone: 323-860-0319
Email: *mcq@8thwonderent.com*

9.14 PICTURES

1804 Chestnut Street, Suite 2
Philadelphia, PA 19103

Phone: 215-238-0707
Fax: 215-238-0663
Email: *info@914pictures.com*

Submission Policy: Accepts Query Letter from unproduced, unrepresented writers via email
Year Established: 2002

Don Argott
Title: Owner/Producer
Phone: ext. 12#
IMDB: *www.imdb.com/name/nm0034531*

Sheena M. Joyce
Title: Owner
Phone: ext. #11
IMDB: *www.imdb.com/name/nm1852224*

900 FILMS

1611A South Melrose Drive, #362
Vista, CA 92081

Phone: 760-477-2470
Fax: 760-477-2478
Email: *asst@900films.com*

Submission Policy: Accepts Query Letter from unproduced, unrepresented writers via email
Genre: Socio-cultural, Reality
Company Focus: Feature Films, TV, Post-Production (Editing, Special Effects), Reality Programming (Reality TV, Documentaries, Special Events, Sporting Events), Media (Commercials/Branding/Marketing)

Tony Hawk
Title: Principle/Professional Skateboarder

Jesse Fritsch
Title: Director of New Media/Producer

Angela Rhodehamel
Title: Production Manager/Producer

A LIKELY STORY

150 West 22nd Street, 9th Floor
New York, NY 10011

Phone: 917-484-8931
Email: *info@likely-story.com*

Submission Policy: Does not accept any unsolicited material
Company Focus: Feature Films

Anthony Bregman
Title: Producer/Founder
IMDB: *www.imdb.com/name/nm0106835*

A-LINE PICTURES

2231 Broadway #19
New York, NY 10024

Phone: 212-496-9496
Fax: 212-496-9497
Email: *info@a-linepictures.com*

Submission Policy: Does not accept any unsolicited material
Year Established: 2005

Caroline Baron
Title: Producer
IMDB: *www.imdb.com/name/nm0056205*

A-MARK ENTERTAINMENT

233 Wilshire Boulevard, Suite 200
Santa Monica, CA 90401

Phone: 310-255-0900
Email: *info@amarkentertainment.com*

Submission Policy: Does not accept any unsolicited material
Year Established: 2004

Bruce McNall
Title: Co-Chair
IMDB: *www.imdb.com/name/nm1557652*

A. SMITH & COMPANY PRODUCTIONS

9911 West Pico Boulevard, Suite 250
Los Angeles, CA 90035

Phone: 310-432-4800
Fax: 310-551-3085
Email: *info@asmithco.com*

Submission Policy: Accepts Query Letter from unproduced, unrepresented writers via email

Arthur Smith
Title: CEO

A.C. LYLES PRODUCTIONS, INC.

5555 Melrose Avenue
Hart Building 409
Hollywood, CA 90038-3197

Phone: 323-956-5819

Submission Policy: Accepts Query Letter from unproduced, unrepresented writers via email

A.C. Lyles
Title: Producer
Email: *ac_lyles@paramount.com*

A&E NETWORK

235 East 45th Street
New York, NY 10017

Phone: 212-210-1400
Fax: 212-210-9755
Email: *feedback@aetv.com*

Submission Policy: Does not accept any unsolicited material

Thomas Moody
Title: Senior Vice-President Programming, Planning & Acquisitions

AARDMAN ANIMATIONS

Gas Ferry Road
Bristol BS1 6UN
United Kingdom

Phone: +44 117-984-8485
Fax: +44 117-984-8486
Email: *mail@aardman.com*

Submission Policy: Accepts Query Letter from unproduced, unrepresented writers

Susan Breen
Title: Head of Development, Features

ABANDON PICTURES, INC.

711 Route 302
Pine Bush, NY 12566

Phone: 845-361-9317
Fax: 845-361-9150
Email: *investments@aecap.com*

Submission Policy: Does not accept any unsolicited material

Karen Lauder
Title: President & CEO

ABERRATION FILMS

1425 North Crescent Heights Boulevard, #203
West Hollywood, CA 90046

Phone: 323-656-1830
Email: *aberrationfilms@yahoo.com*

Submission Policy: Accepts Query Letter from unproduced, unrepresented writers
Genre: Drama
Company Focus: Feature Films

Susan Dynner
Title: Director/Producer
IMDB: *www.imdb.com/name/nm1309839*

ACAPPELLA PICTURES

8271 Melrose Avenue, Suite 101
Los Angeles, CA 90046

Phone: 323-782-8200
Fax: 323-782-8210

Submission Policy: Accepts Query Letter from unproduced, unrepresented writers via email

Charles Evans Jr.
Title: President
IMDB: *www.imdb.com/name/nm0262509*

ACCELERATED ENTERTAINMENT LLC

10201 West Pico Boulevard, Building 6
Los Angeles, CA 90064

Submission Policy: Accepts Query Letter from unproduced, unrepresented writers via email
Genre: Memoir & True Stories, Drama,

Socio-cultural
Company Focus: Feature Films

Jason Perr
Title: Partner/Executive Producer
Email: *jperr@acceleratedent.com*
IMDB: *www.imdb.com/name/nm1280790*

Christina Lee Storm
Title: Partner/Producer
Email: *cleestorm@acceleratedent.com*
IMDB: *www.imdb.com/name/nm0497028*

Allison Calleri
Title: Partner/Producer
Email: *acalleri@acceleratedent.com*
IMDB: *www.imdb.com/name/nm1819857*

ACT III PRODUCTIONS

100 North Crescent Dr, Suite 250
Beverly Hills, CA 90210

Phone: 310-385-4111
Fax: 310-385-4148

Submission Policy: Accepts Query Letter from unproduced, unrepresented writers

Norman Lear
Title: Chairman/CEO
Email: *normanl@actiii.com*
IMDB: *www.imdb.com/name/nm0005131*

ACTUAL REALITY PICTURES

Phone: 310-202-1272
Fax: 310-202-1502
Email: *questions@arp.tv*

Submission Policy: Does not accept any unsolicited material

R.J. Cutler
Title: President
IMDB: *www.imdb.com/name/nm0191712*

AD HOMINEM ENTERPRISES

506 Santa Monica Boulevard, Suite 400
Santa Monica, CA 90401

Phone: 310-394-1444
Fax: 310-394-5401

Submission Policy: Does not accept any unsolicited material
Company Focus: Feature Films

Alexander Payne
Title: Partner
Phone: 310-394-1444
IMDB: *www.imdb.com/name/nm0668247*
Assistant: Anna Musso

Jim Burke
Title: Partner
Phone: 310-394-1444
Email: *jwb@adhominem.us*
IMDB: *www.imdb.com/name/nm0121724*
Assistant: Adam Wagner

Evan Endicott
Title: Director of Development
Phone: 310-394-1444
IMDB: *www.imdb.com/name/nm1529002*

ADAM FIELDS PRODUCTIONS

8899 Beverly Boulevard, Suite 821
West Hollywood, CA 90048

Phone: 310-859-9300
Fax: 310-859-4795

Submission Policy: Accepts Query Letter from unproduced, unrepresented writers

Adam Fields
Title: President
IMDB: *www.imdb.com/name/nm0276178*

ADELSTEIN PRODUCTIONS

144 South Beverly Dr, Suite 500
Beverly Hills, CA 90212

Phone: 310-860-5502

Submission Policy: Does not accept any unsolicited material

Marty Adelstein
Title: Producer
Phone: 310-270-4570
IMDB: *www.imdb.com/name/nm1374351*

ADULT SWIM

1065 Williams St NW
Atlanta, GA 30309

Phone: 404-827-1500

Submission Policy: Does not accept any unsolicited material

Keith Crofford
Title: Vice-President Production
IMDB: *www.imdb.com/name/nm0188443*

AEI—ATCHITY ENTERTAINMENT INTERNATIONAL, INC.

9601 Wilshire Boulevard, #1202
Beverly Hills, CA 90210

Phone: 323-932-0407
Fax: 323-932-0321
Email: *submissions@aeionline.com*

Submission Policy: Accepts Query Letter from unproduced, unrepresented writers

Jennifer Pope
Title: Submissions Coordinator
Phone: 323-932-0407
Email: *jp@aeionline.com*

AFTER DARK FILMS

8967 Sunset Boulevard
West Hollywood, CA 90069

Phone: 310-270-4260
Fax: 310-270-4262
Email: *info@afterdarkfilms.com*

Submission Policy: Does not accept any unsolicited material
Genre: Horror

Stephanie Caleb
Title: Executive Vice-President Acquisitions & Creative Affairs
IMDB: *www.imdb.com/name/nm2554487*

AGAMEMNON FILMS, INC.

650 North Bronson Avenue, Suite B225
Los Angeles, CA 90004

Phone: 323-960-4066
Fax: 323-960-4067

Submission Policy: Accepts Query Letter from unproduced, unrepresented writers via email
Genre: Action, Thriller, TV Drama, Family,

Drama, Reality
Company Focus: TV, Reality Programming (Reality TV, Documentaries, Special Events, Sporting Events)

Fraser Clarke Heston
Title: President, CEO and Co-Founder
IMDB: *www.imdb.com/name/nm0381699*
Assistant: Heather Thomas

Alex Butler
Title: Senior Partner and Producer
IMDB: *www.imdb.com/name/nm0124808*

AGILITY STUDIOS

11928 1/2 Ventura Boulevard
Studio City, CA 91604

Phone: 310-314-1440
Fax: 310-496-3292
Email: *info@agilitystudios.com*

Submission Policy: Accepts Query Letter from unproduced, unrepresented writers via email
Year Established: 2008

Scott Ehrlich
Title: CEO
IMDB: *www.imdb.com/name/nm3796990*

AHIMSA FILMS

6671 Sunset Boulevard, Suite 1593
Los Angeles, CA 90028

Phone: 323-464-8500
Fax: 323-464-8535

Submission Policy: Accepts Query Letter from unproduced, unrepresented writers

Rebecca Yeldham
Title: President
IMDB: *www.imdb.com/name/nm0947344*

AHIMSA MEDIA

8060 Colonial Drive, Suite 204
Richmond, BC V7C 4V1
Canada

Phone: 604-785-3602
Email: *info@ahimsamedia.com*

Submission Policy: Accepts Query Letter from

unproduced, unrepresented writers via email
Company Focus: Media

Erica Hargreave
Title: President/Head of Creative and
Interactive
IMDB: *www.imdb.com/name/nm2988128*

AIRMONT PICTURES

344 Mesa Road
Santa Monica, CA 90402

Phone: 310-985-3896

Submission Policy: Accepts Query Letter from
unproduced, unrepresented writers

Matthew Gannon
Title: Producer
IMDB: *www.imdb.com/name/nm0304478*

AL ROKER PRODUCTIONS

250 West 57th Street, Suite 1525
New York, NY 10019

Phone: 212-757-8500
Fax: 212-757-8513
Email: *info@alroker.com*

Submission Policy: Does not accept any
unsolicited material
Company Focus: Post-Production (Editing,
Special Effects)
Year Established: 1994

Al Roker
Title: CEO
IMDB: *www.imdb.com/name/nm0737963*

ALAN BARNETTE PRODUCTIONS

100 Universal City Plaza
Building 2352, Suite 101
Universal City, CA 91608

Phone: 818-733-0993
Fax: 818-733-3172
Email: *dabarnette@aol.com*

Submission Policy: Does not accept any
unsolicited material

Alan Barnette
Title: Executive Producer
IMDB: *www.imdb.com/name/nm0056002*

ALAN DAVID GROUP

8840 Wilshire Boulevard, Suite 200
Beverly Hills, CA 90211

Phone: 310-358-3155
Fax: 310-358-3256
Email: *ad@adgmp.com*

Submission Policy: Does not accept any
unsolicited material

Alan David
Title: President
IMDB: *www.imdb.com/name/nm2220960*

ALAN SACKS PRODUCTIONS, INC.

11684 Ventura Boulevard, Suite 809
Studio City, CA 91604

Phone: 818-752-6999
Fax: 818-752-6985
Email: *asacks@pacbell.net*

Submission Policy: Does not accept any
unsolicited material

Alan Sacks
Title: Executive Producer
IMDB: *www.imdb.com/name/nm0755286*

ALCHEMY ENTERTAINMENT

7024 Melrose Ave, Suite 420
Los Angeles, CA 90038

Phone: 323-937-6100
Fax: 323-937-6102

Submission Policy: Does not accept any
unsolicited material

Jason Barrett
Title: Manager/Producer
IMDB: *www.imdb.com/name/nm2249074*

ALCON ENTERTAINMENT, LLC

10390 Santa Monica Boulevard, Suite 250
Los Angeles, CA 90025

Phone: 310-789-3040
Fax: 310-789-3060
Email: *info@alconent.com*

Submission Policy: Does not accept any unsolicited material

Broderick Johnson
Title: Co-Founder/Co-CEO
IMDB: *www.imdb.com/name/nm0424663*

ALEX ROSE PRODUCTIONS, INC.

8291 Presson Place
Los Angeles, CA 90069

Phone: 323-654-8662
Fax: 323-654-0196

Submission Policy: Accepts Query Letter from unproduced, unrepresented writers

Alexandra Rose
Title: President/Writer/Producer
IMDB: *www.imdb.com/name/nm0741228*

ALEXANDER/ENRIGHT & ASSOCIATES

201 Wilshire, Boulevard, 3rd Floor
Santa Monica, CA 90401

Phone: 310-458-3003
Fax: 310-393-7238

Submission Policy: Accepts Query Letter from unproduced, unrepresented writers

Les Alexander
Title: Executive Producer
IMDB: *www.imdb.com/name/nm0018573*

ALIANZA FILMS INTERNATIONAL LTD.

11941 Weddington Street, Suite #106
Studio City, CA 91607

Phone: 310-933-6250
Fax: 310-388-0874
Email: *alianza@usa.com*

Submission Policy: Accepts Query Letter from unproduced, unrepresented writers
Year Established: 1984

Shari Hamrick
Title: Executive
Email: *shari@alianzafilms.com*
IMDB: *www.imdb.com/name/nm0359089*

ALLAN MCKEOWN PRESENTS

1534 17th Street, #102
Santa Monica, CA 90404

Phone: 310-264-2474
Fax: 310-264-4663
Email: *info@ampresents.tv*

Submission Policy: Accepts Query Letter from unproduced, unrepresented writers via email
Year Established: 2007

Allan McKeown
Title: CEO/Producer
Email: *info@ampresents.tv*

ALLENTOWN PRODUCTIONS

100 Universal City Plaza
Building 2372B, Suite 114
Universal City, CA 91608

Phone: 818-733-1002
Fax: 818-866-4181
Email: *writetous@allentownproductions.com*

Submission Policy: Does not accept any unsolicited material
Year Established: 1994

James Moll
Title: Founder/Producer/Director
IMDB: *www.imdb.com/name/nm0002224*

ALLOY ENTERTAINMENT

6300 Wilshire Boulevard, Suite 2150
Los Angeles, CA 90048

Phone: 323-801-1373
Fax: 323-801-1355
Email: *LAassistant@alloyentertainment.com*

Submission Policy: Accepts Query Letter from unproduced, unrepresented writers via email

Bob Levy
Title: Executive Vice-President of Film
IMDB: *www.imdb.com/name/nm2145920*

ALOE ENTERTAINMENT/PROUD MARY

433 North Camden Dr, Suite 600
Beverly Hills, CA 90210

Phone: 310-288-1886
Fax: 310-288-1801
Email: *info@aloeentertainment.com*

Submission Policy: Does not accept any
unsolicited material
Year Established: 1999

Mary Aloe
Title: Producer/President
IMDB: *www.imdb.com/name/nm0022053*

ALTA LOMA ENTERTAINMENT

2706 Media Center Drive
Los Angeles, CA 90065-1733

Phone: 323-276-4211
Fax: 323-276-4500

Submission Policy: Does not accept any
unsolicited material

Richard Rosenzweig
Title: Executive Producer
Phone: 323-276-4211
IMDB: *www.imdb.com/name/nm0742866*

ALTURAS FILMS

2403 Main Street
Santa Monica, CA 90405

Phone: 310-230-6100
Fax: 310-314-2135
Email: *info@alturasfilms.com*

Submission Policy: Does not accept any
unsolicited material
Year Established: 2004

Marshall Rawlings
Title: Owner/Producer
Email: *reception@alturasfilms.com*
IMDB: *www.imdb.com/name/nm1987844*

AMBASSADOR ENTERTAINMENT

P. O. Box 1522
Pacific Palisades, CA 90272

Phone: 310-862-5200
Fax: 310-496-3140
Email: *aspeval@ambassadortv.com*

Submission Policy: Does not accept any
unsolicited material
Year Established: 1999

Albert Spevak
Title: President
IMDB: *www.imdb.com/name/nm0818411*

AMBER ENTERTAINMENT

6030 Wilshire Boulevard, Suite 300
Los Angeles, CA 90036
United States

21 Ganton Street, 4th Floor
London
United Kingdom
W1F 98N

Phone: 310-242-6445 or +44 207-292-7170
Email: *info@amberentertainment.com*

Submission Policy: Does not accept any
unsolicited material
Year Established: 2010

Ileen Maisel
Title: Executive (London Office)
IMDB: *www.imdb.com/name/nm0537884*

AMBUSH ENTERTAINMENT

7364-1/2 Melrose Avenue
Los Angeles, CA 90046

Phone: 323-951-9197
Fax: 323-951-9998
Email: *info@ambushentertainment.com*

Submission Policy: Accepts Scripts from
produced or represented writers
Year Established: 2000

Miranda Bailey
Title: Partner/Producer
IMDB: *www.imdb.com/name/nm0047419*

AMERICAN WORK INC.

7030 Delongpre
Los Angeles, CA 90028

Phone: 323-668-1100
Fax: 323-668-1133

Submission Policy: Accepts Query Letter from unproduced, unrepresented writers
Genre: Comedy

Scot Armstrong
Title: Writer/Director/Producer
IMDB: *www.imdb.com/name/nm0035905*

AMERICAN WORLD PICTURES

21700 Oxnard Street, Suite 1770
Woodland Hills, CA 91367

Phone: 818-340-9004
Fax: 818-340-9011
Email: *info@americanworldpictures.com*

Submission Policy: Accepts Scripts from unproduced, unrepresented writers
Genre: Action, Comedy, Horror, Romance, Thriller, Family, Drama
Company Focus: Feature Films

Mark L. Lester
Title: President/CEO
Email: *mark@americanworldpictures.com*
IMDB: *www.imdb.com/name/nm0504495*

Dana Dubovsky
Title: President of Production
Email: *dana@americanworldpictures.com*
IMDB: *www.imdb.com/name/nm0239541*

Dee Camp
Title: Vice-President of Acquisitions
Email: *dee@americanworldpictures.com*
IMDB: *www.imdb.com/name/nm3036636*

AMERICAN ZOETROPE

916 Kearny Street
San Francisco, CA 94133

Phone: 415-788-7500
Fax: 415-989-7910
Email: *contests@zoetrope.com*

Submission Policy: Accepts Scripts from unproduced, unrepresented writers
Genre: Action, Crime, Memoir & True Stories, Thriller
Year Established: 1972

Francis Ford Coppola
Title: Emeritus
IMDB: *www.imdb.com/name/nm0000338*

AMY ROBINSON PRODUCTIONS

101 Broadway, Suite 405
Brooklyn, NY 11211

Fax: 718-408-9553
Email: *arobinsonprod@aol.com*

Submission Policy: Accepts Query Letter from unproduced, unrepresented writers via email

Amy Robinson
IMDB: *www.imdb.com/name/nm0732364*

AN OLIVE BRANCH PRODUCTIONS, INC.

12400 Wilshire Boulevard, Suite 1275
Los Angeles, CA 90025

Phone: 310-860-6088
Email: *info@anolivebranchmedia.com*

Submission Policy: Accepts Scripts from produced or represented writers
Genre: Drama
Company Focus: Feature Films

Cybill Lui
Title: Principal/Producer
Email: *cybill@anolivebranchmedia.com*
IMDB: *www.imdb.com/name/nm3359236*

George Zakk
Title: Principal/Producer
Email: *george@anolivebranchmedia.com*
IMDB: *www.imdb.com/name/nm0952327*

ANCHOR BAY FILMS

2950 North Hollywood Way, 3rd Floor
Burbank, CA 91505

Phone: 818-748-4000
Email: *questions@anchorbayent.com*

Submission Policy: Accepts Query Letter from unproduced, unrepresented writers
Genre: Crime, Horror, Thriller
Year Established: 1997

Bill Clark
Title: President
IMDB: *www.imdb.com/name/nm0163694*

ANDREW LAUREN PRODUCTIONS

36 East 23rd Street, Suite 6F
New York, NY 10010

Phone: 212-475-1600
Fax: 212-529-1095
Email: *query@andrewlaurenproductions.com*

Submission Policy: Accepts Scripts from
unproduced, unrepresented writers
Genre: Drama
Company Focus: Feature Films, TV

Andrew Lauren
Title: Chairman/Founder
IMDB: *www.imdb.com/name/nm0491054*

Daniel Lipski
Email: *dlipski@andrewlaurenproductions.com*
IMDB: *www.imdb.com/name/nm2370474*

Jake Perron
Title: Director of Development
Email: *jperron@andrewlaurenproductions.com*
IMDB: *www.imdb.com/name/nm2889919*

ANGELWORLD ENTERTAINMENT LTD.

Beverly Hills Office
8200 Wilshire Boulevard 2nd Floor
Beverly Hills, CA 900211

London Office
New Bridge House
30–34 New Bridge Street
London
EC4 V6BJ

Malta Office
6 Triq Ta Fuq Il Widien
Mellieha
Malta

Phone: 310-600-7436
Fax: 323-328-1843
Email: *asst@angelworldentertainment.com*

Submission Policy: Accepts Query Letter from
unproduced, unrepresented writers via email
Company Focus: Feature Films
Year Established: 2007

Darby Angel
Title: CEO/Producer
Email: *chris@angelworldentertainment.com*
IMDB: *www.imdb.com/name/nm3786007*
Assistant: Christopher Tisa

John Michaels
Title: Head Production/Executive Producer

Max Mai
Title: Development Associate
Email: *max@angelworldentertainment.com*
IMDB: *www.imdb.com/name/nm4221777*

ANIMUS FILMS

914 Hauser Boulevard
Los Angeles, CA 90036

Phone: 323-988-5557
Fax: 323-571-3361
Email: *info@animusfilms.com*

Submission Policy: Accepts Query Letter from
unproduced, unrepresented writers
Genre: Memoir & True Stories, Thriller
Year Established: 2003

Jim Young
Title: Producer
IMDB: *www.imdb.com/name/nm1209063*

ANNE CARLUCCI PRODUCTIONS

9200 Sunset Boulevard
Penthouse 20
Los Angeles, CA 90069

Phone: 310-550-9545
Fax: 310-550-8471
Email: *acprod@sbcglobal.net*

Submission Policy: Accepts Query Letter from
unproduced, unrepresented writers
Genre: Memoir & True Stories

Anne Carlucci
Title: Executive Producer
Phone: 310-913-5626
IMDB: *www.imdb.com/name/nm0138243*

ANONYMOUS CONTENT

3532 Hayden Avenue
Culver City, CA 90232

Phone: 310-558-3667
Fax: 310-558-4212
Email: *filmtv@anonymouscontent.com*

Submission Policy: Accepts Query Letter from unproduced, unrepresented writers via email
Genre: Action, Comedy, Crime, Memoir & True Stories, Thriller, TV Drama, TV Sitcom, Family, Drama
Company Focus: Feature Films, TV, Media (Commercials/Branding/Marketing)
Year Established: 1999

Steve Golin
Title: CEO

Matt DeRoss
Title: Vice-President, Features
Email: *mattd@anonymouscontent.com*
IMDB: *www.imdb.com/name/nm2249185*

Emmeline Yang
Title: Director of Development
IMDB: *www.imdb.com/name/nm2534779*

APERTURE ENTERTAINMENT

7620 Lexington Avenue
West Hollywood, CA 90046

Phone: 323-848-4069
Email: *agasst@aperture-ent.com*

Submission Policy: Accepts Scripts from unproduced, unrepresented writers
Genre: Action, Fantasy, Horror, Science Fiction, Thriller
Company Focus: Feature Films, TV
Year Established: 2009

Adam Goldworm
Title: Manager/Producer
Email: *adam@aperture-ent.com*
IMDB: *www.imdb.com/name/nm0326411*
Assistant: David Okubo

APPLE AND HONEY FILM CORP

9190 West Olympic Boulevard, Suite 363
Beverly Hills, CA 90212

Phone: 310-556-5639
Fax: 310-556-1295
Email: *quarrel@pacbell.net*

Submission Policy: Accepts Query Letter from unproduced, unrepresented writers via email

David Brandes
Title: Writer, Producer, Director
IMDB: *www.imdb.com/name/nm0104617*

ARC LIGHT FILMS

8447 Wilshire Boulevard, Suite 101
Beverly Hills, CA 90211

Phone: 310-777-8855
Fax: 310-777-8882
Email: *info@arclightfilms.com*

Submission Policy: Accepts Query Letter from unproduced, unrepresented writers via email
Company Focus: Feature Films

Gary Hamilton

Phone: 310-528-5888
Email: *gary@arclightfilms.com*
IMDB: *www.imdb.com/name/nm0357861*

Mike Gabrawy
Title: Vice-President Creative
Phone: 310-475-2330
Email: *info@arclightfilms.com*
IMDB: *www.imdb.com/name/nm0300166*

John Kim
Title: Development Manager
Phone: 310-777-8855
Email: *john@arclightfilms.com*

ARENAS FILMS

3375 Barham Boulevard
Los Angeles, CA 90068

Phone: 323-785-5555
Fax: 323-785-5560
Email: *general@arenasgroup.com*

Submission Policy: Accepts Query Letter from unproduced, unrepresented writers via email
Year Established: 1988

Katherine Borda
Title: Executive Director of Creative and

Production
IMDB: *www.imdb.com/name/nm3248118*

ARS NOVA

511 West 54th Street
New York, NY 10019

Phone: 212-586-4200
Fax: 212-489-1908
Email: *info@arsnovaent.com*

Submission Policy: Accepts Scripts from unproduced, unrepresented writers
Genre: Action, Comedy, Fantasy, Myth, Science Fiction

Jon Steingart
Title: Producer
Email: *japfelbaum@arsnovaent.com*
IMDB: *www.imdb.com/name/nm0826050*

ARTICLE 19 FILMS

247 Centre Street, Suite 7W
New York, NY 10013

Phone: 212-777-1987
Fax: 212-777-2585
Email: *article19films@gmail.com*

Submission Policy: Accepts Query Letter from unproduced, unrepresented writers
Genre: Memoir & True Stories

Filippo Bozotti
Title: Producer-Executive
IMDB: *www.imdb.com/name/nm1828075*

ARTISTS PRODUCTION GROUP (APG)

9348 Civic Center Drive
2nd Floor
Beverly Hills, CA 90210

Phone: 310-300-2400
Fax: 310-300-2424

Submission Policy: Accepts Scripts from produced or represented writers

Chris George
Title: Creative Executive
IMDB: *www.imdb.com/name/nm0313383*

ASYLUM ENTERTAINMENT

7920 Sunset Boulevard, Second Floor
Los Angeles, CA 90046

Phone: 310-696-4600
Fax: 310-696-4891
Email: *info@asylument.com*

Submission Policy: Accepts Scripts from unproduced, unrepresented writers
Genre: Action, Crime, Fantasy, Horror, Memoir & True Stories, Science Fiction, Thriller, TV Drama

Marielle Skouras
Title: Director of Development
IMDB: *www.imdb.com/name/nm4413245*

ATLAS ENTERTAINMENT (PRODUCTION BRANCH OF MOSAIC)

9200 Sunset Boulevard, 10th Floor
Los Angeles, CA 90069

Phone: 310-786-8900
Fax: 310-777-2185

Submission Policy: Does not accept any unsolicited material
Company Focus: Feature Films, TV

Alex Gartner
Title: Producer
Phone: 310-786-8105
IMDB: *www.imdb.com/name/nm0308672*

Jake Kurily
Title: Director of Development
Phone: 310-786-8974
IMDB: *www.imdb.com/name/nm2464228*

Andy Horwitz
Title: Creative Executive
Phone: 310-786-4948
IMDB: *www.imdb.com/name/nm2191045*

ATLAS MEDIA CORPORATION

242 West 36th Street, 11th Floor
New York, NY, 10018

Phone: 212-714-0222
Fax: 212-714-0240
Email: *info@atlasmediacorp.com*

Submission Policy: Accepts Query Letter from produced or represented writers
Genre: Memoir & True Stories

Glen Freyer
Title: Sr. Vice-President Development
IMDB: *www.imdb.com/name/nm0294662*

ATMOSPHERE ENTERTAINMENT MM, LLC

4751 Wilshire, Boulevard, 3rd Floor
Los Angeles, CA, 90010

Phone: 323-549-4350
Fax: 323-549-9832

Submission Policy: Accepts Scripts from produced or represented writers
Genre: Fantasy, Horror, Thriller

David Hopwood
Title: Sr. Vice-President and TV Development
IMDB: *www.imdb.com/name/nm2055027*

AUTOMATIK ENTERTAINMENT

8322 Beverly Boulevard, Suite 303C
Los Angeles, CA 90048

Phone: 323-677-2486
Fax: 323-657-5354
Email: *info@imglobalfilm.com*

Submission Policy: Does not accept any unsolicited material
Genre: Action, Comedy, Fantasy, Thriller, Socio-cultural
Company Focus: Feature Films, TV

Brian Kavanaugh-Jones
Title: President-Producer
Phone: 323-677-2486
Email: *office@automatikent.com*
IMDB: *www.imdb.com/name/nm2271939*
Assistant: Alex Saks

Bailey Conway
Title: Director of Development
Email: *office@automatikent.com*
IMDB: *www.imdb.com/name/nm2811848*

BAD HAT HARRY

10201 West Pico Boulevard
Building 50
Los Angeles, CA 90064

Phone: 310-369-2080
Email: *reception@badhatharry.com*

Submission Policy: Accepts Scripts from produced or represented writers
Genre: Action, Fantasy, Myth, Science Fiction, Thriller, TV Drama

Bryan Singer
Title: CEO/Producer/Director/Writer
IMDB: *www.imdb.com/name/nm0001741*

BAD ROBOT

1221 Olympic Boulevard
Santa Monica, CA 90404

Phone: 310-664-3456
Fax: 310-664-3457

Submission Policy: Does not accept any unsolicited material
Genre: Action, Fantasy, Science Fiction, TV Drama, Drama
Company Focus: Feature Films, TV

Jon Cohen
Title: Development

BALDWIN ENTERTAINMENT GROUP, LTD.

9200 West Sunset Boulevard
Los Angeles, CA 90069
Email: *info@baldwinent.com*

Submission Policy: Does not accept any unsolicited material
Genre: Action, Comedy, Memoir & True Stories, Romance, Drama
Company Focus: Feature Films
Year Established: 2009

Howard Baldwin
Title: Producer/President
IMDB: *www.imdb.com/name/nm0049920*

Karen Baldwin
Title: Senior Vice-President
IMDB: *www.imdb.com/name/nm0049945*

Ryan Wuerfel
Title: Creative Executive
Email: *ryan@baldwinent.com*
IMDB: *www.imdb.com/name/nm3601274*

BALLYWOOD INC.

6738 Wedgewood Place
Los Angeles, CA 90068

Phone: 323-874-3396

Submission Policy: Accepts Scripts from unproduced, unrepresented writers

Michael Besman
Title: Producer
IMDB: *www.imdb.com/name/nm0078698*

BARNSTORM FILMS

73 Market Street
Venice, CA 90291

Phone: 310-396-5937
Fax: 310-450-4988

Submission Policy: Accepts Query Letter from unproduced, unrepresented writers

Tony Bill
Title: Producer/Director
IMDB: *www.imdb.com/name/nm0082300*

BARNSTORM PICTURES LLC

8524 Fontana Street
Downey, CA 90241

Submission Policy: Does not accept any unsolicited material
Company Focus: Feature Films

Justin Lin
Title: Producer/Director
IMDB: *www.imdb.com/name/nm0510912*

BARRY FILMS

4081 Redwood Avenue
Los Angeles, CA 90066

Phone: 310-871-3392
Email: *anna@barryfilms.com*

Submission Policy: Accepts Query Letter from unproduced, unrepresented writers via email
Genre: Action, Fantasy, Romance, Animation
Company Focus: Feature Films

Benito Mueller
Title: Producer
Email: *benito@barryfilms.com*
IMDB: *www.imdb.com/name/nm1762339*

BARSA ENTERTAINMENT

68-444 Perez Road, Suite O
Cathedral City, CA 92234

Phone: 760-324-9855
Fax: 760-324-9035
Email: *info@basraentertainment.com*

Submission Policy: Accepts Query Letter from unproduced, unrepresented writers
Year Established: 2002

Daniela Ryan
Title: Producer
Email: *daniela@basraentertainment.com*
IMDB: *www.imdb.com/name/nm0752491*

BAUER MARTINEZ INTERNATIONAL

601 Cleveland Street, Suite 501
Clearwater, FL 33755

Phone: 727-210-1408
Fax: 727-210-1470

Submission Policy: Accepts Query Letter from unproduced, unrepresented writers

Phillipe Martinez
Title: Producer/CEO
Email: *cindy@cinepropictures.com*
IMDB: *www.imdb.com/name/nm0553662*

BAZELEVS PRODUCTION

Pudovkina Street
6/1
Moscow 119285

Phone: +7 495-223-04-00
Email: *film@bazelevs.ru*

Submission Policy: Does not accept any unsolicited material
Company Focus: Feature Films

Timur Bekmambetov
Title: CEO/Director/Producer
IMDB: *www.imdb.com/name/nm0067457*

BBC FILMS

BBC Television Centre
Wood Lane
London W12 7RJ
United Kingdom

Phone: +44 20-8576-7265
Fax: +44 20-8576-7268

Submission Policy: Accepts Scripts from unproduced, unrepresented writers
Genre: Action, Comedy, Crime, Detective, Fantasy, Horror, Memoir & True Stories, Myth, Romance, Science Fiction, Thriller, TV Drama, TV Sitcom
Company Focus: Feature Films, TV

Ben Stephenson
Title: Head of Drama Commisioning
IMDB: *www.imdb.com/name/nm1254318*

Kate Harwood
Title: Head of Series and Serials
IMDB: *www.imdb.com/name/nm0367825*

Anne Gilchrist
Title: Creative Director
IMDB: *www.imdb.com/name/nm1369889*

BELLADONNA PRODUCTIONS

164 West 25th Street 9th Floor
New York, NY 10001

Phone: 212-807-0108
Fax: 212-807-6263
Email: *mail@belladonna.bz*

Submission Policy: Accepts Query Letter from unproduced, unrepresented writers
Genre: Comedy, Memoir & True Stories, Thriller
Year Established: 1994

René Bastian
Title: Owner/Producer
IMDB: *www.imdb.com/name/nm0060459*

BELLWETHER PICTURES

Submission Policy: Accepts Query Letter from unproduced, unrepresented writers via email
Genre: Action, Comedy, Science Fiction, Drama
Company Focus: Feature Films, Media
Year Established: 2011

Joss Whedon
Title: Writer/Producer/Co-Founder
IMDB: *www.imdb.com/name/nm0923736*

Kai Cole
Title: Producer/Co-Founder
IMDB: *www.imdb.com/name/nm4740874*

Daniel S. Kaminsky
Title: Creative Executive
IMDB: *www.imdb.com/name/nm3354467*

BENAROYA PICTURES

311 North Robertson Boulevard, Suite 686
Beverly Hills, CA 90211

Phone: 323-883-0056
Fax: 866-220-5520
Email: *general@benaroyapics.com*

Submission Policy: Accepts Query Letter from unproduced, unrepresented writers via email
Genre: Drama
Company Focus: Feature Films
Year Established: 2006

Michael Benaroya
Title: Founder-CEO
IMDB: *www.imdb.com/name/nm2918260*

Joe Jenckes
Title: Head of Production
Email: *joel@benaroyapics.com*
IMDB: *www.imdb.com/name/nm3765270*

Clayton Young
Title: Business Development
Email: *clay@benaroyapics.com*
IMDB: *www.imdb.com/name/nm4464240*

BENDERSPINK

5870 West Jefferson Boulevard, Studio E
Los Angeles, CA 90016

Phone: 323-904-1800
Fax: 323-297-2442
Email: *info@benderspink.com*

Submission Policy: Does not accept any unsolicited material
Genre: Action, Comedy, Crime, Detective, Fantasy, Horror, Memoir & True Stories, Myth, Romance, Science Fiction, Thriller, TV Drama, TV Sitcom

Chris Bender
Title: Founder
IMDB: *www.imdb.com/name/nm0070454*

J.C. Spink
Title: Founder
IMDB: *www.imdb.com/name/nm0818940*

BERK LANE ENTERTAINMENT

9595 Wilshire Boulevard, Suitee 900
Beverly Hills, CA 90212

Phone: 310-300-8410

Submission Policy: Does not accept any unsolicited material
Genre: Action, Comedy, Crime

Jason Berk
Title: Co-Chairman
IMDB: *www.imdb.com/name/nm1357809*

BERLANTI TELEVISION

500 South Buena Vista Street
Old Animation Building, 2B-5
Burbank, CA 91521

Phone: 818-560-4536
Fax: 818-560-3931

Submission Policy: Accepts Query Letter from unproduced, unrepresented writers
Genre: TV Drama

Greg Berlanti
Title: Writer-Producer-Director
IMDB: *www.imdb.com/name/nm0075528*

BERMANBRAUN

2900 West Olympic Boulevard, 3rd Floor
Sanata Monica, CA, 90404

Phone: 310-255-7272
Fax: 310-255-7058
Email: *info@bermanbraun.com*

Submission Policy: Does not accept any unsolicited material

Chris Cowan
Title: Executive, Head of Unscripted Television
Phone: 310-255-7272
IMDB: *www.imdb.com/name/nm0184544*

Andrew Mittman
Title: Executive, Head of Feature Film
Phone: 310-255-7272
IMDB: *www.imdb.com/name/nm3879410*

BERNERO PRODUCTIONS

500 South Buena Vista Street
Animation Building 2D-4
Burbank, CA 91521

Phone: 818-560-1442
Email: *info@berneroproductions.com*

Submission Policy: Accepts Query Letter from unproduced, unrepresented writers via email

Bob Kim
Title: Producer
IMDB: *www.imdb.com/name/nm2344755*

BETH GROSSBARD PRODUCTIONS

5168 Otis Avenue
Tarzana, CA 91356

Phone: 818-758-2500
Fax: 818-705-7366
Email: *bgpix@sbcglobal.net*

Submission Policy: Accepts Query Letter from produced or represented writers
Genre: TV Drama, TV Sitcom

Beth Grossbard
Title: Executive Producer
Email: *Kerry@capix.com*
IMDB: *www.imdb.com/name/nm0343526*

BIG FOOT ENTERTAINMENT INC.

1214 Abbot Kinney Boulevard
Los Angeles, CA 90291

Phone: 310-593-4646
Email: *info@bigfoot.com*

Submission Policy: Accepts Query Letter from unproduced, unrepresented writers via email
Genre: Action, Fantasy, Myth, Science Fiction, Thriller, Animation, Drama
Company Focus: Feature Films, TV
Year Established: 2004

Ashley Jordan
Title: CEO
Email: *ashley@bigfootcorp.com*
IMDB: *www.imdb.com/name/nm1248442*

BIG TALK PRODUCTIONS

26 Nassau Street
London
W1W 7AQ

Phone: +44 (0) 20-7255-1131
Fax: +44 (0) 20-7255-1132
Email: *info@bigtalkproductions.com*

Submission Policy: Does not accept any unsolicited material
Genre: Action, Comedy, Crime, Science Fiction, TV Drama, TV Sitcom

Rachael Prior
Title: Head of Development—Fim
IMDB: *www.imdb.com/name/nm0975099*

BIRCH TREE ENTERTAINMENT INC.

10620 Southern Highlands Parkway
Suite 110-418
Las Vegas, NV 89141

Phone: 702-858-2782
Fax: 702-583-7928

Submission Policy: Accepts Scripts from produced or represented writers
Genre: Action
Company Focus: Feature Films

Art Birzneck
Title: President/CEO
IMDB: *www.imdb.com/name/nm1010723*

BISCAYNE PICTURES

500 South Buena Vista Street
Animation Building
Burbank, CA 91521-1802

Phone: 310-777-2007
Email: *info@biscaynepictures.com*

Submission Policy: Accepts Query Letter from unproduced, unrepresented writers via email

Jeff Silver
Title: President-Producer
IMDB: *www.imdb.com/name/nm0798711*

BIX PIX ENTERTAINMENT

3511 West Burbank Boulevard
Burbank, CA 91505

Phone: 818-953-7474
Fax: 818-953-9948
Email: *info@bixpix.com*

Submission Policy: Accepts Query Letter from unproduced, unrepresented writers
Genre: Fantasy
Year Established: 1998

Kelli Bixler
Title: Founder/President/Executive Producer
IMDB: *www.imdb.com/name/nm1064778*

BLACK SHEEP ENTERTAINMENT

11271 Ventura Boulevard, #447
Studio City, CA 91604

Phone: 310-424-5085
Fax: 310-424-7117

Submission Policy: Accepts Query Letter from unproduced, unrepresented writers
Year Established: 2009

Steven Feder
Title: Owner/Writer/Producer/Director
Email: *steven@blacksheepent.com*
IMDB: *www.imdb.com/name/nm0270090*

BLACKLIGHT TRANSMEDIA

9465 Wilshire Boulevard
Beverly Hills, CA 90212

Phone: 310-858-2196
Email: *info@blacklighttransmedia.com*

Submission Policy: Accepts Scripts from produced or represented writers
Company Focus: Feature Films

Zak Kadison
Title: Founder/CEO
IMDB: *www.imdb.com/name/nm1780162*

Justin Catron
Title: Creative Executive
IMDB: *www.imdb.com/name/nm2031037*

BLEIBERG ENTERTAINMENT

225 South Clark Drive
Beverly Hills, CA 90211

Phone: 310-273-0003
Fax: 310-273-0007
Email: *info@bleibergent.com*

Submission Policy: Accepts Query Letter from unproduced, unrepresented writers via email
Company Focus: Feature Films, TV

Ehud Bleiberg
Title: CEO/Founder
Email: *ehud@bleibergent.com*
IMDB: *www.imdb.com/name/nm0088173*

Nicholas Donnermeyer
Title: Vice-President Acquisitions & Development
Email: *nick@bleibergent.com*
IMDB: *www.imdb.com/name/nm2223730*

BLUE SKY STUDIOS

One American Lane
Greenwich, CT 06831

Phone: 203-992-6000
Fax: 203-992-6001
Email: *info@blueskystudios.com*

Submission Policy: Does not accept any unsolicited material
Company Focus: Feature Films
Year Established: 1997

Chris Wedge
Title: Vice-President
Phone: 203-992-6000
IMDB: *www.imdb.com/name/nm0917188*

BLUEGRASS FILMS

100 Universal City Plaza
Bungalow 4171
Universal City, CA 91608

Phone: 818-777-3200

Submission Policy: Accepts Scripts from produced or represented writers
Genre: Action, Crime, Fantasy, Romance, Science Fiction, Thriller, Drama
Company Focus: Feature Films, TV

Scott Stuber
Title: Producer
IMDB: *www.imdb.com/name/nm0835959*

Michael Clear
Title: Creative Executive
Email: *michael.clear@univfilms.com*
IMDB: *www.imdb.com/name/nm2752795*

Nicholas Nesbitt
Title: Creative Executive
Email: *nicholas.nesbitt@univfilms.com*

BLUEPRINT PICTURES

43-45 Charlotte Street
London W1T 1RS
United Kingdom

Phone: +44 0207-580-6915
Fax: +44 0207-580-6934
Email: *asst@blueprintpictures.com*

Submission Policy: Does not accept any unsolicited material
Year Established: 2004

Graham Broadbent
Title: Producer
IMDB: *www.imdb.com/name/nm0110357*

BLUMHOUSE PRODUCTIONS

5555 Melrose Avenue
Lucy Bungalow 103
Los Angeles, CA 90038

Phone: 323-956-4480

Submission Policy: Accepts Query Letter from unproduced, unrepresented writers
Genre: Action, Horror, Thriller
Year Established: 2000

Jason Blum
Title: Producer
IMDB: *www.imdb.com/name/nm0089658*

BOBKER/KRUGAR FILMS

1416 North La Brea Avenue
Hollywood, CA 90028

Phone: 323-469-1440

Submission Policy: Accepts Query Letter from unproduced, unrepresented writers

Daniel Bobker
Title: Producer
IMDB: *www.imdb.com/name/nm0090394*

BOGNER ENTERTAINMENT

269 South Beverly Drive, Suite 8
Beverly Hills, CA 90212

Phone: 310-553-0300
Email: *info.beitv@gmail.com*

Submission Policy: Accepts Scripts from unproduced, unrepresented writers
Genre: Horror, Thriller
Year Established: 2000

Oliver Bogner
Title: Vice-President Development & Casting
Email: *oliverbogner@gmail.com*
IMDB: *www.imdb.com/name/nm3331124*

BOKU FILMS

1438 North Gower Street
Box 87
Hollywood, CA 90028

Phone: 323-860-7710
Fax: 323-860-7706

Submission Policy: Does not accept any unsolicited material
Genre: Thriller, TV Drama

Alan Poul
Title: Producer/Director
IMDB: *www.imdb.com/name/nm0693561*

BOLD FILMS

6464 Sunset Boulevard, Suite 800
Los Angeles, CA 90028

Phone: 323-769-8900
Fax: 323-769-8954
Email: *info@boldfilms.com*

Submission Policy: Does not accept any unsolicited material
Genre: Action, Fantasy, Horror, Thriller
Company Focus: Feature Films, TV

Jon Oakes
Title: Vice-President of Development
IMDB: *www.imdb.com/name/nm1198333*

Garrick Dion
Title: Senior Vice-President of Development
IMDB: *www.imdb.com/name/nm1887182*

Stephanie Wilcox
Title: Creative Executive
IMDB: *www.imdb.com/name/nm3432545*

BONA FIDE PRODUCTIONS

8899 Beverly Boulevard, Suite 804
Los Angeles, CA 90048

Phone: 310-273-6782
Fax: 310-273-7821

Submission Policy: Accepts Query Letter from unproduced, unrepresented writers
Company Focus: Feature Films
Year Established: 1993

Albert Berger
Title: Producer
IMDB: *www.imdb.com/name/nm0074100*

BOSS MEDIA

9440 Santa Monica Boulevard, Suite 400
Beverly Hills, CA 90210

Phone: 310-205-9900
Fax: 310-205-9909

Submission Policy: Does not accept any

unsolicited material

Frank Mancuso, Jr.
Title: President
IMDB: *www.imdb.com/name/nm0541548*

BOXING CAT PRODUCTIONS

11500 Hart Street
North Hollywood, CA 91605

Phone: 818-765-4870
Fax: 818-765-4975

Submission Policy: Accepts Query Letter from
unproduced, unrepresented writers via email
Genre: Comedy, Family
Company Focus: Feature Films, TV

Tim Allen
Title: Actor/Producer
IMDB: *www.imdb.com/name/nm0000741*

Matt Carroll
Email: *matt.carroll@disney.com*

BOY WONDER PRODUCTIONS

68 Jay Street, Suite 423
Brooklyn, NY 11201

Phone: 347-632-2961
Fax: 347-332-6953
Email: *info@boywonderproductions.net*

Submission Policy: Accepts Query Letter from
unproduced, unrepresented writers via email
Genre: Action, Memoir & True Stories, TV
Drama, TV Sitcom
Year Established: 2006

Michael Morrissey
Title: President/Producer
IMDB: *www.imdb.com/name/nm3155184*

BOZ PRODUCTIONS

1822 Camino Palmero
Los Angeles, CA 90046-2202

Phone: 323-876-3232

Submission Policy: Accepts Query Letter from
unproduced, unrepresented writers

Bo Zenga
Title: Writer/Director/Producer
Email: *bozenga@sbcglobal.net*
IMDB: *www.imdb.com/name/nm0954848*

BRANDED FILMS

4000 Warner Boulevard
Building 139, Suite 107
Burbank, CA 91522

Phone: 818-954-7969
Email: *info@branded-films.com*

Submission Policy: Does not accept any
unsolicited material
Genre: Comedy
Company Focus: Feature Films, TV
Year Established: 2011

Russell Brand
Title: Founder/Actor/Producer
IMDB: *www.imdb.com/name/nm1258970*
Assistant: Lee Sacks

Nik Linnen
Title: Partner-Producer
IMDB: *www.imdb.com/name/nm3800556*

Beau Bauman
Title: President
Email: *beau@branded-films.com*
IMDB: *www.imdb.com/name/nm0062149*

BRANDMAN PRODUCTIONS

2062 North Vine Street, Suite 5
Los Angeles, CA 90068

Phone: 323-463-3224
Fax: 323-463-0852

Submission Policy: Accepts Query Letter from
unproduced, unrepresented writers

Michael Bradman
Title: President/Producer
IMDB: *www.imdb.com/name/nm0104701*

BRIGHTLIGHT PICTURES

The Bridge Studios
2400 Boundary Road
Burnaby, BC V5M 3Z3
Canada

Phone: 604-628-3000
Fax: 604-628-3001
Email: *info@brightlightpictures.com*

Submission Policy: Does not accept any unsolicited material
Genre: Comedy, Drama
Company Focus: Feature Films, TV
Year Established: 2001

Stephen Hegyes
Title: Co-Chairman/Producer
IMDB: *www.imdb.com/name/nm0373812*

Shawn Williamson
Title: Co-Chairman/Producer
IMDB: *www.imdb.com/name/nm0932144*

Stephanie Swedlove
Title: Creative Executive
Email: *stephanie@brightlightpictures.com*
IMDB: *www.imdb.com/name/nm2801861*

BURLEIGH FILMWORKS

22287 Mulholland Highway, Suite 129
Calabasas, CA 91302

Phone: 818-224-4686
Fax: 818-223-9089

Submission Policy: Accepts Query Letter from unproduced, unrepresented writers

Steve Burleigh
Email: *steve.burleigh@burleighfilmworks.com*
IMDB: *www.imdb.com/name/nm0122114*

BURNSIDE ENTERTAINMENT INC.

2424 North Ontario Street
Burbank, CA 91504

Phone: 818-565-5986
Email: *mail@burnsideentertainment.com*

Submission Policy: Accepts Query Letter from unproduced, unrepresented writers

Glen Trotiner
Title: Producer/Partner
IMDB: *www.imdb.com/name/nm0873641*

CAMELOT ENTERTAINMENT GROUP

10 Universal City Plaza
NBC/Universal Building, Floor 20
Universal City, CA 91608

Phone: 818-308-8858
Fax: 818-308-8848
Email: *submissions@camelotfilms.com*

Submission Policy: Accepts Scripts from unproduced, unrepresented writers
Genre: Action, Comedy, Horror, Thriller

Ryan Keller
Title: Sales Assistant
IMDB: *www.imdb.com/name/nm2418352*

CAMELOT PICTURES

9255 Sunset Boulevard, Suite 711
Los Angeles, CA 90069

Phone: 310-288-3000
Fax: 310-288-3054
Email: *info@camelot-pictures.com*

Submission Policy: Accepts Query Letter from unproduced, unrepresented writers via email
Genre: Comedy, Family, Drama
Company Focus: Feature Films

Gary Gilbert
Title: President
IMDB: *www.imdb.com/name/nm1344784*

Jordan Horowitz
Title: Vice-President, Production and Development
IMDB: *www.imdb.com/name/nm0395302*

CAPITAL ARTS ENTERTAINMENT

23315 Clifton Plaza
Valencia, CA 91354

Phone: 818-343-8950
Fax: 818-343-8962
Email: *info@capitalarts.com*

Submission Policy: Accepts Query Letter from unproduced, unrepresented writers via email
Genre: Action, Comedy, Horror, Thriller
Year Established: 1995

Mike Elliot
Title: Partner/Producer
IMDB: *www.imdb.com/name/nm0254291*

CAPTIVATE ENTERTAINMENT

100 Universal City Plaza
Bungalow 4111
Universal City, CA 91608

Phone: 818-777-6711
Fax: 818-733-4303

Submission Policy: Does not accept any
unsolicited material
Genre: Action, Comedy, Fantasy, Myth,
Romance, Science Fiction, Thriller, Drama
Company Focus: Feature Films, TV

Jeffrey M. Weiner
Title: Chairman/CEO
IMDB: *www.imdb.com/name/nm1788648*

Ben Smith
Title: Producer
IMDB: *www.imdb.com/name/nm3328356*

Tony Shaw
Title: Creative Executive
Email: *tony.shaw@univfilms.com*
IMDB: *www.imdb.com/name/nm4130192*

CASEY SILVER PRODUCTIONS

506 Santa Monica Boulevard, Suite 322
Santa Monica, CA 90401

Phone: 310-566-3750
Fax: 310-566-3751

Submission Policy: Does not accept any
unsolicited material
Genre: Action, Comedy, Thriller, Family,
Drama
Company Focus: Feature Films

Casey Silver
Title: Chairman
Email: *casey@caseysilver.com*
IMDB: *www.imdb.com/name/nm0798661*

Matthew Reynolds
Title: Creative Executive
Email: *matthew@caseysilver.com*
IMDB: *www.imdb.com/name/nm2303863*

CASTLE ROCK ENTERTAINMENT

335 North Maple Drive, Suite 350
Beverly Hills, CA 90210-3867

Phone: 310-285-2300
Fax: 310-285-2345

Submission Policy: Accepts Scripts from
produced or represented writers

Rob Reiner
Title: Director/Producer/Writer
Email: *rob.reiner@castle-rock.com*
IMDB: *www.imdb.com/name/nm0001661*

CATAPULT FILMS

832 Third Street, Suite 303
Santa Monica, CA 90403-1155

Phone: 310-395-1470
Fax: 310-401-0122

Submission Policy: Accepts Scripts from
produced or represented writers

Lisa Josefsberg
Title: Producer
IMDB: *www.imdb.com/name/nm2248853*

CELADOR FILMS

39 Long Acre
London, WC2E 9LG
United Kingdom

Phone: +44 20-7845-6800
Fax: +44 20-7845-6801

Submission Policy: Accepts Scripts from
produced or represented writers
Year Established: 1989

Paul Smith
Title: Chairman/Executive Producer
Email: *psmith@celador.co.uk*
IMDB: *www.imdb.com/name/nm0809531*

CENTROPOLIS ENTERTAINMENT

1445 North Stanley
3rd Floor
Los Angeles, CA 90046

Phone: 323-850-1212
Fax: 323-850-1201
Email: *info@centropolis.com*

Submission Policy: Accepts Scripts from produced or represented writers
Genre: Action, Fantasy, Memoir & True Stories, Myth, Romance
Year Established: 1985

Roland Emmerich
Title: Partner/Producer
IMDB: *www.imdb.com/name/nm0000386*

Ute Emmerich
Title: Partner/Producer
IMDB: *www.imdb.com/name/nm0256498*

CHAIKEN FILMS

802 Potrero Avenue
San Francisco, CA 94110

Phone: 415-826-7880
Fax: 415-826-7882
Email: *info@chaikenfilms.com*

Submission Policy: Accepts Query Letter from unproduced, unrepresented writers
Genre: Memoir & True Stories
Year Established: 1998

Jennifer Chaiken
Title: Producer
Email: *jen@chaikenfilms.com*
IMDB: *www.imdb.com/name/nm0149671*

CHARTOFF PRODUCTIONS

1250 Sixth Street, Suite 101
Santa Monica, CA 90401

Phone: 310-319-1960
Fax: 310-319-3469
Email: *chartoffprod@cs.com*

Submission Policy: Accepts Scripts from produced or represented writers
Year Established: 1986

Robert Chartoff
Title: CEO/Producer
IMDB: *www.imdb.com/name/nm0153590*

CHERNIN ENTERTAINMENT

1733 Ocean Avenue, Suite 300
Santa Monica, CA 90401

Phone: 310-899-1205

Submission Policy: Accepts Scripts from produced or represented writers
Genre: Action, Comedy, TV Drama, TV Sitcom
Company Focus: Feature Films
Year Established: 2009

Peter Chernin
Title: Principle
IMDB: *www.imdb.com/name/nm1858656*

Dylan Clark
Email: *dc@cherninent.com*
IMDB: *www.imdb.com/name/nm1249995*

Jenno Topping
Title: Executive Vice-President
Email: *jt@cherninent.com*
IMDB: *www.imdb.com/name/nm0867768*

CHESTNUT RIDGE PRODUCTIONS

8899 Beverly Boulevard, Suite 800
Los Angeles, CA

Phone: 310-285-7011

Submission Policy: Does not accept any unsolicited material
Year Established: 2009

Paula Wagner
Title: Owner/Producer
IMDB: *www.imdb.com/name/nm0906048*

CHEYENNE ENTERPRISES LLC

406 Wilshire Boulevard
Santa Monica, CA 90401

Phone: 310-455-5000
Fax: 310-688-8000

Submission Policy: Accepts Scripts from produced or represented writers
Year Established: 2000

Arnold Rifkin
Title: President/Producer
IMDB: *www.imdb.com/name/nm0726476*

CHICAGO FILMS

101 Fith Avenue
8th Floor
New York, NY 10003

Phone: 212-645-3000
Fax: 212-645-3014

Submission Policy: Accepts Scripts from produced or represented writers

Bob Balaban
Title: Actor/Producer
IMDB: *www.imdb.com/name/nm0000837*

CHICKFLICKS

8861 St Ives Drive
Los Angeles, CA 90069

Phone: 310-854-7210
Email: *info@chickflicksinc.com*

Submission Policy: Accepts Scripts from produced or represented writers
Genre: Comedy, Fantasy, Memoir & True Stories, Myth, Romance

Sara Risher
Title: Partner/Producer
Phone: 310-854-7210
Email: *sara@chickflicksinc.com*
IMDB: *www.imdb.com/name/nm0728260*

CHOTZEN/JENNER PRODUCTIONS

1626 North Wilcox Avenue, Ste1381
Hollywood, CA 90028

Phone: 323-465-9877
Fax: 323-460-6451

Submission Policy: Accepts Scripts from produced or represented writers
Genre: TV Drama, TV Sitcom
Year Established: 1990

Yvonne E. Chotzen
Title: Producer/Partner
IMDB: *www.imdb.com/name/nm0159278*

William Jenner
Title: Producer/Partner
IMDB: *www.imdb.com/name/nm0421076*

CHRIS/ROSE PRODUCTIONS

3131 Torreyson Place
Los Angeles, CA 90046

Phone: 310-418-1017
Email: *crproductions@att.net*

Submission Policy: Accepts Scripts from produced or represented writers
Genre: Memoir & True Stories, TV Drama, TV Sitcom

Robert W. Christiansen
Title: Executive Producer
Phone: 310-781-0833
IMDB: *www.imdb.com/name/nm0160222*

CHUBBCO FILMCO

373 North Kenter Avenue
Los Angeles, CA 90049

Phone: 310-729-5858
Fax: 310-933-1704

Submission Policy: Does not accept any unsolicited material
Genre: Action, Crime, Memoir & True Stories

Caldecot Chubb
Title: Producer
Email: *chubbco@gmail.com*
IMDB: *www.imdb.com/name/nm0160941*

CHUCK FRIES

9903 Santa Monica Boulevard, Suite 870
Beverly Hills, CA 90212

Phone: 310-203-9520
Fax: 310-203-9519

Submission Policy: Accepts Scripts from produced or represented writers
Genre: Crime, Detective

Charles W. Fries
Title: Chairman/President/CEO
IMDB: *www.imdb.com/name/nm0295594*

CINDY COWAN ENTERTAINMENT, INC.

8265 West Sunset Boulevard, Suite 205
Los Angeles, CA 90046

Phone: 323-822-1082
Fax: 323-822-1086
Email: *info@cowanent.com*

Submission Policy: Accepts Scripts from produced or represented writers
Year Established: 1999

Cindy Cowan
Title: President
IMDB: *www.imdb.com/name/nm0184546*

CINE MOSAIC

130 West 25th Street, 12th Floor
New York, NY 10001

Phone: 212-625-3797
Fax: 212-625-3571
Email: *info@cinemosaic.net*

Submission Policy: Accepts Scripts from produced or represented writers
Genre: Action, Memoir & True Stories, TV Drama
Year Established: 2002

Lydia Dean Pilcher
Title: Independent Producer/Founder
IMDB: *www.imdb.com/name/nm0212990*

CINEMA EPHOCH

10 Universal City Plaza, 20th Floor
Universal City, CA 91608

Phone: 818-753-2345
Email: *acquisitions@cinemaepoch.com*

Submission Policy: Accepts Query Letter from unproduced, unrepresented writers
Genre: Action, Comedy, Crime, Detective, Horror, Memoir & True Stories, Myth, Thriller
Year Established: 2001

Gregory Hatanaka
Title: President/Distributor/Producer
IMDB: *www.imdb.com/name/nm0368693*

CINEMA LIBRE STUDIO

8328 De Soto Avenue
Canoga Park, CA 91304

Phone: 818-349-8822
Fax: 818-349-9922
Email: *project@CinemaLibreStudio.com*

Submission Policy: Accepts Query Letter from unproduced, unrepresented writers
Year Established: 2003

Philippe Diaz
Title: Producer/Owner
IMDB: *www.imdb.com/name/nm0225034*

CINEMAGIC ENTERTAINMENT

9229 Sunset Boulevard, Suite 610
West Hollywood, CA 90069

Phone: 310-385-9322
Fax: 310-385-9347

Submission Policy: Accepts Query Letter from unproduced, unrepresented writers
Genre: Action, Crime, Detective, Fantasy, Horror, Myth, Science Fiction, Thriller

Lee Cohn
Title: Vice-President, Development

CINETELE FILMS

8255 Sunset Boulevard
Los Angeles, CA 90046

Phone: 323-654-4000
Fax: 323-650-6400
Email: *info@cinetelfilms.com*

Submission Policy: Does not accept any unsolicited material
Genre: Crime, Horror, Thriller, TV Drama
Year Established: 1985

Paul Hertzberg
Title: President/CEO
IMDB: *www.imdb.com/name/nm0078473*

CINEVILLE

3400 Airport Avenue
Santa Monica, CA 90405

Phone: 310-397-7150
Fax: 310-397-7155
Email: *info@cineville.com*

Submission Policy: Accepts Query Letter from

unproduced, unrepresented writers
Genre: Comedy, Memoir & True Stories, Romance
Year Established: 1990

Carl Colpaert
Title: Partner
IMDB: *www.imdb.com/name/nm0173207*

CIRCLE OF CONFUSION PRODUCTIONS

8548 Washington Boulevard
Culver City, CA 90232

Phone: 310-253-7777
Fax: 310-253-9065
Email: *queries@circleofconfusion.com*

Submission Policy: Accepts Query Letter from unproduced, unrepresented writers
Genre: Action, Comedy, Crime, Detective, Fantasy, Horror, Memoir & True Stories, Myth, Romance, Science Fiction, Thriller, TV Drama, TV Sitcom

Stephen Emery
Title: Executive Vice-President Production and Development
Email: *stephen@circleofconfusion.com*
IMDB: *www.imdb.com/name/nm1765323*

CITY ENTERTAINMENT

266 1/2 South Rexford Drive
Beverly Hills, CA 90212

Phone: 310-273-3101
Fax: 310-273-3676

Submission Policy: Does not accept any unsolicited material

Joshua D. Maurer
Title: President/Producer
IMDB: *www.imdb.com/name/nm0561027*

CLASS 5 FILMS

200 Park Avenue South
8th Floor
New York, NY 10003

Phone: 917-414-9404

Submission Policy: Accepts Query Letter from

produced or represented writers

Edward Norton
Title: Producer/Actor/Director/Writer
IMDB: *www.imdb.com/name/nm0001570*

CLEAR PICTURES ENTERTAINMENT

12400 Ventura Boulevard, Suite 306
Studio City, CA 91604

Phone: 818-980-5460
Fax: 818-980-4716
Email: *clearpicturesinc@aol.com*

Submission Policy: Accepts Query Letter from unproduced, unrepresented writers via email
Genre: Memoir & True Stories, TV Drama, Drama, Socio-cultural
Company Focus: Feature Films, TV
Year Established: 2009

Elizabeth Fowler
Title: Principle
IMDB: *www.imdb.com/name/nm2085583*

CLEARVIEW PRODUCTIONS

1180 South Beverly Drive, Suite 700
Los Angeles, CA 90035

Phone: 310-271-7698
Fax: 310-278-9978

Submission Policy: Does not accept any unsolicited material

Albert S. Ruddy
Title: Producer
IMDB: *www.imdb.com/name/nm0748665*

CLIFFORD WERBER PRODUCTIONS

232 South Beverly Drive, Suite 224
Beverly Hills, CA 90212

Phone: 310-288-0900
Fax: 310-288-0600

Submission Policy: Accepts Query Letter from produced or represented writers

Clifford Werber
Title: Producer
IMDB: *www.imdb.com/name/nm0921222*

CLOSED ON MONDAYS ENTERTAINMENT

4024 Radford Avenue
CBS Bungalow #1
Studio City, CA 91604

Phone: 818-655-7450

Submission Policy: Does not accept any
unsolicited material
Year Established: 2003

Joe Nozemack
Title: Prodocer/Co-founder
IMDB: *www.imdb.com/name/nm1060496*

CLOUD EIGHT FILMS

39 Long Acre
London WC2E 9LG
United Kingdom

Phone: +44 20-7845-6877

Submission Policy: Accepts Scripts from
produced or represented writers
Year Established: 2009

Christian Colson
Title: Chairman/Producer
Phone: +44 20 7845 6988
IMDB: *www.imdb.com/name/nm1384503*

CODE ENTERTAINMENT

9229 Sunset Boulevard, Suite 615
Los Angeles, CA 90069

Phone: 310-772-0008
Fax: 310-772-0006
Email: *contact@codeentertainment.com*

Submission Policy: Accepts Scripts from
produced or represented writers
Year Established: 2005

Bart Rosenblatt
Title: Producer
Phone: 310-772-0008 ext. 3
IMDB: *www.imdb.com/name/nm0742386*

CODEBLACK ENTERTAINMENT

111 Universal Hollywood Dr, Suite 2260
Universal City, CA 91608

Phone: 818-286-8600
Fax: 818-286-8649
Email: *info@codeblackentertainment.com*

Submission Policy: Does not accept any
unsolicited material
Year Established: 2005

Jeff Clanagan
Title: CEO
IMDB: *www.imdb.com/name/nm0163335*

COLLEEN CAMP PRODUCTIONS

6464 Sunset Boulevard, Suite 800
Los Angeles, CA 90028

Phone: 323-463-1434
Fax: 323-463-4379
Email: *asst@ccprods.com*

Submission Policy: Accepts Query Letter from
unproduced, unrepresented writers

Colleen Camp
Title: Producer
IMDB: *www.imdb.com/name/nm0131974*

COLOR FORCE

1524 Cloverfield Boulevard, Suite C
Santa Monica, CA 90404

Phone: 310-828-0641
Fax: 310-828-0672

Submission Policy: Accepts Query Letter from
unproduced, unrepresented writers
Genre: Action, Comedy
Year Established: 2007

Nina Jacobson
Title: Producer
Email: *nina.jacobson@colorforce.com*
IMDB: *www.imdb.com/name/nm1749221*

COLOSSAL ENTERTAINMENT

PO Box 461010
Los Angeles, CA 90046

Phone: 323-656-6647
Email: *clsslent@aol.com*

Submission Policy: Accepts Query Letter from
unproduced, unrepresented writers

Kelly Rowan
Title: Producer
IMDB: *www.imdb.com/name/nm0746414*

COLUCCI FILMS/ZIEGER PRODUCTIONS

Phone: 310-476-1679
Fax: 310-476-7928

Submission Policy: Accepts Query Letter from unproduced, unrepresented writers

Michele Colucci Zieger
Title: Producer
IMDB: *www.imdb.com/name/nm1024135*

COMEDY ARTS STUDIOS

2500 Broadway
Santa Monica, CA 90404

Phone: 310-382-3677
Fax: 310-382-3170

Submission Policy: Accepts Query Letter from unproduced, unrepresented writers
Genre: TV Drama, TV Sitcom

Stu Smiley
Title: Owner/Executive Producer
IMDB: *www.imdb.com/name/nm0806979*

COMPLETION FILMS

60 East 42nd Street, Suite 4600
New York, NY 10165

Phone: 718-693-2057
Fax: 888-693-4133
Email: *info@completionfilms.com*

Submission Policy: Accepts Query Letter from unproduced, unrepresented writers
Genre: Memoir & True Stories

Kisha Cameron-Dingle
Title: President

CONCEPT ENTERTAINMENT

334 1/2 North Sierra Bonita Avenue
Los Angeles, CA 90036

Phone: 323-937-5700
Email: *enquiries@conceptentertainment.biz*

Submission Policy: Accepts Query Letter from unproduced, unrepresented writers
Genre: Action, Comedy, Crime, Detective, Fantasy, Horror, Memoir & True Stories, Myth, Romance, Science Fiction, Thriller, TV Drama, TV Sitcom

David Faigenblum
Title: Producer/Manager
IMDB: *www.imdb.com/name/nm1584960*

CONSTATIN FILM

US Office:
9200 West Sunset Boulevard, Suite 800
West Hollywood, CA 90069

European Office:
Feilitzschstr. 6
Munich, Bavaria D-80802
Germany

Phone: 310-247-0300
Fax: 310-247-0305
Email: *zentrale@constantin-film.de*

Submission Policy: Accepts Query Letter from produced or represented writers
Year Established: 1950

Robert Kultzer
Title: Executive
Phone: 310-247-0300 ext. 3
Email: *robert.kultzer@constantin-film.de*
IMDB: *www.imdb.com/name/nm0474709*

CONTENT MEDIA CORPORATION PLC

225 Arizona Ave, Suite #250
Santa Monica
CA 90401

Phone: 310-576-1059
Fax: 310-576-1859
Email: *scriptsubmissions@contentmediacorp.com*

Submission Policy: Accepts Query Letter from unproduced, unrepresented writers

Jamie Carmichael
Title: President, Film Division
Email: *jamie.carmichael@contentmediacorp.com*
IMDB: *www.imdb.com/name/nm0138430*

CONUNDRUM ENTERTAINMENT

325 Wilshire Boulevard, Suite 201
Santa Monica, CA 90401

Phone: 310-319-2800
Fax: 310-319-2808

Submission Policy: Accepts Scripts from
produced or represented writers
Genre: Comedy

Peter Farrelly
Title: President
IMDB: *www.imdb.com/name/nm0268380*

COOPER'S TOWN PRODUCTIONS

302A West 12th Street, Suite 214
New York, NY 10014

Phone: 212-255-7566
Fax: 212-255-0211
Email: *info@copperstownproductions.com*

Submission Policy: Accepts Query Letter from
unproduced, unrepresented writers
Genre: Memoir & True Stories
Company Focus: Feature Films

Phillip Seymour Hoffman
Title: Partner
IMDB: *www.imdb.com/name/nm0000450*

CREANSPEAK PRODUCTIONS LLC

120 South El Camino Drive
Beverly Hills, CA 90212

Phone: 310-273-8217
Email: *info@creanspeak.com*

Submission Policy: Accepts Query Letter from
unproduced, unrepresented writers via email
Genre: Action, Comedy, Memoir & True
Stories, Family, Drama, Socio-cultural
Company Focus: Feature Films, TV, Post-
Production (Editing, Special Effects), Reality
Programming (Reality TV, Documentaries,
Special Events, Sporting Events), Media
(Commercials/Branding/Marketing)

Kelly Crean
Title: Founder/Executive
Phone: 310-273-8217
Email: *info@creanspeak.com*
IMDB: *www.imdb.com/name/nm1047631*

Jon H. Freis, Esq.
Title: Vice-President/Executive
Phone: 310-273-8217
Email: *info@creanspeak.com*
IMDB: *www.imdb.com/name/nm2045371*

CRAVE FILMS

3312 Sunset Boulevard
Los Angeles, CA 90026

Phone: 323-669-9000
Fax: 323-669-9002

Submission Policy: Does not accept any
unsolicited material
Genre: Drama
Company Focus: Feature Films

David Ayer
Title: Writer/Director/Producer
Email: *david@cravefilms.com*
IMDB: *www.imdb.com/name/nm0043742*

Alex Ott
Title: Vice-President, Productions
Email: *alex@cravefilms.com*
IMDB: *www.imdb.com/name/nm1944773*

CRESCENDO PRODUCTIONS

252 North Larchmont Boulevard, Suite 200
Los Angeles, CA 90004

Phone: 323-465-2222
Fax: 323-464-3750

Submission Policy: Accepts Query Letter from
unproduced, unrepresented writers
Genre: Action, Comedy, Crime, Thriller, Drama
Company Focus: Feature Films, TV, Reality
Programming (Reality TV, Documentaries,
Special Events, Sporting Events)

Don Cheadle
Title: Actor/Executive
Phone: 323-465-2222
IMDB: *www.imdb.com/name/nm0000332*

Kay Liberman
Title: Executive/Producer
Phone: 323-465-2222
IMDB: *www.imdb.com/name/nm2248796*

Lenore Zerman
Title: Executive/Producer
Phone: 323-465-2222 or 323-464-0870
IMDB: *www.imdb.com/name/nm2251256*

CREST ANIMATION PRODUCTIONS

333 North Glenoaks Boulevard, Suite 300
Burbank, CA 91502

Phone: 818-846-0166
Fax: 818-846-6074
Email: *info@crestcgi.com*

Submission Policy: Accepts Query Letter from
unproduced, unrepresented writers via email
Genre: Animation
Company Focus: Feature Films

Richard Rich
Title: President/Writer
Phone: 818-846-0166
Email: *info@crestcgi.com*
IMDB: *www.imdb.com/name/nm0723704*

Gregory J.M. Kasunich
Title: Production Coordinator/Manager
Phone: 818-846-0166
Email: *gkasunich@crestcgi.com*
IMDB: *www.imdb.com/name/nm3215310*

CRIME SCENE PICTURES

3450 Cahuenga Boulevard W, Suite 701
Los Angeles, CA 90068

Phone: 323-963-5136
Email: *info@crimescenepictures.net*

Submission Policy: Does not accept any
unsolicited material
Company Focus: Feature Films
Year Established: 2010

Adam Ripp
Title: Writer/Producer/Director
IMDB: *www.imdb.com/name/nm0728063*

Brett Hedblom
Title: Director of Development
IMDB: *www.imdb.com/name/nm3916261*

Jennifer Marmor
Title: Creative Executive
IMDB: *www.imdb.com/name/nm4420063*

CROSS CREEK PICTURES

9220 West Sunset Boulevard, Suite 100
West Hollywood, CA 90069

Phone: 310-248-4061
Fax: 310-248-4068
Email: *info@crosscreekpictures.com*

Submission Policy: Accepts Query Letter from
unproduced, unrepresented writers via email
Genre: Drama
Company Focus: Feature Films, TV

Brian Oliver
Title: President
Email: *brian@crosscreekpicture.com*
IMDB: *www.imdb.com/name/nm1003922*

John Hilary Shepherd
Title: Creative Executive
Phone: 310-248-4061
Email: *info@crosscreekpicture.com*
IMDB: *www.imdb.com/name/nm3005173*

Stephanie Hall
Title: Development
Email: *stephanie@crosscreekpicture.com*
IMDB: *www.imdb.com/name/nm2420653*

CROSSROADS FILMS

1722 Whitley Avenue
Los Angeles, CA 90028

Phone: 310-659-6220
Fax: 310-659-3105

Submission Policy: Accepts Query Letter from
unproduced, unrepresented writers
Genre: Comedy, Crime, Romance, Thriller,
Drama
Company Focus: Feature Films, TV, Media
(Commercials/Branding/Marketing)

Camille "Cami" Taylor
Title: Producer/Partner
Phone: 310-659-6220
IMDB: *www.imdb.com/name/nm0852088*

CRUCIAL FILMS

2220 Colorado Avenue, 5th Floor
Santa Monica, CA 90404

Phone: 310-865-8249
Fax: 310-865-7068
Email: *crucialfilms.asst@gmail.com*

Submission Policy: Does not accept any
unsolicited material
Genre: Action, Comedy, Crime, Fantasy,
Horror, Romance, Thriller, Drama
Company Focus: Feature Films, TV

Daniel Schnider
Title: Head of Production & Development/
Producer
Phone: 310-865-8249
Email: *crucialfilms.asst@gmail.com*
IMDB: *www.imdb.com/name/nm3045845*

Dr. Dre
Title: Principal/Executive
Phone: 310-865-8249
IMDB: *www.imdb.com/name/nm0236564*
Assistant: *crucialfilms.asst@gmail.com*

CRYSTAL LAKE ENTERTAINMENT, INC.

4420 Hayvenhurst Avenue
Encino, CA 91436

Phone: 818-995-1585
Fax: 818-995-1677
Email: *sscfilms@earthlink.net*

Submission Policy: Accepts Query Letter from
unproduced, unrepresented writers via email
Genre: Horror, Science Fiction, Thriller
Company Focus: Feature Films, TV

Sean S. Cunningham
Title: Producer/Director/Writer
Phone: 818-995-1585
Email: *sscfilms@earthlink.net*
IMDB: *www.imdb.com/name/nm0192446*

Geoff Garrett
Title: Creative Executive/Producer/Production
Manager/Cinematographer
Phone: 818-995-1585
Email: *sscfilms@earthlink.net*
IMDB: *www.imdb.com/name/nm0308117*

CRYSTAL SKY PICTURES, LLC

10203 Santa Monica Boulevard, 5th Floor
Los Angeles, CA 90067

Phone: 310-843-0223
Fax: 310-553-9895
Email: *info@crystalsky.com*

Submission Policy: Accepts Query Letter from
unproduced, unrepresented writers via email
Genre: Action, Comedy, Crime, Fantasy,
Horror, Science Fiction, Thriller, Family,
Drama
Company Focus: Feature Films

Steven Paul
Title: Executive/CEO
Phone: 310-843-0223
Email: *info@crystalsky.com*
IMDB: *www.imdb.com/name/nm0666999*

Eric M. Breiman
Title: Executive/Producer/Production
Manager/Actor
Phone: 310-843-0223
Email: *info@crystalsky.com*

Florent Gaglio
Title: Executive
Phone: 310-843-0223
Email: *info@crystalsky.com*
IMDB: *www.imdb.com/name/nm2904382*

CUBE VISION

9000 West Sunset Boulevard
West Hollywood, CA 90069

Phone: 310-461-3490
Fax: 310-461-3491

Submission Policy: Accepts Query Letter from
unproduced, unrepresented writers
Genre: Action, Comedy, Crime, Romance,
Thriller, Family, Animation, Drama
Company Focus: Feature Films, TV, Reality

Programming (Reality TV, Documentaries, Special Events, Sporting Events)

Ice Cube
Title: Owner/Partner
Phone: 310-461-3495
IMDB: *www.imdb.com/name/nm0001084*
Assistant: Nancy Leiviska

Matt Alvarez
Title: Partner
Phone: 310-461-3490
IMDB: *www.imdb.com/name/nm0023297*
Assistant: Lawtisha Fletcher

David Hebenstreit
Title: Partner
Phone: 310-461-3481
IMDB: *www.imdb.com/name/nm0372843*

CURB ENTERTAINMENT

3907 West Alameda Avenue
Burbank, CA 91505

Phone: 818-843-8580
Fax: 818-566-1719
Email: *info@curbentertainment.com*

Submission Policy: Accepts Query Letter from unproduced, unrepresented writers via email
Genre: Comedy, Crime, Horror, Romance, Science Fiction, Thriller, Family, Animation, Drama
Company Focus: Feature Films, TV
Year Established: 1984

Carole Curb Nemoy
Title: President/Executive Producer
Phone: 818-843-8580
Email: *ccurb@curb.com*
IMDB: *www.imdb.com/name/nm0626002*

Mona Kirton
Title: Director/Head, Distribution Services
Phone: 818-843-8580
Email: *mkirton@curb.com*
IMDB: *www.imdb.com/name/nm1310398*

Christy Peterson
Title: Acquisitions
Phone: 818-843-8580
Email: *cpeterson@curb.com*

CYAN PICTURES

410 Park Avenue, 15th Floor
New York, NY 10022

Phone: 212-274-1085
Email: *info@cyanpictures.com*

Submission Policy: Accepts Query Letter from unproduced, unrepresented writers via email
Genre: Comedy, Crime, Horror, Memoir & True Stories, Romance, Science Fiction, Thriller, Drama
Company Focus: Feature Films, Reality Programming (Reality TV, Documentaries, Special Events, Sporting Events)

Joshua Bryce Newman
Title: CEO
Phone: 212-274-1085
Email: *newman@cyanpictures.com*
IMDB: *www.imdb.com/name/nm1243333*

Alexander Burns
Title: CFO
Phone: 212-274-1085
Email: *info@cyanpictures.com*

Wes Schrader
Title: Vice-President of Distribution
Phone: 212-274-1085
Email: *schrader@cyanpictures.com*

CYPRESS FILMS, INC.

630 Ninth Avenue, Suite 415
New York, NY 10036

Phone: 212-262-3900
Fax: 212-262-3925

Submission Policy: Accepts Query Letter from unproduced, unrepresented writers via email
Genre: Comedy, Romance, Science Fiction, Family, Drama
Company Focus: Feature Films

Joseph Pierson
Title: President/Director/Producer
Phone: 212-262-3900
Email: *joseph@cypressfilms.com*
IMDB: *www.imdb.com/name/nm0682777*

Jon Glascoe
Title: Co-Founder/Executive Producer/Writer
Phone: 212-262-3900
Email: *jglascoe@cypressfilms.com*
IMDB: *www.imdb.com/name/nm0321797*

Jessica Forsythe
Title: Submissions Director
Email: *jforsythe@cypressfilms.com*

CYPRESS POINT PRODUCTIONS

3000 Olympic Boulevard
Santa Monica, CA 90404

Phone: 310-315-4787
Fax: 310-315-4785
Email: *cppfilms@earthlink.net*

Submission Policy: Accepts Query Letter from
unproduced, unrepresented writers via email
Genre: Action, Comedy, Crime, Memoir
& True Stories, Romance, Science Fiction,
Thriller, Family, Drama
Company Focus: TV

Gerald W. Abrams
Title: Chairman
Phone: 310-315-4787
Email: *cppfilms@earthlink.net*
IMDB: *www.imdb.com/name/nm0009181*

Michael Waldron
Title: Director, Development
Phone: 310-315-4787
Email: *cppfilms@earthlink.net*
IMDB: *www.imdb.com/name/nm1707236*

D. PETRIE PRODUCTIONS, INC.

13201 Haney Place
Los Angeles, CA 90049

Phone: 310-394-2608
Fax: 310-395-8530
Email: *dgpetrie@aol.com*

Submission Policy: Accepts Query Letter from
unproduced, unrepresented writers via email
Genre: Drama
Company Focus: TV

Dorothea G. Petrie
Title: Owner/Executive Producer
Phone: 310-394-2608
Email: *dgpetrie@aol.com*
IMDB: *www.imdb.com/name/nm0677955*
Assistant: John Cockrell

June Petrie
Title: Producer/Co-Producer
Phone: 310-394-2608
IMDB: *www.imdb.com/name/nm0677968*

DAKOTA PICTURES

4133 Lankershim Boulevard
North Hollywood, CA 91602

Phone: 818-760-0099
Fax: 818-760-1070
Email: *info@dakotafilms.com*

Submission Policy: Does not accept any
unsolicited material
Genre: Action, Comedy, Crime, Fantasy,
Memoir & True Stories, Thriller, Family,
Animation, Drama
Company Focus: Feature Films, TV, Reality
Programming (Reality TV, Documentaries,
Special Events, Sporting Events)

Troy Miller
Title: Founder/Director/Producer
Phone: 818-760-0099
Email: *info@dakotafilms.com*
IMDB: *www.imdb.com/name/nm0003474*

A.J. DiAntonio
Title: Producer/Production Executive
Phone: 818-760-0099
Email: *info@dakotafilms.com*
IMDB: *www.imdb.com/name/nm1472504*

Matt Magielnicki
Title: Producer/Development Executive
Phone: 818-760-0099
Email: *info@dakotafilms.com*
IMDB: *www.imdb.com/name/nm2616148*

DAN LUPOVITZ PRODUCTIONS

936 South Alandele Avenue
Los Angeles, CA 90036

Phone: 323-930-0769
Fax: 310-385-0196
Email: *dlupovitz@aol.com*

Submission Policy: Accepts Query Letter from unproduced, unrepresented writers via email
Genre: Comedy, Romance, Drama
Company Focus: Feature Films, TV

Dan Lupovitz
Title: Executive/Producer
Phone: 323-930-0769
Email: *dlupovitz@aol.com*
IMDB: *www.imdb.com/name/nm0526991*

Randy Albelda
Title: Development
Phone: 323-930-0769

DAN WINGUTOW PRODUCTIONS

534 Laguardia Pl., Suite 3
New York, NY 10012

Phone: 212-477-1328
Fax: 212-254-6902

Submission Policy: Accepts Query Letter from unproduced, unrepresented writers
Genre: Comedy, Crime, Fantasy, Horror, Romance, Science Fiction, Thriller, Drama
Company Focus: Feature Films, TV

Dan Wigutow
Title: Executive Producer
Phone: 212-477-1328
IMDB: *www.imdb.com/name/nm0927887*

Caroline Moore
Title: Co-Producer
Phone: 212-477-1328
IMDB: *www.imdb.com/name/nm0601006*

DANIEL SLADEK ENTERTAINMENT CORPORATION

8306 Wilshire Boulevard, Suite 510
Beverly Hills, CA 90211

Phone: 323-934-9268
Fax: 323-934-7362
Email: *danielsladek@mac.com*

Submission Policy: Does not accept any

unsolicited material
Genre: Action, Comedy, Crime, Fantasy, Horror, Memoir & True Stories, Romance, Science Fiction, Thriller, Drama, Reality
Company Focus: Feature Films, TV, Reality Programming (Reality TV, Documentaries, Special Events, Sporting Events)
Year Established: 1998

Daniel Sladek
Title: President/Producer
Phone: 323-934-9268
Email: *danielsladek@mac.com*
IMDB: *www.imdb.com/name/nm0805202*

Chris Taaffe
Title: Producer/Actor
Phone: 323-934-9268
IMDB: *www.imdb.com/name/nm0845815*

Jamie King
Title: Manager/Art Department
Phone: 323-934-9268
IMDB: *www.imdb.com/name/nm1414386*

DANIEL L. PAULSON PRODUCTIONS

9056 Santa Monica Boulevard, Suite 203A
West Hollywood, CA 90069

Phone: 310-278-9747
Fax: 310-278-3751
Email: *dlpprods@sbcglobal.net*

Submission Policy: Does not accept any unsolicited material
Genre: Action, Comedy, Crime, Detective, Romance, Thriller, TV Sitcom, Family, Drama, Reality
Company Focus: Feature Films, TV, Reality Programming (Reality TV, Documentaries, Special Events, Sporting Events)

Daniel L. "Dan" Paulson
Title: President/Executive
Phone: 310-278-9747
Email: *dlpprods@sbcglobal.net*
IMDB: *www.imdb.com/name/nm0667340*

Steve A. Kennedy
Title: Director/Adminstration
Phone: 310-278-9747
Email: *dlpprods@sbcglobal.net*
IMDB: *www.imdb.com/name/nm0448346*

DANIEL OSTROFF PRODUCTIONS

2046 North Hillhurst Ave. #120
Los Angeles, CA 90027

Phone: 323-284-8824
Email: *oteamthe@gmail.com*

Submission Policy: Accepts Query Letter from
unproduced, unrepresented writers
Genre: TV Sitcom
Company Focus: Feature Films, TV, Reality
Programming (Reality TV, Documentaries,
Special Events, Sporting Events)

Daniel Ostroff
Title: Producer
Phone: 323-284-8824
Email: *oteamthe@gmail.com*
IMDB: *www.imdb.com/name/nm0652491*

DANIEL PETRIE JR. & COMPANY

18034 Ventura Boulevard, Suite 445
Encino, CA 91316

Phone: 818-708-1602
Fax: 818-774-0345

Submission Policy: Accepts Query Letter from
unproduced, unrepresented writers
Genre: Action, Comedy, Crime, Detective,
Horror, Romance, Science Fiction, Thriller,
Drama
Company Focus: Feature Films, TV

Daniel Petrie, Jr.
Title: Director/Writer/Producer
Phone: 818-708-1602
IMDB: *www.imdb.com/name/nm0677943*

Rick Dugdale
Title: Vice-President/Executive/Producer/
Production Manager
Phone: 818-708-1602
IMDB: *www.imdb.com/name/nm1067987*

DARIUS FILMS INCORPORATED

1020 Cole Avenue, Suite 4363
Los Angeles, CA 90038

Phone: 310-728-1342
Fax: 310-494-0575
Email: *info@dariusfilms.com*

Submission Policy: Accepts Query Letter from
produced or represented writers
Genre: Comedy, Crime, Detective, Fantasy,
Memoir & True Stories, Romance, Science
Fiction, Thriller, Drama
Company Focus: Feature Films, TV

Nicholas Tabarrok
Title: President/Actor/Producer
Phone: 310-728-1342
Email: *info@dariusfilms.com*
IMDB: *www.imdb.com/name/nm0002431*

Daniel Baruela
Title: Development
Phone: 310-728-1342
Email: *info@dariusfilms.com*
IMDB: *www.imdb.com/name/nm3758990*

DARK HORSE ENTERTAINMENT

8425 West 3rd Street, Suite 400
Los Angeles, CA 90048

Phone: 323-655-3600
Fax: 323-655-2430

Submission Policy: Does not accept any
unsolicited material
Genre: Action, Comedy, Crime, Fantasy,
Horror, Memoir & True Stories, Romance,
Science Fiction, Thriller, Family, Animation,
Drama
Company Focus: Feature Films

Mike Richardson
Title: President/Producer
Phone: 323-655-3600
Email: *miker@darkhorse.com*
IMDB: *www.imdb.com/name/nm0724700*
Assistant: Pete Cacioppo

Keith Goldberg

Title: Senior Vice-President Production
Phone: 323-655-3600
Email: *keithg@darkhorse.com*
IMDB: *www.imdb.com/name/nm1378991*

Chris Tongue

Title: Vice-President, Creative Affairs
Phone: 323-655-3600
Email: *christ@darkhorse.com*
IMDB: *www.imdb.com/name/nm1142896*

DARKO ENTERTAINMENT

1041 North Formosa Avenue, Suite I
West Hollywood, CA 90046

Phone: 323-850-2480
Fax: 323-850-2481
Email: *info@darko-entertainment.com*

Submission Policy: Does not accept any
unsolicited material
Genre: Fantasy, Horror, Thriller
Company Focus: Feature Films, TV

DARKWOODS PRODUCTIONS

301 East Colorado Boulevard, Suite 705
Pasadena, CA 91101

Phone: 323-454-4580
Fax: 323-454-4581

Submission Policy: Does not accept any
unsolicited material
Genre: Comedy, Crime, Fantasy, Horror,
Memoir & True Stories, Romance, Science
Fiction, Thriller, Drama
Company Focus: Feature Films

Frank Darobont

Title: Partner/Director/Writer/Producer
Phone: 323-454-4582
IMDB: *www.imdb.com/name/nm0001104*
Assistant: Alex White

Denise Huth

Title: Vice-President, Production
Phone: 323-454-4580
IMDB: *www.imdb.com/name/nm1040337*

Jess Clark

Title: Creative Executive
Phone: 323-454-4580
IMDB: *www.imdb.com/name/nm1042404*

DARREN STARR PRODUCTIONS

9200 Sunset Boulevard, Suite 430
Los Angeles, CA 90069

Phone: 310-274-2145
Fax: 310-274-1455

Submission Policy: Accepts Query Letter from
unproduced, unrepresented writers
Genre: Crime, Memoir & True Stories,
Romance, TV Drama, TV Sitcom, Drama
Company Focus: Feature Films, TV

Darren Star

Title: Creator/Executive Producer/Writer
Phone: 310-274-2145
IMDB: *www.imdb.com/name/nm0823015*

Charles Pugliese

Title: Vice-President Production and
Development
Phone: 310-274-2145
IMDB: *www.imdb.com/name/nm1551399*

DAVE BELL ASSOCIATES

3211 Cahuenga Boulevard West
Los Angeles, CA 90068

Phone: 323-851-7801
Fax: 323-851-9349
Email: *dbamovies@aol.com*

Submission Policy: Accepts Query Letter from
unproduced, unrepresented writers via email
Genre: Horror, Memoir & True Stories,
Romance, Science Fiction, Family, Drama,
Socio-cultural
Company Focus: Feature Films, TV, Reality
Programming (Reality TV, Documentaries,
Special Events, Sporting Events)

Dave Bell

Title: President
Phone: 323-851-7801
Email: *dbamovies@aol.com*
IMDB: *www.imdb.com/name/nm0068132*

Ted Weiant
Title: Director, Motion Pictures
Phone: 323-851-7801
Email: *dbamovies@aol.com*
IMDB: *www.imdb.com/name/nm1059707*

Fred Putman
Title: Director, TV
Phone: 323-851-7801
IMDB: *www.imdb.com/name/nm1729656*

DAVID EICK PRODUCTIONS

100 Universal City Plaza
Universal City, CA 91608

Phone: 818-501-0146
Fax: 818-733-2522

Submission Policy: Accepts Query Letter from
unproduced, unrepresented writers
Genre: Action, Science Fiction, Thriller, Drama
Company Focus: TV

David Eick
Title: President
Phone: 818-501-0146
IMDB: *www.imdb.com/name/nm0251594*

DAVIS ENTERTAINMENT

150 South Barrington Place
Los Angeles, CA 90049

Phone: 310-556-3550
Fax: 310-556-3688

Submission Policy: Accepts Scripts from
produced or represented writers

John Davis
Title: Executive/Chairman/Founder
IMDB: *www.imdb.com/name/nm0204862*

Kyle Franke
Title: Director of Development
IMDB: *www.imdb.com/name/nm4677569*

John Fox
Title: President of Production

DEED FILMS

Phone: 310-924-5329

Submission Policy: Accepts Query Letter from
unproduced, unrepresented writers via email
Genre: Comedy, Crime
Company Focus: Feature Films
Year Established: 2008

Scott Donley
Title: President
IMDB: *www.imdb.com/name/nm4238094*

Judith Barrett Lawson
Email: *jlawson@deedfilms.com*
IMDB: *www.imdb.com/name/nm4238122*

Robert Louis Love II
IMDB: *www.imdb.com/name/nm2871637*

DEFIANCE ENTERTAINMENT

6605 Hollywood Boulevard, Suite 100
Los Angeles, CA 91401

Phone: 323-393-0132
Email: *info@defiance-ent.com*

Submission Policy: Accepts Query Letter from
unproduced, unrepresented writers via email
Genre: Action, Comedy, Crime, Fantasy,
Horror, Myth, Science Fiction, Thriller, Drama
Company Focus: Feature Films, TV, Media
(Commercials/Branding/Marketing)
Year Established: 2006

Brian R. Keathley
Title: President/CEO
Email: *brian@defiance-ent.com*
IMDB: *www.imdb.com/name/nm0444080*

Clare Kramer
Title: COO
Email: *clare@defiance-ent.com*
IMDB: *www.imdb.com/name/nm0004456*

DEPTH OF FIELD

1724 Whitley Avenue
Los Angeles, CA 90028

Phone: 323-466-6500
Fax: 323-466-6501

Submission Policy: Accepts Scripts from
produced or represented writers
Company Focus: Feature Films

DIBONAVENTURA PICTURES

5555 Melrose Avenue
DeMille Building, 2nd Floor
Los Angeles, CA 90038

Phone: 323-956-5454
Fax: 323-862-2288

Submission Policy: Does not accept any
unsolicited material
Genre: Action, Fantasy, Science Fiction, Thriller
Company Focus: Feature Films

Lorenzo di Bonaventura
Title: President/Producer
IMDB: *www.imdb.com/name/nm0225146*

Erik Howsam
Title: Senior Vice-President Production
IMDB: *www.imdb.com/name/nm1857184*

DINOVI PICTURES

720 Wilshire Boulevard, Suite 300
Santa Monica, CA 90401

Phone: 310-458-7200
Fax: 310-458-7211

Submission Policy: Accepts Scripts from
produced or represented writers
Company Focus: Feature Films
Year Established: 1993

Denise DiNovi
IMDB: *www.imdb.com/name/nm0224145*

DNA FILMS

10 Amwell Street
London EC1R 1UQ

Phone: +44 020-7843-4410
Fax: +44 020-7843-4411
Email: *info@dnafilms.com*

Submission Policy: Does not accept any
unsolicited material
Company Focus: Feature Films
Year Established: 1999

Andrew Macdonald
Title: Partner
Phone: +44 020 7843 4410
IMDB: *www.imdb.com/name/nm0531602*

Allon Reich
Title: Partner
Phone: +44 020 7843 4410
IMDB: *www.imdb.com/name/nm0716924*

DOBRE FILMS

Phone: 310-926-6439
Email: *dobrefilms@dobrefilms.com*

Submission Policy: Accepts Scripts from
unproduced, unrepresented writers
Genre: Action, Comedy, Crime, Detective,
Fantasy, Horror, Myth, Romance, Science
Fiction, TV Drama, TV Sitcom, Drama,
Socio-cultural
Company Focus: Feature Films, TV

Christopher D'Elia
Title: CEO Director/Producer
Phone: 310-926-6439
Email: *cdelia@dobrefilms.com*
IMDB: *www.imdb.com/name/nm3179988*

Michael Klein
Title: President—Producer/Manager
Phone: 323-510-0818
Email: *mklein@dobrefilms.com*
IMDB: *www.imdb.com/name/nm3180840*

DOUBLE FEATURE FILMS

9320 Wilshire Boulevard #200
Beverly Hills, CA 90212

Phone: 310-887-1100
Email: *dffproducerdesk@gmail.com*

Submission Policy: Does not accept any
unsolicited material
Genre: Action, Comedy, Fantasy, Myth,
Thriller, Drama
Company Focus: Feature Films
Year Established: 2005

Michael Shamberg
Title: Co-Chair/Partner
IMDB: *www.imdb.com/name/nm0787834*

Stacey Sher
Title: Co-Chari/Partner
IMDB: *www.imdb.com/name/nm0792049*

Ameet Shukla
Title: Creative Executive
IMDB: *www.imdb.com/name/nm2627415*

DOUBLE NICKEL ENTERTAINMENT

234 West 138th Street
New York, NY 10030

Phone: 646-435-4390
Fax: 212-694-6205
Email: *admin@doublenickelentertainment.com*

Submission Policy: Accepts Query Letter from unproduced, unrepresented writers via email
Genre: Drama
Company Focus: Feature Films

Jenette Kahn
Title: Partner/Producer
IMDB: *www.imdb.com/name/nm1986495*

Adam Richman
Title: Partner/Producer
IMDB: *www.imdb.com/name/nm0725013*

ECHO BRIDGE ENTERTAINMENT

8383 Wilshire Boulevard, Suite 530
Beverly Hills, CA 90211

Phone: 323-658-7900
Fax: 323-658-7922

Submission Policy: Accepts Query Letter from unproduced, unrepresented writers via email
Company Focus: Feature Films

ECHO FILMS

c/o Allen Keshishian/Brillstein Entertainment Partners
9150 Wilshire Boulevard, Suite 350
Beverly Hills, CA 90212

Phone: 323-935-2909

Submission Policy: Does not accept any unsolicited material
Genre: Comedy, Romance, Drama
Company Focus: Feature Films

Jennifer Aniston
Title: Producer

Kristin Hahn
Title: Producer

ECHO LAKE ENTERTAINMENT

421 South Beverly Drive
8th Floor
Beverly Hills, CA 90212

Phone: 310-789-4790
Fax: 310-789-4791
Email: *contact@echolakeproductions.com*

Submission Policy: Does not accept any unsolicited material
Genre: Thriller, Drama, Reality
Company Focus: Feature Films, TV, Reality Programming (Reality TV, Documentaries, Special Events, Sporting Events)

Doug Mankoff
Title: President

Andrew Spaulding
Title: President, Production

Ilda Diffley
Title: Director, Development/Creative Executive

ECLECTIC PICTURES

7119 Sunset Boulevard, Suite 375
Los Angeles, CA 90046

Phone: 323-656-7555
Fax: 323-848-7761
Email: *info@eclecticpictures.com*

Submission Policy: Accepts Query Letter from unproduced, unrepresented writers via email
Company Focus: Feature Films

Benjamin Scott
Title: Head of Development and Production
Email: *benjamin@eclecticpictures.com*
IMDB: *www.imdb.com/name/nm2623559*

John Yarincik
Title: Development
Email: *john@eclecticpictures.com*
IMDB: *www.imdb.com/name/nm2432490*

EDEN ROCK MEDIA, INC.

1416 North LaBrea Avenue
Hollywood, CA 90028

Phone: 323-802-1718
Fax: 323-802-1832
Email: *taugsberger@edenrockmedia.com*

Submission Policy: Does not accept any
unsolicited material
Genre: Crime, Memoir & True Stories, Science
Fiction, Thriller, Family, Drama
Company Focus: Feature Films, TV, Media
(Commercials/Branding/Marketing)

Thomas Ausberger
Title: Producer

Jana Ausberger
Title: Development

EDMONDS ENTERTAINMENT

1635 North Cahuenga Boulevard, 6th Floor
Los Angeles, CA 90028

Phone: 323-860-1550
Fax: 323-860-1537

Submission Policy: Accepts Scripts from
produced or represented writers
Genre: Romance, Family, Drama,
Socio-cultural
Company Focus: Feature Films, TV, Reality
Programming (Reality TV, Documentaries,
Special Events, Sporting Events)

Tracey Edmonds
Title: President/CEO
Assistant: Amy Ficken

Sheila Ducksworth
Title: Sr. Vice-President, TV & Film

EDWARD R. PRESSMAN FILM CORPORATION

1639 11th Street, Suite 251
Santa Monica, CA 90404

Phone: 310-450-9692
Fax: 310-450-9705

Submission Policy: Does not accept any
unsolicited material
Genre: Action, Comedy, Fantasy, Myth,
Thriller, Drama
Company Focus: Feature Films

Edward Pressman
Title: CEO/Chairman
Assistant: Melissa Glassman

Jon Katz
Title: COO/Business & Legal Affairs

Sarah Ramey
Title: Head, Development & Creative Affairs

EDWARD SAXON PRODUCTIONS

1526 14th Street #105
Santa Monica, CA 90404

Phone: 310-893-0903
Email: *esaxon@saxonproductions.net*

Submission Policy: Accepts Query Letter from
unproduced, unrepresented writers via email
Genre: Action, Memoir & True Stories,
Romance, Family, Drama
Company Focus: Feature Films, TV

Ed Saxon
Title: Producer

EFISH ENTERTAINMENT, INC.

4236 Arch Street, Suite 407
Studio City, CA 91604

Phone: 818-509-9377
Email: *info@efishentertainment.com*

Submission Policy: Accepts Query Letter from
unproduced, unrepresented writers via email
Genre: Action, Crime, Horror, Science Fiction
Company Focus: Feature Films
Year Established: 2009

Eric Fischer
Title: CEO/Producer
Email: *ericasst@efishentertainment.com*
IMDB: *www.imdb.com/name/nm2737789*

Brianna Lee Johnson
Email: *briannaasst@efishentertainment.com*
IMDB: *www.imdb.com/name/nm3776636*

Mike Williams
Title: Development
Assistant: *mikeasst@efishentertainment.com*

EIGHTH SQUARE ENTERTAINMENT

606 North Larchmont Boulevard, Suite 307
Los Angeles, CA 90004

Phone: 323-469-1003
Fax: 323-469-1516

Submission Policy: Does not accept any
unsolicited material
Genre: Comedy, Crime, Thriller, Drama
Company Focus: Feature Films, TV, Theater

Jeff Melnick
Title: Producer

Janette Jenson 'JJ' Hoffman
Title: Producer

ELECTRIC DYNAMITE

1741 Ivar Avenue
Los Angeles, CA 90028

Phone: 323-790-8040

Submission Policy: Accepts Query Letter from
unproduced, unrepresented writers
Genre: Comedy, Fantasy, Science Fiction, TV
Sitcom
Company Focus: Feature Films, TV, Media
(Commercials/Branding/Marketing)

Jack Black
Title: Principal

Ben Cooley
Title: Development

Priyanka Mattoo
Title: Development

ELECTRIC ENTERTAINMENT

940 North Highland Ave, Suite A
Los Angeles, CA 90038

Phone: 323-817-1300
Fax: 323-467-7155

Submission Policy: Does not accept any

unsolicited material
Genre: Action, Comedy, Memoir & True
Stories, Science Fiction, Thriller, Animation,
Drama, Socio-cultural, Reality
Company Focus: Feature Films, TV, Reality
Programming (Reality TV, Documentaries,
Special Events, Sporting Events), Media
(Commercials/Branding/Marketing)

Dean Devlin
Title: President

Jose Behar
Title: Vice-President, Business Development

Jenn Court
Title: Creative Executive

ELECTRIC FARM ENTERTAINMENT

3000 Olympic Boulevard
Building 3, Suite 1366
Santa Monica, CA 90404

Phone: 310-264-4199
Fax: 310-264-4196
Email: *contact@electricfarment.com*

Submission Policy: Accepts Query Letter from
unproduced, unrepresented writers via email
Genre: Action, Fantasy, Science Fiction, Drama
Company Focus: Feature Films, TV, Media
(Commercials/Branding/Marketing)

Stan Rogow
Title: Principal/Executive Producer
Assistant: Allison Lurie

Brent Friedman
Title: Principal/Executive Producer

Katrina Moran
Title: Sr. Vice-President, Business Development

ELECTRIC SHEPHERD PRODUCTIONS

8306 Wilshire Boulevard, #2016
Beverly Hills, CA 90211

Phone: 310-433-5282
Fax: 323-315-7170
Email: *admin@electricshepherdproductions.com*

Submission Policy: Accepts Query Letter from

unproduced, unrepresented writers via email
Genre: Action, Fantasy, Myth, Science Fiction, Thriller, Drama
Company Focus: Feature Films, TV, Media (Commercials/Branding/Marketing)

Isa Dick Hackett
Title: CEO/President

Kalen Egan
Title: Development Associate

ELEPHANT EYE FILMS

27 West 20th Street, Suite 607
New York, NY 10011

Phone: 212-488-8877
Fax: 212-488-8878
Email: *info@elephanteyefilms.com*

Submission Policy: Does not accept any unsolicited material
Genre: Action, Comedy, Fantasy, Memoir & True Stories, Drama, Socio-cultural
Company Focus: Feature Films

Kim Jose
Title: Principal
Email: *Kim@elephanteyefilms.com*

Dave Robinson
Title: Principal
Email: *Dave@elephanteyefilms.com*

Toni Branson
Title: Production/Development Executive
Email: *Toni@elephanteyefilms.com*

ELEVATE ENTERTAINMENT

1925 Century Park East, Suite 2320
Los Angeles, CA 90067

Phone: 310-557-0100
Fax: 310-788-3490
Email: *info@elevate-ent.com*

Submission Policy: Accepts Query Letter from unproduced, unrepresented writers via email
Genre: Action, Comedy, Crime, Fantasy, Memoir & True Stories, Romance, Science Fiction, Family, Animation, Drama, Socio-cultural
Company Focus: Feature Films, TV

Alex Cole
Title: President/Manager
Phone: 310-557-0100
Email: *acole@elevate-ent.com*
IMDB: *www.imdb.com/name/nm2251162*

Tom Spriggs
Title: Manager/Producer
Phone: 310-651-9935
Email: *tspriggs@elevate-ent.com*
IMDB: *www.imdb.com/name/nm3136570*

ELIXIR FILMS

8033 West Sunset Boulevard, Suite 867
West Hollywood, CA 90046

Phone: 323-848-9867
Fax: 323-848-5945
Email: *info@elixirfilms.com*

Submission Policy: Does not accept any unsolicited material
Genre: Family, Drama
Company Focus: Feature Films

David Alexanian
Title: Producer

Alexis Alexanian
Title: Producer
Assistant: Joe Brinkman

ELKINS ENTERTAINMENT

8306 Wilshre Boulevard
PMB 3643
Beverly Hills, CA 90211

Phone: 323-932-0400
Fax: 323-932-6400
Email: *info@elkinsent.com*

Submission Policy: Accepts Query Letter from unproduced, unrepresented writers via email
Genre: Comedy, Memoir & True Stories, Romance, Drama, Reality
Company Focus: Feature Films, TV, Reality Programming (Reality TV, Documentaries, Special Events, Sporting Events)

Hillard Elkins
Title: President/Producer/Manager

Sandi Love
Title: Vice-President/Manager

EMBASSY ROW LLC

6565 Sunset Boulevard, Suite 200
Los Angeles, CA 90028

Phone: 323-417-6560
Fax: 323-469-0015
Email: *info@embassyrow.com*

Submission Policy: Does not accept any
unsolicited material
Genre: Action, Comedy, Fantasy, Science
Fiction, TV Sitcom, Drama
Company Focus: Feature Films, TV, Reality
Programming (Reality TV, Documentaries,
Special Events, Sporting Events), Media
(Commercials/Branding/Marketing)

Michael Davies
Title: President, Production

Tammy Johnston
Title: Sr. Vice-President, Production/General
Manager

Samantha Repp
Title: Manager, Production

EMBER ENTERTAINMENT GROUP

11718 Barrington Court, Suite 116
Los Angeles, CA 90049

Phone: 310-498-5585
Fax: 310-589-4850
Email: *eeg.bronson@verizon.net*

Submission Policy: Accepts Query Letter from
unproduced, unrepresented writers via email
Genre: Action, Comedy, Fantasy, Science
Fiction, Drama
Company Focus: Feature Films, TV

T.S. Goldberg
Title: President, Physical Production

J.A. Keller
Title: Finance

EMERALD CITY PRODUCTIONS, INC.

c/o Stankevich-Gochman
9777 Wilshire Boulevard, Suite 550
Beverly Hills, CA 90212

Phone: 310-859-8825
Fax: 310-859-8830

Submission Policy: Does not accept any
unsolicited material
Genre: Fantasy, Science Fiction, Drama,
Socio-cultural
Company Focus: Feature Films

Barrie Osborne
Title: Producer

ENDGAME ENTERTAINMENT

9100 Wilshire Boulevard, Suite 100W
Beverly Hills, CA 90212

Phone: 310-432-7300
Fax: 310-432-7301
Email: *reception@endgameent.com*

Submission Policy: Does not accept any
unsolicited material
Genre: Action, Comedy, Crime, Detective,
Memoir & True Stories, Romance, Science
Fiction, Thriller, Animation, Drama,
Socio-cultural
Company Focus: Feature Films, TV, Reality
Programming (Reality TV, Documentaries,
Special Events, Sporting Events), Theater

James Stern
Title: Chairman & CEO

Adam Del Deo
Title: Sr. Vice-President, Production

Lucas Smith
Title: Sr. Vice-President, Development

ENERGY ENTERTAINMENT

9348 Civic Center Drive
Mezzanine Level
Beverly Hills, CA 90210

Phone: 310-746-4872
Email: *info@energyentertainment.net*

Submission Policy: Does not accept any

unsolicited material
Genre: Comedy, Memoir & True Stories, Science Fiction, Drama
Company Focus: Feature Films

Brooklyn Weaver
Title: Owner/Manager
Assistant: David Binns

Angelina Chen
Title: Manager

ENTERTAINMENT ONE

9465 Wilshire Boulevard, Suite 500
Los Angeles, CA 90212

Phone: 310-407-0960
Email: *eonetv@entonegroup.com*

Submission Policy: Does not accept any unsolicited material
Genre: Comedy, TV Drama, TV Sitcom, Animation, Drama
Company Focus: TV, Reality Programming (Reality TV, Documentaries, Special Events, Sporting Events), Media (Commercials/Branding/Marketing)

Frank Saperstein
Title: Senior Vice President Television/Family—Los Angeles office

Monica Hoge
Title: Development Coordinator (LA)

Swin Chang
Title: Director of Development (Toronto)

ENTITLED ENTERTAINMENT

2038 Redcliff Street
Los Angeles, CA 90039

Phone: 323-469-9000
Fax: 323-660-5292

Submission Policy: Does not accept any unsolicited material
Genre: Memoir & True Stories, Family, Drama
Company Focus: Feature Films, Theater

James Burke
Title: Partner

Scott Disharoon
Title: Partner

ENVISION MEDIA ARTS

5555 Melrose Avenue
Building 221, Suite 110
Los Angeles, CA 90038

Phone: 323-956-9687
Fax: 323-862-2205
Email: *info@envisionma.com*

Submission Policy: Accepts Query Letter from unproduced, unrepresented writers via email
Genre: Action, Comedy, Fantasy, Myth, Romance, TV Drama, TV Sitcom, Family, Drama, Socio-cultural
Company Focus: Feature Films, TV
Year Established: 2002

Lee Nelson
Title: CEO
Phone: 323-956-9687
Email: *lnelson@envisionma.com*
IMDB: *www.imdb.com/name/nm0625540*

David Buelow
Title: President of Film & TV
Phone: 323-956-9687
Email: *dbuelow@envisionma.com*
IMDB: *www.imdb.com/name/nm2149164*

David Tish
Title: Director of Development
Phone: 323-956-9687
Email: *dtish@envisionma.com*
IMDB: *www.imdb.com/name/nm2953843*

EPIC LEVEL ENTERTAINMENT, LTD.

7095 Hollywood Boulevard #688
Hollywood, CA 91604

Phone: 818-752-6800
Fax: 818-752-6814
Email: *info@epiclevel.com*

Submission Policy: Accepts Query Letter from unproduced, unrepresented writers via email
Genre: Action, Fantasy, Horror, Myth, Science Fiction, Thriller, Animation
Company Focus: Feature Films, TV, Reality Programming (Reality TV, Documentaries,

Special Events, Sporting Events), Media (Commercials/Branding/Marketing)

John Frank Rosenblum
Title: Producer

Cindi Rice
Title: Producer

Paige Barnett
Title: Associate Producer

EPIGRAM ENTERTAINMENT

3745 Longview Valley Road
Sherman Oaks, CA 91423

Phone: 818-461-8937
Fax: 818-461-8919
Email: *epigrament@sbcglobal.net*

Submission Policy: Accepts Query Letter from unproduced, unrepresented writers via email
Genre: Comedy, Romance, Drama
Company Focus: Feature Films, TV, Media (Commercials/Branding/Marketing)

Doug Draizin
Title: Partner

Val McLeroy
Title: Partner

Ellen Baskin
Title: Vice-President, Development

EPIPHANY PICTURES, INC.

10625 Esther Avenue
Los Angeles, CA 90064

Phone: 310-815-1266
Fax: 310-815-1269
Email: *epiphanysubmissions@gmail.com*

Submission Policy: Accepts Query Letter from unproduced, unrepresented writers via email
Genre: Action, Comedy, Crime, Fantasy, Memoir & True Stories, Myth, Romance, Science Fiction, Thriller, TV Drama, TV Sitcom, Family, Animation, Drama, Socio-cultural, Reality
Company Focus: Feature Films, TV, Reality Programming (Reality TV, Documentaries, Special Events, Sporting Events), Media

(Commercials/Branding/Marketing)

Scott Frank
Title: Producer/Director
Email: *scott@epiphanypictures.com*

Dan Halperin
Title: Producer/Director
Phone: 310-452-0242
Email: *dan@epiphanypictures.com*

Dave Schilling
Title: Story Editor
Email: *dwsreader@gmail.com*

ESCAPE ARTISTS

10202 West Washington Boulevard
Astaire Building, 3rd Floor
Culver City, CA 90232

Phone: 310-244-8833
Fax: 310-204-2151
Email: *info@escapeartistsent.com*

Submission Policy: Does not accept any unsolicited material
Genre: Action, Comedy, Fantasy, Myth, Romance, Science Fiction, Drama, Reality
Company Focus: Feature Films, TV

Todd Black
Title: Partner/Producer
Email: *todd_black@spe.sony.com*
IMDB: *www.imdb.com/name/nm0085542*

Jason Blumenthal
Title: Partner/Producer
Email: *jason_blumenthal@spe.sony.com*
IMDB: *www.imdb.com/name/nm0089820*

Steve Tisch
Title: Partner/Producer
Email: *steve_tisch@spe.sony.com*
IMDB: *www.imdb.com/name/nm0005494*

EVERYMAN PICTURES

3000 West Olympic Boulevard, Suite 1500
Santa Monica, CA 90404

Phone: 310-460-7080
Fax: 310-460-7081

Submission Policy: Does not accept any

unsolicited material
Genre: Comedy, Drama
Company Focus: Feature Films

Jay Roach
Title: Director/Chairman/CEO
Email: *jay.roach@fox.com*
IMDB: *www.imdb.com/name/nm0005366*

FACE PRODUCTIONS

335 North Maple Drive, Suite 135
Beverly Hills, CA 90210

Phone: 310-205-2746
Fax: 310-285-2386

Submission Policy: Does not accept any
unsolicited material
Genre: Action, Comedy, Drama
Company Focus: Feature Films

Billy Crystal
Title: Actor/Writer/Producer
IMDB: *www.imdb.com/name/nm0000345*

Carol Sidlow
Title: Development
IMDB: *www.imdb.com/name/nm0796623*

FAKE EMPIRE FEATURES

5555 Melrose Avenue
Marx Brothers Building #207
Hollywood, CA 90038

Phone: 323-956-8766

Submission Policy: Accepts Scripts from
produced or represented writers
Company Focus: Feature Films

Lisbeth Rowinski
Title: Vice-President-Feature Film
IMDB: *www.imdb.com/name/nm2925164*

Jay Marcus
Title: Creative Executive
IMDB: *www.imdb.com/name/nm1682408*

FAKE EMPIRE TELEVISION

400 Warner Boulevard
Building 138, Room 1101
Burbank, CA 91522

Phone: 818-954-2420

Submission Policy: Accepts Scripts from
produced or represented writers
Company Focus: TV

Josh Schwatz
Title: Founder/Producer/Writer/Director
IMDB: *www.imdb.com/name/nm0777300*

Leonard Goldstein
Title: Head, Television
IMDB: *www.imdb.com/name/nm2325264*

FARRELL PAURA PRODUCTIONS

11150 Santa Monica Boulevard, Suite 450
Los Angeles, CA 90025

Submission Policy: Accepts Query Letter from
unproduced, unrepresented writers via email
Company Focus: Feature Films

Catherine Paura
Title: CEO

Wayne Kline
Title: Vice-President

FEDERATOR STUDIOS

Frederator Studios
231 West Olive Avenue
Burbank, CA 91502

Phone: 818-736-3606
Fax: 818-736 3449
Email: *hey@frederator.com*

Submission Policy: Accepts Query Letter from
unproduced, unrepresented writers via email
Company Focus: Feature Films, TV
Year Established: 1998

Fred Seibert
Title: President-Producer
Phone: 646-274-4601
Email: *fred@frederator.com*
IMDB: *www.imdb.com/name/nm0782288*
Assistant: Zoe Barton—*zoe@frederator.com*

Eric Homan
Title: Vice-President, Development
Email: *eric@frederator.com*
IMDB: *www.imdb.com/name/nm2302704*

FILMNATION ENTERTAINMENT

345 North Maple Dr, Suite 202
Beverly Hills, CA 90210

Phone: 310-859-0088
Fax: 310-859-0089

Submission Policy: Accepts Query Letter from unproduced, unrepresented writers
Genre: Action, Crime, Fantasy, Horror, Thriller, Drama
Company Focus: Feature Films
Year Established: 2008

Glen Basner
Title: Founder/CEO
Email: *gbasner@wearefilmnation.com*
IMDB: *www.imdb.com/name/nm0059984*

Patrick Chu
Title: Director of Development
Email: *pchu@wearefilmnation.com*
IMDB: *www.imdb.com/name/nm1776958*

FIVE BY EIGHT PRODUCTIONS

4312 Clarissa Avenue
Los Angeles, CA 90027

Submission Policy: Accepts Query Letter from unproduced, unrepresented writers via email
Genre: Drama, Socio-cultural
Company Focus: Feature Films, TV
Year Established: 2006

Michael Connors
Email: *mike@fivebyeight.com*
IMDB: *www.imdb.com/name/nm2155421*

Sean Mullen
Email: *sean@fivebyeight.com*
IMDB: *www.imdb.com/name/nm2013693*

FIVE SMOOTH STONE PRODUCTIONS

106 Oakland Hills Court
Duluth, GA 30097

Phone: 770-476-7171

Submission Policy: Does not accept any unsolicited material
Genre: Memoir & True Stories
Company Focus: Feature Films

Rich Middlemas
Title: Producer

FLASHPOINT ENTERTAINMENT

9150 Wilshire Boulevard, Suite 247
Beverly Hills, CA 90212

Phone: 310-205-6300
Email: *info@flashpointent.com*

Submission Policy: Does not accept any unsolicited material
Company Focus: Feature Films, TV

Andrew Tennenbaum
Title: Manager/Producer
IMDB: *www.imdb.com/name/nm0990025*

Tom Johnson
Title: Director/Development
Phone: 310-205-6300
IMDB: *www.imdb.com/name/nm1927361*

Laura Roman-Rockhold
Title: Assistant
Phone: 310-205-6300
Email: *info@flashpointent.com*
IMDB: *www.imdb.com/name/nm4099178*

FLAVOR UNIT ENTERTAINMENT

119 Washington Avenue, Suite 400
Miami Beach, FL 33139

Phone: 201-333-4883
Fax: 973-556-1770
Email: *Billy@flavorentertainment.com*

Submission Policy: Accepts Query Letter from unproduced, unrepresented writers via email
Company Focus: Feature Films

Queen Latifah
Title: CEO
Phone: 201-333-4883
IMDB: *www.imdb.com/name/nm0001451*

Shakim Compere
Title: CEO
Phone: 201-333-4883
IMDB: *www.imdb.com/name/nm1406277*

Otis Best
Title: Producer/General Manager
Phone: 201-333-4883
IMDB: *www.imdb.com/name/nm1454006*

FLOWER FILMS INC.

7360 Santa Monica Boulevard
West Hollywood, CA 90046

Phone: 323-876-7400
Fax: 323-876-7401

Submission Policy: Accepts Scripts from produced or represented writers
Company Focus: Feature Films
Year Established: 1995

Drew Barrymore
Title: Partner
Phone: 323-876-7400
IMDB: *www.imdb.com/name/nm0000106*

Chris Miller
Title: Vice-President/Producer
Phone: 323-876-7400
IMDB: *www.imdb.com/name/nm0588091*
Assistant: Steven Acosta

Ember Truesdell
Title: Vice-President Development
Phone: 323-876-7400
Email: *ember@flowerfilms.com*
IMDB: *www.imdb.com/name/nm1456092*

FORENSIC FILMS, INC

1 Worth Street, 2nd Floor
New York, NY 10013

Phone: 212-966-1110
Email: *forensicfilms@gmail.com*

Submission Policy: Accepts Query Letter from unproduced, unrepresented writers via email
Company Focus: Feature Films

Scott Macauley
Title: Producer
Phone: 212-966-1110
IMDB: *www.imdb.com/name/nm0531337*

Robin O'Hara
Title: Producer
Phone: 212-966-1110
IMDB: *www.imdb.com/name/nm0641327*

FORESIGHT UNLIMITED

2934 1/2 Beverly Glen Circle, Suite 900
Bel Air, CA 90077

Phone: 310-275-5222
Fax: 310-275-5202
Email: *info@foresight-unltd.com*

Submission Policy: Accepts Query Letter from unproduced, unrepresented writers via email
Genre: Drama
Company Focus: Feature Films

Mark Damon
Title: CEO
IMDB: *www.imdb.com/name/nm0198941*

Tamara Stuparich de la Barra
Title: President and COO
IMDB: *www.imdb.com/name/nm1736077*

FOREST PARK PICTURES

11210 Briarcliff Lane
Studio City, CA 91604-4277

Phone: 323-654-2735
Fax: 323-654-2735

Submission Policy: Accepts Query Letter from unproduced, unrepresented writers
Company Focus: Feature Films
Year Established: 2002

Hayden Christensen
Title: Partner
Phone: 323-848-2942 ext. 265
IMDB: *www.imdb.com/name/nm0159789*

Tove Christensen
Title: Partner
Phone: 323-848-2942 ext. 265
IMDB: *www.imdb.com/name/nm0159922*

FORGET ME NOT PRODUCTIONS

Email: *info@4getmenotproductions.com*

Submission Policy: Accepts Query Letter from

unproduced, unrepresented writers via email
Genre: Drama
Company Focus: Feature Films

Jennifer Gargano
Title: President/CEO/Producer
Email: *jennifergargano@4getmenotproductions.com*
IMDB: *www.imdb.com/name/nm2470854*

FORTIS FILMS

8581 Santa Monica Boulevard, Suite 1
West Hollywood, CA 90069

Phone: 310-659-4533
Fax: 310-659-4373

Submission Policy: Accepts Query Letter from unproduced, unrepresented writers
Genre: Comedy, Romance, Drama
Company Focus: Feature Films, TV

Sandra Bullock
Title: Partner
Phone: 310-659-4533
IMDB: *www.imdb.com/name/nm0000113*

Maggie Biggar
Title: Partner
Phone: 310-659-4533
IMDB: *www.imdb.com/name/nm0081772*

FORTRESS FEATURES

2727 Main Street, Suite E
Santa Monica, CA 90405

Phone: 323-467-4700

Submission Policy: Does not accept any unsolicited material
Company Focus: Feature Films, TV
Year Established: 2004

Brett Forbes
Title: Partner
Phone: 323-467-4700
IMDB: *www.imdb.com/name/nm1771405*

Patrick Rizzotti
Title: Partner
Phone: 323-467-4700
IMDB: *www.imdb.com/name/nm0729948*

Bonnie Forbes
Title: Producer/Development
Phone: 323-467-4700
IMDB: *www.imdb.com/name/nm1424832*

FORWARD ENTERTAINMENT

9255 Sunset Boulevard, Suite 805
West Hollywood, CA 90069

Phone: 310-278-6700
Fax: 310-278-6770

Submission Policy: Accepts Query Letter from unproduced, unrepresented writers via email
Company Focus: Feature Films, TV

Connie Tavel
Title: Partner
Phone: 310-278-6700
Email: *ctavel@forward-ent.com*
IMDB: *www.imdb.com/name/nm0851679*

Vera Mihailovich
Title: Partner
Phone: 310-278-6700
Email: *vmihailovich@forward-ent.com*
IMDB: *www.imdb.com/name/nm2250568*

Adrienne Sandoval
Title: Executive Assistant
Phone: 310-278-6700
Email: *asandoval@forward-ent.com*
IMDB: *www.imdb.com/name/nm2302898*

FOURBOYS FILMS

4000 Warner Boulevard
Burbank, CA 91522

Phone: 818-954-4378
Fax: 818-954-5359
Email: *info@fourboysfilms.com*

Submission Policy: Does not accept any unsolicited material
Genre: Comedy, TV Drama, TV Sitcom, Animation
Company Focus: Feature Films, TV

Patricia Heaton
Title: Partner
Phone: 818-954-4378
IMDB: *www.imdb.com/name/nm0005004*

David Hunt
Title: Partner
Phone: 818-954-4378
IMDB: *www.imdb.com/name/nm0402408*

A.J. Morewitz
Title: President
Phone: 818-954-4378
IMDB: *www.imdb.com/name/nm1031450*

FOX 2000 PICTURES

10201 West Pico Boulevard
Building 7B
Los Angeles, CA 90035

Phone: 310-369-2000
Fax: 310-369-4258

Submission Policy: Does not accept any
unsolicited material
Genre: Action, Comedy, Fantasy, Myth,
Romance, Thriller, Family, Drama
Year Established: 1996

Elizabeth Gabler
Title: President, Production
Phone: 310-369-2000
Email: *elizabeth.gabler@fox.com*
IMDB: *www.imdb.com/name/nm1992894*

FOX INTERNATIONAL PRODUCTIONS

10201 West Pico Boulevard
Los Angeles, CA 90035

Phone: 310-369-1000

Submission Policy: Does not accept any
unsolicited material
Genre: Action, Romance, Drama
Year Established: 2008

Sanford Panitch
Title: President
Phone: 310-369-1000
Email: *sanford.panitch@fox.com*
IMDB: *www.imdb.com/name/nm0659529*

FOX SEARCHLIGHT PICTURES

10201 West Pico Boulevard
Building 38
Los Angeles, CA 90035

Phone: 310-369-1000
Fax: 310-369-2359

Submission Policy: Does not accept any
unsolicited material
Genre: Action, Comedy, Fantasy, Romance,
Thriller, Family, Drama
Year Established: 1994

Stephen Gilula
Title: Co-President
Phone: 310-369-1000
Email: *stephen.gilula@fox.com*
IMDB: *www.imdb.com/name/nm2322989*

FR PRODUCTIONS

2980 Beverly Glenn Cir., Suite 200
Los Angeles, CA 90077

Phone: 310-470-9212
Fax: 310-470-4905
Email: *frprod@earthlink.net*

Submission Policy: Accepts Query Letter from
unproduced, unrepresented writers via email
Genre: Crime, Family, Drama
Company Focus: Feature Films

Fred Roos
Title: Producer/President
Phone: 310-470-9212
Email: *frprod@earthlink.net*
IMDB: *www.imdb.com/name/nm0740407*

FRED KUENERT PRODUCTIONS

1601 Hilts Ave. #2
Los Angeles, CA 90024

Phone: 310-470-3363
Fax: 310-470-0060

Submission Policy: Accepts Query Letter from
unproduced, unrepresented writers via email
Genre: Action, Fantasy, Horror, Science Fiction,
Thriller
Company Focus: Feature Films

Fred Kuenert
Email: *fkuehnert@earthlink.net*
IMDB: *www.imdb.com/name/nm0473896*

Sandra Chouinard
Title: Partner

FREDERIC GOLCHAN PRODUCTIONS

c/o Radar Pictures
10900 Wilshire Boulevard, 14th Floor
Los Angeles, CA 90024

Phone: 310-208-8525
Fax: 310-208-1764
Email: *fgfilm@aol.com*

Submission Policy: Does not accept any unsolicited material
Genre: Action, Drama

Frederic Golchan
Title: President-Producer
Email: *asstgolchan@gmail.com*
IMDB: *www.imdb.com/name/nm0324907*
Assistant: Gaillaume Chiasoda

Cody Stallings
Title: Development
IMDB: *www.imdb.com/name/nm3225268*

FRESH & SMOKED

3500 West Olive Avenue, Suite 300
Burbank, CA 91505

Phone: 818-505-1311
Fax: 818-301-2135
Email: *development@freshandsmoked.com*

Submission Policy: Accepts Scripts from unproduced, unrepresented writers
Genre: Action, Comedy, Crime, Detective, Fantasy, Horror, Memoir & True Stories, Myth, Romance, Science Fiction, Thriller, TV Drama, TV Sitcom, Family, Animation, Drama, Socio-cultural
Company Focus: Feature Films, TV, Post-Production (Editing, Special Effects), Reality Programming (Reality TV, Documentaries, Special Events, Sporting Events), Media (Commercials/Branding/Marketing)

Monika Gosch
Title: Producer
Email: *monika@freshandsmoked.com*
IMDB: *www.imdb.com/name/nm2815838*

Jeremy Gosch
Title: Director
Email: *jeremy@freshandsmoked.com*
IMDB: *www.imdb.com/name/nm0331443*

Angela McIntyre
Title: Internal Development
Email: *angela@freshandsmoked.com*

FRIED FILMS

100 North Crescent Drive, Suite 350
Beverly Hills, CA 90210

Phone: 310-694-8150
Fax: 310-861-5454

Submission Policy: Accepts Query Letter from unproduced, unrepresented writers
Genre: Action, Crime, Detective, Thriller, Drama
Company Focus: Feature Films, TV
Year Established: 1990

Robert Fried
Title: Producer
IMDB: *www.imdb.com/name/nm0294975*

Tyrrell Shaffner
Title: Development Executive
IMDB: *www.imdb.com/name/nm1656222*

FRIENDLY FILMS

100 North Crescent Drive, Suite 350
Beverly Hills, CA 90210

Phone: 310-432-1818
Fax: 310-432-1801
Email: *info@friendly-films.com*

Submission Policy: Accepts Query Letter from unproduced, unrepresented writers
Genre: Comedy, Family
Company Focus: Feature Films
Year Established: 2006

David T. Friendly
Title: Founder, Producer
IMDB: *www.imdb.com/name/nm0295560*

Drew Comins
Title: Creative Executive
Email: *dc@friendly-films.com*

FULLER FILMS

P.O. BOX 976
Venice, CA 90294

Phone: 310-717-8842

Submission Policy: Does not accept any unsolicited material
Company Focus: Feature Films

Paul De Souza
Title: Producer
Email: *gopics@verizon.net*
IMDB: *www.imdb.com/name/nm0996278*

Henry Beean
Title: Writer/Director/Producer
IMDB: *www.imdb.com/name/nm0063785*

FURST FILMS/OLÉ

8954 West Pico Boulevard
2nd Floor
Los Angeles, CA 90035

Phone: 310-278-6468
Fax: 310-278-7401
Email: *info@furstfilms.com*

Submission Policy: Accepts Query Letter from unproduced, unrepresented writers via email
Genre: Action, Crime, Detective, Horror, Thriller, Drama
Company Focus: Feature Films, TV, Reality Programming (Reality TV, Documentaries, Special Events, Sporting Events)

Bryan Furst
Title: Principal/Producer
IMDB: *www.imdb.com/name/nm1227576*

Jan-Willem van der Vaart
Title: Creative Executive

Meredith L. Ditlow
Title: Manager, Creative Affairs
Email: *meredith@furstfilms.com*
IMDB: *www.imdb.com/name/nm1902828*

FURTHUR FILMS

100 Universal City Plaza
Building 5174
Universal City, CA 91608

Phone: 818-777-6700
Fax: 818-866-1278

Submission Policy: Accepts Query Letter from unproduced, unrepresented writers
Genre: Action, Comedy, Crime, Detective, Thriller, Drama
Company Focus: Feature Films

Michael Douglas
Title: Producer
IMDB: *www.imdb.com/name/nm0000140*

Andy Ziskin
Title: Development

FUSEFRAME

2332 Cotner Ave, Suite 200
Los Angeles, CA 90064

Phone: 424-208-1765

Submission Policy: Does not accept any unsolicited material
Genre: Horror, Thriller
Company Focus: Feature Films
Year Established: 2011

Marcus Chait
Title: Director of Film and New Media
IMDB: *www.imdb.com/name/nm1483939*

Eva Konstantopoulos
Title: Book to Screen Coordinator
IMDB: *www.imdb.com/name/nm2192285*

FUSION FILMS

2355 Westwood Boulevard, Suite 117
Los Angeles, CA 90064

Phone: 310-441-1496

Submission Policy: Accepts Query Letter from unproduced, unrepresented writers
Genre: Comedy, Horror, Thriller, Animation, Drama
Company Focus: Feature Films, TV

John Baldecchi
Title: Co-CEO, Producer
IMDB: *www.imdb.com/name/nm0049689*

Jay Judah
Title: Creative Executive

GAETA/ROSENZWEIG FILMS

150 Ocean Park Boulevard #322
Santa Monica, CA 90405-3572

Phone: 310-399-7101

Submission Policy: Accepts Query Letter from unproduced, unrepresented writers
Genre: Thriller, TV Drama, Drama
Company Focus: Feature Films, TV

Alison Rosenzweig
IMDB: *www.imdb.com/name/nm0742851*

GALATÉE FILMS

19 Avenue de Messine
Paris, France 75008

Phone: +33 1 44 29 21 40
Fax: +33 1 44 29 25 90
Email: *mail@galateefilms.com*

Submission Policy: Accepts Query Letter from unproduced, unrepresented writers via email
Company Focus: Feature Films

Jacques Perrin
Title: Producer/CEO
IMDB: *www.imdb.com/name/nm0674742*

Nicolas Mauvernay
Title: Producer
IMDB: *www.imdb.com/name/nm1241814*

Christophe Barratier
Title: Producer
IMDB: *www.imdb.com/name/nm0056725*

GALLANT ENTERTAINMENT

16161 Ventura Boulevard, Suite 664
Encino, CA 91436

Phone: 818-905-9848
Fax: 818-906-9965
Email: *mog@gallantentertainment.com*

Submission Policy: Accepts Query Letter from unproduced, unrepresented writers via email
Genre: Romance, Thriller, TV Drama, Family, Drama
Company Focus: Feature Films, TV, Reality Programming (Reality TV, Documentaries, Special Events, Sporting Events), Media

(Commercials/Branding/Marketing)
Year Established: 1992

Michael Gallant
Title: President/Producer
IMDB: *www.imdb.com/name/nm0302572*

K.R. Gallant
Title: Operations
Email: *krg@gallantentertainment.com*

GARY HOFFMAN PRODUCTIONS

3931 Puerco Canyon Road
Malibu, CA 90265

Phone: 310-456-1830
Fax: 310-456-8866
Email: *garyhofprods@charter.net*

Submission Policy: Accepts Query Letter from unproduced, unrepresented writers via email
Genre: Action, Comedy, Drama
Company Focus: Feature Films, TV

Gary Hoffman
Title: Producer/President
IMDB: *www.imdb.com/name/nm0388888*

Ann P. Ryan
Title: Development

GARY SANCHEZ PRODUCTIONS

Phone: 323-465-4600
Fax: 323-465-0782
Email: *gary@garysanchezprods.com*

Submission Policy: Does not accept any unsolicited material
Genre: Comedy
Company Focus: Feature Films, TV

Will Ferrell
Title: Founder/Executive Producer/Actor
IMDB: *www.imdb.com/name/nm0002071*

GENEXT FILMS

5610 Soto Street
Huntington Park, CA 90255
Email: *contact@genextfilms.com*

Submission Policy: Accepts Query Letter from

unproduced, unrepresented writers via email
Genre: Socio-cultural
Company Focus: Feature Films, TV

Carlos A. Salas
Title: CEO/Producer
IMDB: *www.imdb.com/name/nm2972624*
Assistant: Kathy Snyder

Rossana Salas
Title: CFO/Producer
IMDB: *www.imdb.com/name/nm2970664*

GENREBEND PRODUCTIONS, INC.

233 Wilshire Boulevard, Suite 400
Santa Monica, CA 90401

Phone: 310-860-0878
Email: *genrebend@elvis.com*

Submission Policy: Accepts Query Letter from unproduced, unrepresented writers via email
Genre: TV Drama, TV Sitcom
Company Focus: Feature Films, TV

David Nutter
Title: President/Director
IMDB: *www.imdb.com/name/nm0638354*

Tom Lavagnino
Title: Vice-President Creative Affairs, Writer
IMDB: *www.imdb.com/name/nm0491706*

GEORGE LITTO PRODUCTIONS, INC.

339 North Orange Drive
Los Angeles, CA 90036

Phone: 323-936-6350
Fax: 323-936-6762

Submission Policy: Accepts Query Letter from unproduced, unrepresented writers
Company Focus: Feature Films
Year Established: 1997

George Litto
Title: CEO/Owner
IMDB: *www.imdb.com/name/nm0514788*

Linda Lee
Title: Executive Assistant

GERARD BUTLER ALAN SIEGEL ENTERTAINMENT

345 North Maple Drive
Beverly Hills, CA 90210

Phone: 310-278-8400

Submission Policy: Does not accept any unsolicited material
Company Focus: Feature Films

Gerard Butler
Title: Producer/Actor
IMDB: *www.imdb.com/name/nm0124930*

Danielle Robinson
Title: Director of Development

GERBER PICTURES

4000 Warner Boulevard
Building 138, Suite 1202
Burbank, CA 91522

Phone: 818-954-3046
Fax: 818-954-3706

Submission Policy: Does not accept any unsolicited material
Genre: Comedy, TV Drama, TV Sitcom, Family, Animation, Drama
Company Focus: Feature Films, TV

Carrie Gillogly
Title: Creative Executive
IMDB: *www.imdb.com/name/nm2235655*

James Leffler
Title: Development Assistant

Daphne Fei
Title: Development Coordinator

GHOST HOUSE PICTURES

315 South Beverly Dr, Suite 216
Beverly Hills, CA 90212

Phone: 310-785-3900
Fax: 310-785-9176
Email: *info@ghosthousepictures.com*

Submission Policy: Does not accept any

unsolicited material
Genre: Horror, Thriller, TV Drama, TV Sitcom
Company Focus: Feature Films, TV

Sam Raimi
Title: Director/Executive Producer
IMDB: *www.imdb.com/name/nm0000600*

Aaron Lam
Title: Executive
IMDB: *www.imdb.com/name/nm1725478*

GIGANTIC PICTURES

895 1/2 South Lucerne Boulevard
Los Angeles, CA 90005

Phone: 323-936-6117

Submission Policy: Accepts Query Letter from produced or represented writers
Company Focus: Feature Films, TV

Edward J. Bates
Title: Producer
IMDB: *www.imdb.com/name/nm0060901*

GIL ADLER PRODUCTIONS

c/o Peter Franciosa's Office/United Talent Agency
9560 Wilshire Boulevard, Suite 500
Beverly Hills, CA 90212

Submission Policy: Does not accept any unsolicited material
Genre: Action, Horror, Thriller
Company Focus: Feature Films, TV, Reality Programming (Reality TV, Documentaries, Special Events, Sporting Events), Media (Commercials/Branding/Marketing)

Gil Adler
Title: Producer
IMDB: *www.imdb.com/name/nm0012155*
Assistant: Ryan Lough

GIL NETTER PRODUCTIONS

1645 Abbot Kinney Boulevard, Suite 320
Venice, CA 90291

Phone: 310-566-5477

Submission Policy: Does not accept any

unsolicited material
Genre: Comedy, Family
Company Focus: Feature Films

Gil Netter
Title: Producer
IMDB: *www.imdb.com/name/nm0626696*
Assistant: Jennifer Ho

Tom Carstens
Title: Development Executive

Charles Thompson

GILBERT FILMS

8409 Santa Monica Boulevard
West Hollywood, CA 90069

Phone: 323-650-6800
Fax: 323-650-6810
Email: *info@gilbertfilms.com*

Submission Policy: Does not accept any unsolicited material
Company Focus: Feature Films

Gary Gilbert
Title: CEO/President
IMDB: *www.imdb.com/name/nm1344784*

Shauna Bogetz
Title: Director of Development
IMDB: *www.imdb.com/name/nm2868191*

Katie Slovon
Title: Assistant
IMDB: *www.imdb.com/name/nm4244578*

GIRLS CLUB ENTERTAINMENT

1806 Belles Street 3A
The Presidio
San Francisco, CA 94117

Fax: 415-398-2668
Email: *info@girlsclubentertainment.com*

Submission Policy: Does not accept any unsolicited material
Company Focus: Feature Films, TV, Reality Programming (Reality TV, Documentaries, Special Events, Sporting Events)

Jennifer Siebel Newsom
Title: Founder
IMDB: *www.imdb.com/name/nm1308076*

GITLIN PRODUCTIONS

11661 San Vicente Boulevard, Suite 609
Los Angeles, CA 90049

Phone: 310-209-8443
Email: *gitlinproduction@aol.com*

Submission Policy: Accepts Query Letter from
unproduced, unrepresented writers via email
Genre: Action, Comedy, Drama
Company Focus: Feature Films, TV, Reality
Programming (Reality TV, Documentaries,
Special Events, Sporting Events)

Mimi Polk Gitlin
Title: President/Producer
IMDB: *www.imdb.com/name/nm0689316*

GITTES, INC.

10202 West Washington Boulevard
Poitier Building, Suite 1200
Culver City, CA 90232-3195

Phone: 310-244-4333
Fax: 310-244-1711

Submission Policy: Accepts Query Letter from
unproduced, unrepresented writers
Genre: Comedy, Drama
Company Focus: Feature Films

Harry Gittes
Title: Producer
Email: *harry_gittes@spe.sony.com*
IMDB: *www.imdb.com/name/nm0321228*

Edward C. Wang
Title: Director of Development
Phone: 310-244-4334
Email: *edward_wang@spe.sony.com*
IMDB: *www.imdb.com/name/nm0910882*

GK FILMS

1540 2nd Street, Suite 200
Santa Monica, CA 90401

Phone: 310-315-1722
Fax: 310-315-1723
Email: *contact@gk-films.com*

Submission Policy: Does not accept any
unsolicited material
Genre: Comedy, Memoir & True Stories,
Family, Animation, Drama, Socio-cultural
Company Focus: Feature Films, TV
Year Established: 2007

Graham King
Title: CEO
IMDB: *www.imdb.com/name/nm0454752*
Assistant: Leah Williams, Michelle Reed

David Crocket
Title: Creative Executive

GO GIRL MEDIA

3450 Cahuenga Boulevard West #802
Los Angeles, CA 90068

Phone: 310-472-8910
Fax: 818-924-9369
Email: *info@gogirlmedia.com*

Submission Policy: Accepts Query Letter from
unproduced, unrepresented writers via email
Genre: Comedy, Memoir & True Stories, TV
Drama, TV Sitcom, Family, Animation, Drama
Company Focus: Feature Films, TV, Reality
Programming (Reality TV, Documentaries,
Special Events, Sporting Events)
Year Established: 2004

Don Priess
Title: Head of Production. Writer/Producer/
Editor
IMDB: *www.imdb.com/name/nm1043744*

Susie Singer Carter
Title: Owner/Producer/Writer
Email: *Susie@gogirlmedia.com*
IMDB: *www.imdb.com/name/nm0802053*

GOFF-KELLAM PRODUCTIONS

8491 Sunset Boulevard, Suite 1000
West Hollywood, CA 90069

Phone: 310-666-9082
Fax: 323-656-1002
Email: *goffkellam@aol.com*

Submission Policy: Accepts Query Letter from unproduced, unrepresented writers via email
Genre: Comedy, Memoir & True Stories, Romance, Thriller, Socio-cultural
Company Focus: Feature Films
Year Established: 1998

Gina G. Goff
Title: Producer
IMDB: *www.imdb.com/name/nm0324574*

Laura Kellam
Title: Producer
IMDB: *www.imdb.com/name/nm0445496*

GOLD CIRCLE FILMS

233 Wilshire Boulevard, Suite 650
Santa Monica, CA 90401

Phone: 310-278-4800
Fax: 310-278-0885
Email: *info@goldcirclefilms.com*

Submission Policy: Does not accept any unsolicited material
Genre: Comedy, Horror, Romance, Thriller, Family
Company Focus: Feature Films
Year Established: 2000

Rayne Roberts
Title: Creative Executive

GOLDCREST FILMS

65/66 Dean Street
London W1D 4PL
United Kingdom

Phone: +44 207-437-8696
Fax: +44 207-437-4448
Email: *info@goldcrestfilms.com*

Submission Policy: Does not accept any unsolicited material
Genre: Memoir & True Stories, TV Drama, TV Sitcom, Animation
Company Focus: Feature Films, TV, Post-Production (Editing, Special Effects), Reality

Programming (Reality TV, Documentaries, Special Events, Sporting Events)
Year Established: 1977

Stephen Johnston
Title: President
IMDB: *www.imdb.com/name/nm1158125*

GOLDENRING PRODUCTIONS

4804 Laurel Canyon Boulevard
Rm. 570
Valley Village, CA 91607

Phone: 818-508-7425
Email: *info@goldenringproductions.net*

Submission Policy: Accepts Query Letter from unproduced, unrepresented writers via email
Genre: Comedy, Memoir & True Stories, TV Drama, TV Sitcom, Family, Animation
Company Focus: Feature Films, TV

Jane Goldenring
Title: President/Producer
IMDB: *www.imdb.com/name/nm0325553*

Jon King
Title: Development
Email: *jonnyfking@gmail.com*

GOLDSMITH-THOMAS PRODUCTIONS

239 Central Park West, Suite 6A
New York, NY 10024

Phone: 212-243-4147 or 212-242-6741
Fax: 212-799-2545

Submission Policy: Accepts Query Letter from unproduced, unrepresented writers
Genre: Comedy, Memoir & True Stories, Romance, TV Drama, TV Sitcom, Family, Drama
Company Focus: Feature Films, TV

Elaine Goldsmith-Thomas
Title: President/Producer
IMDB: *www.imdb.com/name/nm0326063*

GOOD HUMOR TELEVISION

9255 West Sunset Boulevard #1040
West Hollywood, CA 90069

Phone: 310-205-7361
Fax: 310-550-7962

Submission Policy: Accepts Query Letter from unproduced, unrepresented writers
Genre: Comedy, Animation
Company Focus: TV

Tom Werner
Title: Owner/Executive Producer
IMDB: *www.imdb.com/name/nm0921492*

Mike Clements
Title: President/Executive Producer
IMDB: *www.imdb.com/name/nm2540547*

GORILLA PICTURES

2000 West Olive Avenue
Burbank, CA 91506

Phone: 818-848-2198
Fax: 818-848-2232
Email: *info@gorillapictures.net*

Submission Policy: Does not accept any unsolicited material
Genre: Animation
Company Focus: Feature Films
Year Established: 1999

Bill J. Gottlieb
Title: CEO
Email: *bill.gottlieb@gorillapictures.net*
IMDB: *www.imdb.com/name/nm1539281*

Crystal Roberts
Title: Operations Manager
Email: *Crystal.roberts@gorillapictures.net*

Don Wilson
Title: Executive Vice-President of Developement
Email: *don.wilson@gorillapictures.net*

GOTHAM ENTERTAINMENT GROUP

99 John Street, Suite 1609
New York, NY 10038

Phone: 814-253-5151
Email: *development@ gothamentertainmentgroup.com*

Submission Policy: Accepts Query Letter from unproduced, unrepresented writers via email
Company Focus: Feature Films, TV, Reality Programming (Reality TV, Documentaries, Special Events, Sporting Events)

Joel Roodman
Title: Partner
Email: *joel@gothamentertainmentgroup.com*
IMDB: *www.imdb.com/name/nm0740211*

GRACIE FILMS

c/o Sony Pictures Entertainment
10202 Washington Boulevard, Poitier Building
Culver City, CA 90232

Phone: 310-369-7222

Submission Policy: Does not accept any unsolicited material
Genre: Comedy, Memoir & True Stories, Romance, Family, Animation, Drama
Company Focus: Feature Films, TV

James L. Brooks
Title: Producer/Writer/Director
IMDB: *www.imdb.com/name/nm0000985*

GRADE A ENTERTAINMENT

149 South Barrington Ave, Suite 719
Los Angeles, CA 90049

Phone: 310-358-8600
Fax: 310-919-2998
Email: *development@gradeaent.com*

Submission Policy: Accepts Query Letter from unproduced, unrepresented writers via email
Company Focus: Feature Films, TV

Andy Cohen
Title: Producer/Manager
Email: *andy@gradeaent.com*
IMDB: *www.imdb.com/name/nm2221597*

GRAMMNET PRODUCTIONS

2461 Santa Monica Boulevard #521
Santa Monica, CA 90404

Phone: 310-317-4231
Fax: 310-317-4260

Submission Policy: Does not accept any

unsolicited material
Genre: Comedy, TV Drama, TV Sitcom, Family
Company Focus: Feature Films, TV, Reality
Programming (Reality TV, Documentaries,
Special Events, Sporting Events), Theater

Kelsey Grammar
Title: Actor/Producer/CEO
IMDB: *www.imdb.com/name/nm0001288*
Assistant: Xochitl L. Olivas

Stella Bulochnikov
Title: Executive
Phone: 310-255-5089
Assistant: Melissa Panzer, *mpanzer@lionsgate. com*

GRAN VIA PRODUCTIONS

1888 Century Park East
14th Floor
Los Angeles, CA 90067

Phone: 310-859-3060
Fax: 310-859-3066

Submission Policy: Does not accept any
unsolicited material
Genre: Comedy, Fantasy, Science Fiction, TV
Drama, TV Sitcom, Drama
Company Focus: Feature Films, TV

Mark Johnson
Title: President/Producer
IMDB: *www.imdb.com/name/nm0425741*
Assistant: Emily Eckert (Story Editor)

Mark Ceryak
Title: Creative Executive
IMDB: *www.imdb.com/name/nm1641437*

GRAND CANAL FILM WORKS

1187 Coast Village Road
Montecito, CA 93108
11135 Magnolia
SU 160
North Hollywood, CA 91601

Phone: 818-259-8237

Submission Policy: Does not accept any
unsolicited material
Company Focus: Feature Films, TV, Reality

Programming (Reality TV, Documentaries,
Special Events, Sporting Events), Theater

Craig Haffner
Title: Partner
Email: *CHaffner@GrandCanalFW.com*
IMDB: *www.imdb.com/name/nm0353121*

Rick Brookwell
Title: Partner
Email: *RBrookwell@GrandCanalFW.com*

GRAND PRODUCTIONS, INC.

16255 Venture Boulevard, Suite 400
Encino, CA 91436

Phone: 818-981-1497
Email: *grandproductions@me.cmo*

Submission Policy: Does not accept any
unsolicited material
Genre: TV Drama, TV Sitcom
Company Focus: Feature Films, TV

Gary A. Randall
Title: President/Owner/Executive Producer
IMDB: *www.imdb.com/name/nm0709592*

Jennifer Stempell
Title: Development Executive
IMDB: *www.imdb.com/name/nm4009105*

GRAY ANGEL PRODUCTIONS

69 Windward Avenue
Venice, CA 90291

Phone: 310-581-0010
Fax: 310-396-0551

Submission Policy: Accepts Query Letter from
unproduced, unrepresented writers
Company Focus: Feature Films

Anjelica Huston
Title: CEO/Producer
IMDB: *www.imdb.com/name/nm0001378*

Jaclyn Bashoff
Title: President/Manager
IMDB: *www.imdb.com/name/nm1902472*

GRAZKA TAYLOR PRODUCTIONS

409 North Camden Drive, Suite 202
Beverly Hills, CA 90210

Phone: 310-246-1107

Submission Policy: Does not accept any
unsolicited material
Company Focus: Feature Films, TV, Reality
Programming (Reality TV, Documentaries,
Special Events, Sporting Events)

Grazka Taylor
Title: Producer
Email: *grazka@grazkat.com*
IMDB: *www.imdb.com/name/nm0852429*

GREASY ENTERTAINMENT

6345 Balboa Boulevard
Building 4, Suite 375
Encino, CA 91316

Phone: 310-586-2300
Email: *info@greasy.biz*

Submission Policy: Accepts Query Letter from
unproduced, unrepresented writers via email
Genre: Comedy
Company Focus: Feature Films, TV

Jon Heder
Title: CFO/Actor/Executive
IMDB: *www.imdb.com/name/nm1417647*

Doug Heder
Title: CFO/Executive

Dan Heder
Title: Executive

GREEN HAT FILMS

4000 Warner Boulevard
Building 66
Burbank, CA 91522

Phone: 818-954-3210

Submission Policy: Does not accept any
unsolicited material
Genre: Comedy
Company Focus: Feature Films

Todd Phillips
Title: President/Director
IMDB: *www.imdb.com/name/nm0680846*
Assistant: Joseph Garner

Mark O'Connor
Title: Director of Development

GREENESTREET FILMS

609 Greenwich Street
6th Floor
New York, NY 10014

Phone: 212-609-9000
Fax: 212-609-9099
Email: *info@greenestreetfilms.com*

Submission Policy: Accepts Query Letter from
unproduced, unrepresented writers via email
Company Focus: Feature Films

Amanda Essick
Title: Vice-President, Development
IMDB: *www.imdb.com/name/nm2302699*

Ben Webster
Title: Development Assistant

GREENTREES FILMS

854-A 5th Street
Santa Monica, CA 90403

Phone: 310-899-1522
Fax: 310-496-2082
Email: *info@greentreesfilms.com*

Submission Policy: Accepts Query Letter from
unproduced, unrepresented writers via email
Company Focus: Feature Films, TV, Reality
Programming (Reality TV, Documentaries,
Special Events, Sporting Events), Media
(Commercials/Branding/Marketing)

Jack Binder
Title: Producer/President
IMDB: *www.imdb.com/name/nm0082784*

GRIZZLY ADAMS

PO Box 2438
Coeur d'Alene ID 83816

Phone: 208-683-0593
Email: *admin@grizzlyadams.tv*

Submission Policy: Does not accept any unsolicited material
Company Focus: TV

Julie Magnuson
Title: President/Executive Producer

Tod Swindell
Title: Executive Producer/CCO

GROSS-WESTON PRODUCTIONS

10560 Wilshire Boulevard, Suite 801
Los Angeles, CA 90024

Phone: 310-777-0010
Fax: 310-777-0016
Email: *gross-weston@sbcglobal.net*

Submission Policy: Accepts Scripts from produced or represented writers
Company Focus: Feature Films, TV, Reality Programming (Reality TV, Documentaries, Special Events, Sporting Events), Theater

Mary Gross
Title: Executive Producer

Ann Weston
Title: Executive Producer

GROSSO JACOBSON COMMUNICATIONS CORP.

1801 Avenue of the Stars, Suite 911
Los Angeles, CA 90067

767 Third Avenue
New York, NY 10017

373 Front Street East
Toronto, Ontario MSA 1G4
Canada

Phone: 310-788-8900 (LA)
Email: *grossojacobson@grossojacobson.com*

Submission Policy: Accepts Query Letter from unproduced, unrepresented writers via email
Company Focus: Feature Films, TV, Reality Programming (Reality TV, Documentaries, Special Events, Sporting Events), Theater
Year Established: 1999

Sonny Grosso
Title: Executive Producer

GROUNDSWELL PRODUCTIONS

11925 Wilshire Boulevard, Suite 310
Los Angeles, CA 90025

Phone: 310-385-7540
Fax: 310-385-7541
Email: *info@groundswellfilms.com*

Submission Policy: Does not accept any unsolicited material
Genre: Memoir & True Stories, Drama, Socio-cultural
Company Focus: Feature Films, TV, Theater
Year Established: 2006

Janice Williams
Title: Vice-President of Production
IMDB: *www.imdb.com/name/nm1003921*

Kelly Mullen
Title: Vice-President
IMDB: *www.imdb.com/name/nm4133402*

GUARDIAN ENTERTAINMENT, LTD.

71 5th Avenue
New York, NY 10003

Phone: 212-727-4729
Fax: 212-727-4713
Email: *guardian@guardianltd.com*

Submission Policy: Accepts Query Letter from unproduced, unrepresented writers via email
Company Focus: Feature Films, TV, Reality Programming (Reality TV, Documentaries, Special Events, Sporting Events), Media (Commercials/Branding/Marketing)

Richard Miller
Title: CEO/Executive Producer
Email: *rmiller@guardianltd.com*

Anita Agair
Title: Production Coordinator
Email: *agair@guardianltd.com*

GUNN FILMS

500 South Buena Vista Street
Old Animation Building, Suite 3-A7
Burbank, CA 91521

Phone: 818-560-6156
Fax: 818-842-8394

Submission Policy: Does not accept any
unsolicited material
Genre: Comedy, Family
Company Focus: Feature Films, TV
Year Established: 2001

Andrew Gunn
Title: Producer
Email: *andrew.gunn@disney.com*
IMDB: *www.imdb.com/name/nm0348151*

Heather Hutt
Title: Creative Executive

GUY WALKS INTO A BAR

236 West 27th Street #1000
New York, NY 10001

Phone: 212-941-1509
Email: *info@guywalks.com*

Submission Policy: Does not accept any
unsolicited material
Genre: Comedy, Family, Animation
Company Focus: Feature Films, TV, Media
(Commercials/Branding/Marketing)

Todd Komarnicki
Title: Partner/Producer
IMDB: *www.imdb.com/name/nm0464548*

Jonathan Coleman
Title: Director of Development

H2F ENTERTAINMENT

644 North Cherokee Avenue
Melrose Gate
Los Angeles, CA 90004

Phone: 310-275-3750
Fax: 310-275-3770

Submission Policy: Accepts Query Letter from
unproduced, unrepresented writers
Company Focus: Feature Films, TV

Chris Cowles
Title: Producer
IMDB: *www.imdb.com/name/nm1038319*

Brian McCurly
Title: Assistant

H2O MOTION PICTURES

8549 Hedges Place
Los Angeles, CA 90069, Suite 8
111 East 10th Street
New York
NY 10003

Phone: 323-654-5920
Fax: 323-654-5923
Email: *h2o@h2omotionpictures.com*

Submission Policy: Accepts Query Letter from
unproduced, unrepresented writers via email
Company Focus: Feature Films

Andras Hamori
Title: Producer
IMDB: *www.imdb.com/name/nm0358877*

HAND PICKED FILMS

2893 Sea Ridge Drive
Malibu, CA 90265

Phone: 310-361-6832
Email: *info@handpickedfilms.net*

Submission Policy: Does not accept any
unsolicited material
Genre: Comedy, Detective, Memoir & True
Stories, Animation, Drama
Company Focus: Feature Films, TV, Reality
Programming (Reality TV, Documentaries,
Special Events, Sporting Events), Media
(Commercials/Branding/Marketing)
Year Established: 2005

Anthony Romano
Title: Producer
IMDB: *www.imdb.com/name/nm0738853*

Michel Shane
IMDB: *www.imdb.com/name/nm0788062*

HANDSOME CHARLIE FILMS

1720-1/2 Whitley Avenue
Los Angeles, CA 90028

Phone: 323-462-6013

Submission Policy: Does not accept any
unsolicited material
Company Focus: Feature Films

Natalie Portman
Title: President
IMDB: *www.imdb.com/name/nm0000204*

Kimberly Barton
Title: Creative Executive

HANNIBAL PICTURES

8265 Sunset Boulevard, Suite 107
West Hollywood, CA 90046

Phone: 323-848-2945
Fax: 323-848-2946
Email: *contactus@hannibalpictures.com*

Submission Policy: Accepts Query Letter from
unproduced, unrepresented writers via email
Company Focus: Feature Films
Year Established: 1999

Richard Rionda Del Castro
Title: Chairman/CEO/Producer
IMDB: *www.imdb.com/name/nm0215502*

Cam Canoon
Title: Director of Development
IMDB: *www.imdb.com/name/nm1359191*

HAPPY GIRL PRODUCTIONS

2629 Main Street #211
Santa Monica, CA 90405

Phone: 310-396-6013

Submission Policy: Does not accept any
unsolicited material
Company Focus: Feature Films

Amy Salko Robertson
Title: Film and TV Producer
IMDB: *www.imdb.com/name/nm1516144*

HARPO FILMS, INC.

345 North Maple Dr, Suite 315
Beverly Hills, CA 90210

Phone: 310-278-5559

Submission Policy: Does not accept any
unsolicited material
Company Focus: Feature Films, TV

Oprah Winfrey
Title: Chairman/CEO/Producer
IMDB: *www.imdb.com/name/nm0001856*

HASBRO, INC./HASBRO FILMS

100 Universal City Plaza
Building 5184
Universal City, CA 91608

Phone: 818-777-3431

Submission Policy: Accepts Query Letter from
unproduced, unrepresented writers
Company Focus: Feature Films

Daniel Persitz
Title: Creative Executive
IMDB: *www.imdb.com/name/nm1974626*

HAZY MILLS PRODUCTIONS

4024 Radford Avenue
Building 7—2nd Floor
Studio City, CA 91604

Phone: 818-840-7568

Submission Policy: Does not accept any
unsolicited material
Company Focus: Feature Films, TV, Reality
Programming (Reality TV, Documentaries,
Special Events, Sporting Events)
Year Established: 2004

Sean Hayes
IMDB: *www.imdb.com/name/nm0005003*
Assistant: Jessie Kalick

Kiel Elliott
Title: Development Executive

HBO FILMS & MINISERIES

2500 Broadway, Suite 400
Santa Monica, CA 90404

Phone: 310-382-3000
Fax: 310-382-3552

Submission Policy: Does not accept any unsolicited material
Company Focus: TV

Len Amato
Title: President, Films
IMDB: *www.imdb.com/name/nm0024163*

Kary Antholis
Title: President, HBO Miniseries
IMDB: *www.imdb.com/name/nm0030794*

HEAVY DUTY ENTERTAINMENT

6121 Sunset Boulevard, Suite 103
Los Angeles, CA 90028

Phone: 323-209-3545
Fax: 323-653-1720
Email: *info@heavydutyentertainment.com*

Submission Policy: Does not accept any unsolicited material
Company Focus: Feature Films, TV

Jeff Balis
Title: Producer
IMDB: *www.imdb.com/name/nm0050276*

Rhoades Rader
Title: Producer
IMDB: *www.imdb.com/name/nm0705476*

HEEL AND TOE FILMS

2058 Broadway
Santa Monica, CA 90404

Phone: 310-264-1866
Fax: 310-264-1865

Submission Policy: Does not accept any unsolicited material
Genre: Action, Romance, TV Drama, Drama
Company Focus: Feature Films, TV

Paul Attanasio
Title: Writer/Executive Producer
Email: *paul.attanasio@fox.com*
IMDB: *www.imdb.com/name/nm0001921*

Katie Jacobs
Title: Executive Producer
Email: *katie.jacobs@fox.com*
IMDB: *www.imdb.com/name/nm0414498*

HENCEFORTH PICTURES

1411 Fifth Street, Suite 200
Santa Monica, CA 90401

Phone: 424-832-5517
Fax: 424-832-5564

Submission Policy: Does not accept any unsolicited material
Company Focus: Feature Films, TV

William Monahan
Title: Producer/Writer
IMDB: *www.imdb.com/name/nm1184258*

Justine Suzanne Jones
Title: Vice-President of Development
IMDB: *www.imdb.com/name/nm3540960*

HENDERSON PRODUCTIONS, INC.

4252 Riverside Drive
Burbank, CA 91505

Phone: 818-955-5702

Submission Policy: Does not accept any unsolicited material
Company Focus: Feature Films, Theater

Garry Marshall
Title: Producer/Writer/Director
IMDB: *www.imdb.com/name/nm0005190*

HEYDAY FILMS

4000 Warner Boulevard
Building 81, Room 207
Burbank, CA 91522

Phone: 818-954-3004
Fax: 818-954-3017

Submission Policy: Does not accept any

unsolicited material
Company Focus: Feature Films, TV

Jeffrey Clifford
Title: President
IMDB: *www.imdb.com/name/nm0166641*

HIGH HORSE FILMS

100 Universal City Plaza
Building 2128, Suite E
Universal City, CA 91608

Phone: 323-939-8802
Fax: 323-939-8832

Submission Policy: Accepts Query Letter from
unproduced, unrepresented writers
Genre: TV Drama, TV Sitcom
Company Focus: Feature Films, TV
Year Established: 1990

William Petersen
Title: Actor/Producer
IMDB: *www.imdb.com/name/nm0676973*

Cynthia Chvatal
Title: Producer
IMDB: *www.imdb.com/name/nm0161558*

HOLLYWOOD GANG PRODUCTIONS, LLC

4000 Warner Boulevard
Building 139, Room 201
Burbank, CA 91522

Phone: 818-954-4999
Fax: 818-954-4448

Submission Policy: Does not accept any
unsolicited material
Company Focus: Feature Films

Gianni Nunnari
Title: President/Producer
IMDB: *www.imdb.com/name/nm0638089*

HOWARD BRAUNSTEIN FILMS

1631 21st Street
Santa Monica, CA 90404

Phone: 310-207-6600

Submission Policy: Accepts Scripts from

produced or represented writers
Company Focus: TV

Howard Braunstein
Title: Owner/Executive Producer
IMDB: *www.imdb.com/name/nm0105946*

HUGHES CAPITAL ENTERTAINMENT

22817 Ventura Boulevard, Suite 471
Woodland Hills, CA 91364

Phone: 818-484-3205
Email: *info@trihughes.com*

Submission Policy: Accepts Scripts from
produced or represented writers
Company Focus: Feature Films

Patrick Hughes
Title: President/Producer

Jacob Clymore
Title: Executive Assistant
Email: *jc@trihughes.com*

HUTCH PARKER'S ENTERTAINMENT

10201 West Pico Boulevard
Los Angeles, CA 90064

Email: *hutchparkerentertainment@gmail.com*

Submission Policy: Accepts Scripts from
produced or represented writers
Company Focus: Feature Films
Year Established: 2012

Hutch Parker
Title: Founder

Aaron Ensweiler
Title: Vice-President
IMDB: *www.imdb.com/name/nm3943221*

HYDE PARK ENTERTAINMENT

3500 West Olive Avenue, Suite 300
Burbank, CA 91505

Phone: 818-783-6060
Fax: 818-783-6319
Email: *contact@hydeparkentertainment.com*

Submission Policy: Accepts Query Letter from

unproduced, unrepresented writers via email
Company Focus: Feature Films
Year Established: 1999

Ashtok Amiraj
Title: Chairman/CEO
IMDB: *www.imdb.com/name/nm0002170*

Mike Dougherty
Title: Creative Executive

Marc Fiorentino
Title: Development and Production Executive

Yee Yeo Chang
Title: Executive Development/Production
(Singapore Office)
IMDB: *www.imdb.com/name/nm2303875*

HYPNOTIC FILMS & TELEVISION

12233 West Olympic Boulevard, Suite 255
Los Angeles, CA 90064

Phone: 310-806-6930
Fax: 310-806-6931

Submission Policy: Does not accept any
unsolicited material
Company Focus: Feature Films, TV

Doug Liman
Title: Vice Chairman/Producer
IMDB: *www.imdb.com/name/nm0510731*

Lindsay Sloane
Title: Development Executive

ICON PRODUCTIONS, LLC

808 Wilshire Boulevard, Suite 400
Santa Monica, CA 90401

Phone: 310-434-7300
Fax: 310-434-7377

Submission Policy: Does not accept any
unsolicited material
Company Focus: Feature Films

Mel Gibson
Title: Actor/Producer/Writer
IMDB: *www.imdb.com/name/nm0000154*

IMAGINE ENTERTAINMENT

9465 Wilshire Boulevard
7th Floor
Beverly Hills, CA 90212

Phone: 310-858-2000
Fax: 310-858-2020

Submission Policy: Does not accept any
unsolicited material

Ron Howard
Title: Chairman/Director
IMDB: *www.imdb.com/name/nm0000165*

Erin Fredman
Title: Creative Executive

IMAGINE TELEVISION

9465 Wilshire Boulevard
7th Floor
Beverly Hills, CA 90212

Phone: 310-858-2000
Fax: 310-858-2011

Submission Policy: Does not accept any
unsolicited material
Genre: TV Drama, TV Sitcom
Company Focus: TV

Ron Howard
IMDB: *www.imdb.com/name/nm0000165*

Erin Gunn
Title: Senior Vice-President, Comedy
Development and Current Programming
IMDB: *www.imdb.com/name/nm3838484*

IMPACT PICTURES

9200 West Sunset Boulevard, Suite 800
West Hollywood, CA 90069

Phone: 310-247-1803

Submission Policy: Accepts Query Letter from
unproduced, unrepresented writers via email
Company Focus: Feature Films

Paul W. S. Anderson
Title: Producer/Writer
IMDB: *www.imdb.com/name/nm0027271*
Assistant: Sarah Crompton

Jeremy Bolt
Title: Producer
IMDB: *www.imdb.com/name/nm0093337*

IMPRINT ENTERTAINMENT

100 Universal City Plaza
Bungalow 7125
Universal City, CA 91608

Phone: 818-733-5410
Email: *info@imprint-ent.com*

Submission Policy: Does not accept any
unsolicited material
Company Focus: Feature Films, TV, Reality
Programming (Reality TV, Documentaries,
Special Events, Sporting Events), Media
(Commercials/Branding/Marketing)
Year Established: 2008

Sean McCarthy
Title: Creative Executive

Lee Arter
Title: Executive Assistant
Email: *larter@imprint-ent.com*

IN CAHOOTS

4024 Radford Avenue
Editorial Building 2, Suite 7
Studio City, CA 91604

Phone: 818-655-6482
Fax: 818-655-8472

Submission Policy: Does not accept any
unsolicited material
Genre: TV Drama, TV Sitcom
Company Focus: Feature Films, TV

Ken Kwapis
IMDB: *www.imdb.com/name/nm0477129*

Reynolds Anderson
Title: Creative Executive
IMDB: *www.imdb.com/name/nm1568030*

INDIAN PAINTBRUSH

1660 Euclid Street
Santa Monica, CA 90404

Phone: 310-566-0160
Fax: 310-566-0161
Email: *info@indianpaintbrush.com*

Submission Policy: Does not accept any
unsolicited material
Company Focus: Feature Films

Mark Roybal
Title: President, Production
IMDB: *www.imdb.com/name/nm0747287*

Adam Draves
Title: Creative Executive

INDICAN PRODUCTIONS

2565 Broadway, Suite 138
New York, NY 10025

Phone: 212-666-1500

Submission Policy: Does not accept any
unsolicited material
Company Focus: Feature Films

Julia Ormond
Email: *julia.ormond@fox.com*
IMDB: *www.imdb.com/name/nm0000566*

INDOMITABLE ENTERTAINMENT

1920 Main Street, Suite A
Santa Monica, CA 90405

225 Varick Street, Suite 304
New York, NY 10014

Phone: 310-664-8700 or 212-352-1071
Fax: 310-664-8711 or 212-727-3860
Email: *info@indomitable.com*

Submission Policy: Accepts Query Letter from
unproduced, unrepresented writers via email

Dominic Ianno
Title: Founder, CEO
IMDB: *www.imdb.com/name/nm1746156*

Robert Deege
Title: Vice President of Business & Creative
Affairs
IMDB: *www.imdb.com/name/nm1830098*

Chris Mirosevic
Title: Director of Film Services

IMDB: *www.imdb.com/name/nm1746156*

INDUSTRY ENTERTAINMENT PARTNERS

955 South Carrillo Drive, Suite 300
Los Angeles, CA 90048

Phone: 323-954-9000
Fax: 323-954-9009

Submission Policy: Accepts Scripts from produced or represented writers
Company Focus: Feature Films, TV

INFERNO

1888 Century Park East, Suite 1540
Los Angeles, CA 90067

Phone: 310-598-2550
Fax: 310-598-2551

Submission Policy: Does not accept any unsolicited material
Company Focus: Feature Films

Campbell McInnes
Title: Production Development Executive
IMDB: *www.imdb.com/name/nm0570577*

D.J. Gugenheim
Title: Vice President of Production
IMDB: *www.imdb.com/name/nm1486759*

INFORMANT MEDIA

10866 Wilshire Boulevard
4th Floor, Suite 422
Los Angeles, CA 90024

Phone: 310-470-9309
Fax: 310-347-4497
Email: *development@informantmedia.com*

Submission Policy: Accepts Query Letter from unproduced, unrepresented writers via email
Company Focus: Feature Films, TV

Rick Bitzelberger
Title: Development
Email: *development@informantmedia.com*

INK FACTORY

9 Greek Street
London W1D 4DQ
United Kingdom

Phone: +44 20-7734-7372
Fax: +44 20-7287-5228

Submission Policy: Does not accept any unsolicited material
Genre: Drama
Company Focus: Feature Films
Year Established: 2010

Steven Cornwell
Title: Writer/Producer/Founder
Email: *steven@inkonscreen.co.uk*
IMDB: *www.imdb.com/name/nm4051169*

Rhodri Thomas
Email: *rhodri@inkonscreen.co.uk*
IMDB: *www.imdb.com/name/nm2905579*

INPHENATE

9701 Wilshire Boulevard
10th Floor
Beverly Hills, CA 90212

Phone: 310-601-7117

Submission Policy: Does not accept any unsolicited material
Company Focus: Feature Films, TV, Reality Programming (Reality TV, Documentaries, Special Events, Sporting Events)

Glenn Rigberg
Title: Producer
IMDB: *www.imdb.com/name/nm0726572*

IRISH DREAMTIME

3000 West Olympic Boulevard
Building 3, Suite 2332
Santa Monica, CA 90404

Phone: 310-449-4081
Email: *info@irishdreamtime.com*

Submission Policy: Does not accept any unsolicited material
Company Focus: Feature Films, TV
Year Established: 1996

Pierce Brosnan
Title: Partner/Producer
IMDB: *www.imdb.com/name/nm0000112*

IRONWORKS PRODUCTION

295 Greenwich Street, Suite 391
New York, NY 10007

Phone: 212-486-9829
Fax: 917-757-6988
Email: *ironworksproductions@pobox.com*

Submission Policy: Accepts Query Letter from
unproduced, unrepresented writers via email
Company Focus: Feature Films, TV, Reality
Programming (Reality TV, Documentaries,
Special Events, Sporting Events)

Bruce Weiss
Title: President/Producer
IMDB: *www.imdb.com/name/nm0918933*

ITHACA PICTURES

8711 Bonner Drive
West Hollywood, CA 90048

Phone: 310-967-0112
Fax: 310-967-3053

Submission Policy: Does not accept any
unsolicited material
Genre: Memoir & True Stories, Drama,
Socio-cultural
Company Focus: Feature Films

Michael Fitzgerald
Title: Executive
IMDB: *www.imdb.com/name/nm028033*

Richard Romero
Title: Producer
IMDB: *www.imdb.com/name/nm2484143*

JANE STARTZ PRODUCTIONS, INC.

244 Fifth Avenue
11th Floor
New York, NY 10001

Phone: 212-545-8910
Fax: 212-545-8909

Submission Policy: Accepts Query Letter from

unproduced, unrepresented writers
Company Focus: Feature Films, TV

Jane Startz
Title: President/Producer
IMDB: *www.imdb.com/name/nm0823661*

Carolyn Mao
Title: Development Assistant
Email: *cmao@janestartzproductions.com*

JEFF MORTON PRODUCTIONS

10201 West Pico Boulevard Building 226
Los Angeles, CA 90035

Submission Policy: Does not accept any
unsolicited material
Company Focus: Feature Films, TV

Jeff Morton
Title: Producer
Phone: 310-467-1123
IMDB: *www.imdb.com/name/nm0608005*

JERRY BRUCKHEIMER FILMS & TELEVISION

1631 10th Street
Santa Monica, CA 90404

Phone: 310-664-6260
Fax: 310-664-6261
IMDB: *www.imdb.com/company/co0217391*

Submission Policy: Accepts Query Letter from
unproduced, unrepresented writers
Genre: Action, Comedy, Crime, Detective,
Fantasy, Horror, Memoir & True Stories, Myth,
Science Fiction, Thriller, TV Drama, Family,
Drama, Socio-cultural, Reality
Company Focus: Feature Films, TV, Reality
Programming (Reality TV, Documentaries,
Special Events, Sporting Events)

Jerry Bruckheimer
Title: President/Chairman/CEO
IMDB: *www.imdb.com/name/nm0000988*

Charles Vignola
Title: Director, Development
IMDB: *www.imdb.com/name/nm2248505*

Ryan McKeithan
Title: Manager, TV
IMDB: *www.imdb.com/name/nm4915007*

JERRY WEINTRAUB PRODUCTIONS

190 North Canon Drive, Suite 204
Beverly Hills, CA 90210

Phone: 310-273-8800
Fax: 310-273-8502

Submission Policy: Does not accept any
unsolicited material
Genre: Action, Comedy, Thriller, Drama
Company Focus: Feature Films

Jerry Weintraub
Title: Producer
Assistant: Kimberly Pinkstaff

Susan Ekins
Title: Vice-President, Physical Production
Assistant: Betsy Dennis

JERSEY FILMS

PO Box 491246
Los Angeles, CA 90049

Phone: 310-550-3200
Fax: 310-550-3210
IMDB: *www.imdb.com/company/co0010434*

Submission Policy: Accepts Query Letter from
unproduced, unrepresented writers
Genre: Comedy, Memoir & True Stories,
Drama
Company Focus: Feature Films

Danny DeVito
Title: Executive
IMDB: *www.imdb.com/name/nm0000362*

Nikki Allyn Grosso
Title: Business Manager/Legal
Phone: 310-477-7704
IMDB: *www.imdb.com/name/nm0343777*

JET TONE PRODUCTIONS

21/F Park Commercial Centre
No. 180 Tung Lo Wan Road
Hong Kong
China

Phone: 852-2336-1102
Fax: 852-2337-9849
Email: *jettone@netvigator.com*

Submission Policy: Accepts Query Letter from
unproduced, unrepresented writers via email
Genre: Action, Comedy, Crime, Romance,
Science Fiction, Thriller, Animation, Drama
Company Focus: Feature Films

Wong Kar-wai
Title: Producer/Director

JOEL SCHUMACHER PRODUCTIONS

10960 Wilshire Bvld. Suite 1900
Los Angeles, CA 90024

Phone: 310-472-7602
Fax: 310-270-4618

Submission Policy: Does not accept any
unsolicited material
Genre: Action, Fantasy, Science Fiction, Thriller
Company Focus: Feature Films, TV, Media
(Commercials/Branding/Marketing)

Joel Schumacher
Title: Executive/Owner
Phone: 310-472-7602
IMDB: *www.imdb.com/name/nm0001708*
Assistant: Jeff Feuerstein

Aaron Cooley
Title: Producer
Phone: 818-260-6065
IMDB: *www.imdb.com/name/nm0177583*

JOHN CALLEY PRODUCTIONS

10202 West Washington Boulevard
Crawford Building
Culver City, CA 90232

Phone: 310-244-7777
Fax: 310-244-4070

Submission Policy: Does not accept any
unsolicited material
Genre: Action, Detective, Romance, Drama
Company Focus: Feature Films

John Calley
Title: Producer
Phone: 310-244-7777
IMDB: *www.imdb.com/name/nm1886942*

Lisa Medwid
Title: Executive Vice-President
Phone: 310-244-7777

JOHN GOLDWYN PRODUCTIONS

5555 Melrose Avenue, Dressing Room. 112
Los Angeles, CA 90038

Phone: 323-956-5054
Fax: 323-862-0055

Submission Policy: Does not accept any
unsolicited material
Genre: Action, Crime, Detective, Thriller, TV
Drama, Drama
Company Focus: Feature Films, TV
Year Established: 1991

John Goldwyn
Title: President
IMDB: *www.imdb.com/name/nm0326415*
Assistant: Jasen Laks

Hilary Marx
Title: Creative Executive
IMDB: *www.imdb.com/name/nm1020576*
Assistant: Rebecca Crow

Erin David
Title: Creative Executive
IMDB: *www.imdb.com/name/nm1716252*
Assistant: Rebecca Crow

JOHN WELLS PRODUCTIONS

4000 Warner Boulevard
Building 1
Burbank, CA 91522-0001

Phone: 818-954-1687
Fax: 818-954-3657

Submission Policy: Accepts Query Letter from
unproduced, unrepresented writers
Genre: TV Drama, Drama
Company Focus: Feature Films, TV

Claire Rudnick Polstein
Title: President, Features
Phone: 818-954-1687
IMDB: *www.imdb.com/name/nm0689856*

Andrew Stearn
Title: President, TV
Phone: 818-954-1687
IMDB: *www.imdb.com/name/nm1048942*
Assistant: Chris Loveall

Jinny Joung
Title: Director, Development & Production
Phone: 818-954-5276
IMDB: *www.imdb.com/name/nm2187561*

JOSEPHSON ENTERTAINMENT

501 Santa Monica Boulevard, Suite 700
Santa Monica, CA 90401

Phone: 310-566-2500

Submission Policy: Does not accept any
unsolicited material
Genre: Comedy, TV Drama, Family, Drama
Company Focus: Feature Films, TV

Barry Josephson
Title: Producer/Founder

Tia Maggini
Title: Executive-TV

JUNCTION FILMS INC.

9615 Brighton Way, Suite M110
Beverly Hills, CA 90210

Phone: 310-246-9799
Fax: 310-246-3824

Submission Policy: Accepts Query Letter from
unproduced, unrepresented writers
Company Focus: Feature Films, TV, Reality
Programming (Reality TV, Documentaries,
Special Events, Sporting Events)
Year Established: 2001

Brad Wyman
Title: Producer
Phone: 310-246-9799
IMDB: *www.imdb.com/name/nm0943829*

Donald Kushner
Title: Producer
Phone: 310-246-9799
IMDB: *www.imdb.com/name/nm0476291*

Alwyn Kushner
Title: Producer
Phone: 310-246-9799
IMDB: *www.imdb.com/name/nm1672379*

JUNIPER PLACE PRODUCTIONS

4024 Radford Avenue, Bungalow 1
Studio City, CA 91604

Phone: 818-655-5043
Fax: 818-655-8402

Submission Policy: Accepts Query Letter from unproduced, unrepresented writers
Genre: TV Drama
Company Focus: TV

Jeffrey Kramer
Title: President/Executive Producer
Phone: 818-655-5043
IMDB: *www.imdb.com/name/nm0469552*

John Tymus
Title: Director of Development
Phone: 818-655-5302
IMDB: *www.imdb.com/name/nm2002980*

K/O PAPER PRODUCTS (ALSO KNOWN AS: KURTZMAN ORCI PAPER PRODUCTS)

100 Universal City Plaza
Building 5125
Universal City, CA 91608

Phone: 818-733-9645
Fax: 818-733-6988

Submission Policy: Does not accept any unsolicited material
Genre: Action, Science Fiction, Animation
Company Focus: Feature Films, TV
Year Established: 1997

Alex Kurtzman
Title: Producer/Writer
Phone: 818-733-9645
IMDB: *www.imdb.com/name/nm0476064*

Roberto Orci
Title: Producer/Writer
Phone: 818-733-9645
IMDB: *www.imdb.com/name/nm0649460*

KAPLAN PERONE ENTERTAINMENT

9744 Wilshire Boulevard, Suite 300
Beverly Hills, CA 90212

Phone: 310-285-0116

Submission Policy: Accepts Scripts from produced or represented writers
Company Focus: Feature Films, TV

Aaron Kaplan
Title: Executive and Partner

Sean Perrone
Title: Executive and Partner

Tobin Babst
Title: Manager and Partner

Matt Eisenman
Title: Manager

Josh Goldenberg
Title: Manager

Alex Lerner
Title: Manager

KATALYST FILMS

6806 Lexington Avenue
Los Angeles, CA 90038

Phone: 323-785-2700
Fax: 323-785-2715
Email: *info@katalystfilms.com*

Submission Policy: Accepts Scripts from unproduced, unrepresented writers
Company Focus: Feature Films, TV

Ashton Kutcher
Title: Actor/Executive Producer
IMDB: *www.imdb.com/name/nm0005110*

Jason Goldberg
Title: Producer
IMDB: *www.imdb.com/name/nm0325229*

KGB FILMS

5555 Melrose Avenue, Lucy Bungalow 101
Los Angeles, CA 90038

Phone: 323-956-5000
Fax: 323-224-1876
Email: *turbo@kgbfilms.com*

Submission Policy: Accepts Query Letter from unproduced, unrepresented writers via email
Genre: Drama
Company Focus: Feature Films
Year Established: 1994

Rosser Goodman
Title: Producer/Director
Phone: 323-956-5000
Email: *turbo@kgbfilms.com*
IMDB: *www.imdb.com/name/nm0329223*

Justin Hogan
Title: Producer
Phone: 323-956-5000
Email: *turbo@kgbfilms.com*
IMDB: *www.imdb.com/name/nm0389556*

KILLER FILMS INC.

18th East 16th Street, 4th Floor
New York, NY 10003

Phone: 212-473-3950
Fax: 212-807-1456

Submission Policy: Accepts Query Letter from unproduced, unrepresented writers
Genre: TV Drama, Drama
Company Focus: Feature Films, TV
Year Established: 1995

Christine Vachon
Title: Principal/Producer
Phone: 212-473-3950
IMDB: *www.imdb.com/name/nm0882927*
Assistant: Gabrielle Nadig

Pamela Koffler
Title: Principal/Producer
Phone: 212-473-3950
IMDB: *www.imdb.com/name/nm0463025*
Assistant: Gabrielle Nadig

David Hinojosa
Title: Production and Development Executive
Phone: 212-473-3950
IMDB: *www.imdb.com/name/nm3065267*
Assistant: Gabrielle Nadig

KIPPSTER ENTERTAINMENT

420 West End Avenue
1G
New York, NY 10024

Phone: 212-496-1200

Submission Policy: Does not accept any unsolicited material
Company Focus: Feature Films

Perri Kipperman
Title: Producer
IMDB: *www.imdb.com/name/nm1069530*

David A. Sterns
Title: Producer
IMDB: *www.imdb.com/name/nm3992907*

KOMUT ENTERTAINMENT

300 Television Plaza
Building 140, Suite 201
Burbank, CA 91505

Phone: 818-954-7631

Submission Policy: Accepts Query Letter from unproduced, unrepresented writers
Genre: TV Drama, TV Sitcom
Company Focus: TV

David Kohan
Title: Producer
Phone: 818-954-7631
IMDB: *www.imdb.com/name/nm0463172*

Max Mutchnick
Title: Producer
Phone: 818-954-7631
IMDB: *www.imdb.com/name/nm0616083*

Heather Hicks
Title: Executive Assistant
Phone: 818-954-7631
IMDB: *www.imdb.com/name/nm1337402*

KRASNOFF FOSTER PRODUCTIONS

10202 Washington Boulevard
Culver City, CA 90232

Phone: 310-244-3282

Submission Policy: Accepts Query Letter from

unproduced, unrepresented writers
Genre: Memoir & True Stories, Romance, TV Sitcom, Drama
Company Focus: Feature Films, TV

Russ Krasnoff
Title: President/Partner
Phone: 310-244-3282
IMDB: *www.imdb.com/name/nm0469929*
Assistant: Beth Maurer

Krista Carpenter
Title: Vice President Features
Phone: 323-956-3934
IMDB: *www.imdb.com/name/nm1133845*

Heather Petrigala
Title: Vice President of Television
Phone: 310-244-3282
IMDB: *www.imdb.com/name/nm3799159*

LAKESHORE ENTERTAINMENT

9268 West Third Street
Beverly Hills, CA 90210

Phone: 310-867-8000
Fax: 310-300-3015
Email: *info@lakeshoreentertainment.com*

Submission Policy: Accepts Query Letter from produced or represented writers
Genre: Action, Comedy, Romance, Thriller, Drama
Company Focus: Feature Films
Year Established: 1994

Tom Rosenberg
Title: Chairman/CEO
Phone: 310-867-8000
IMDB: *www.imdb.com/name/nm0742347*
Assistant: Tiffany Shinn

Robert McMinn
Title: Senior Vice President of Development
Phone: 310-867-8000
IMDB: *www.imdb.com/name/nm0573372*

Scott Herbst
Title: Creative Executive
Phone: 310-867-8000
IMDB: *www.imdb.com/name/nm2303203*

LANDSCAPE ENTERTAINMENT

1801 Avenue of the Stars, Suite 260
Los Angeles, CA 90067

Phone: 310-248-6200
Fax: 310-248-6300

Submission Policy: Accepts Query Letter from unproduced, unrepresented writers
Genre: Comedy, Memoir & True Stories, Drama
Company Focus: Feature Films, TV
Year Established: 2007

Bob Cooper
Title: Chairman/CEO
Phone: 310-248-6200
IMDB: *www.imdb.com/name/nm0178341*
Assistant: Sandy Shenkman

Tyler Mitchell
Title: Head of Features
Phone: 310-248-6200
IMDB: *www.imdb.com/name/nm1624685*

J.J. Jamieson
Title: Sr. Vice-President, TV
Phone: 310-248-6200
IMDB: *www.imdb.com/name/nm0417121*
Assistant: Anastasia Heur

LANGLEY PARK PRODUCTIONS

4000 Warner Boulevard
Building 144
Burbank, CA 91522

Phone: 818-954-2930

Submission Policy: Does not accept any unsolicited material
Genre: Comedy, Romance, Drama
Company Focus: Feature Films

Kevin McCormick
Title: Producer
Phone: 818-954-2930
IMDB: *www.imdb.com/name/nm0566557*
Assistant: Shamika Pryce

Rory Koslow
Title: Vice President
Phone: 818-954-2930
IMDB: *www.imdb.com/name/nm1739372*
Assistant: Kari Cooper

Aaron Schmidt
Title: Creative Executive
Phone: 818-954-2930
Email: *aaron.schmidt@langleyparkpix.com*
IMDB: *www.imdb.com/name/nm2087164*

LARRIKIN ENTERTAINMENT

1801 Avenue Of The Stars, Suite 921
Los Angeles, CA 90067

Phone: 310-461-3030

Submission Policy: Accepts Scripts from produced or represented writers
Company Focus: Feature Films

David Calvert Jones
Title: Executive/Producer/Partner
IMDB: *www.imdb.com/name/nm1965869*

Greg Coote
Email: *linw@larrikin-ent.com*
Assistant: Wayne Lin

Robert Lundberg
Title: Head, Development & Production
Email: *rll@larrikin-ent.com*

LAURA ZISKIN PRODUCTIONS

10202 West Washington Boulevard
Astaire Building, Suite 1310
Culver City, CA 90232

Phone: 310-244-7373
Fax: 310-244-0073

Submission Policy: Accepts Query Letter from unproduced, unrepresented writers
Genre: Action, Fantasy, Romance, Drama
Company Focus: Feature Films, TV
Year Established: 1995

Pam Oas Williams
Title: President
Phone: 310-244-7373
IMDB: *www.imdb.com/name/nm0931423*
Assistant: David Jacobson

Julia Barry
Title: Director of Development
Phone: 310-244-7373

LAURENCE MARK PRODUCTIONS

10202 West Washington Boulevard
Poitier Building
Culver City, CA 90232

Phone: 310-244-5239
Fax: 310-244-0055

Submission Policy: Accepts Query Letter from unproduced, unrepresented writers
Genre: Action, Comedy, Science Fiction, Drama
Company Focus: Feature Films, TV

Laurence Mark
Title: President/Producer
Phone: 310-244-5239
IMDB: *www.imdb.com/name/nm0548257*

Tamara Chestna
Title: Director of Development
Phone: 310-244-5239
IMDB: *www.imdb.com/name/nm2309894*

David Blackman
Title: Senior Vice President
Phone: 310-244-5239
IMDB: *www.imdb.com/name/nm1844320*
Assistant: Sean Bennett

LAVA BEAR FILMS

3201-B South La Cienega Boulevard
Los Angeles, CA 90016

Phone: 310-815-9600

Submission Policy: Does not accept any unsolicited material
Genre: Action, Comedy, Fantasy, Romance, Family, Drama
Company Focus: Feature Films
Year Established: 2011

David Linde
Title: Principle
Phone: 310-815-9603
Email: *Dlinde@lavabear.com*
IMDB: *www.imdb.com/name/nm0511482*

Tory Metzger
Title: President of Production
Email: *Tmetzger@lavabear.com*
IMDB: *www.imdb.com/name/nm0582762*

Zachary Studin
Title: Vice-President of Production
Email: *Zstudin@lavabear.com*
IMDB: *www.imdb.com/name/nm1713122*

LAWRENCE BENDER PRODUCTIONS

8530 Wilshire Boulevard, Suite 500
Los Angeles, CA 90211

Phone: 323-951-4600
Fax: 323-951-4601

Submission Policy: Accepts Query Letter from unproduced, unrepresented writers
Genre: Action, Drama
Company Focus: Feature Films, TV

Lawrence Bender
Title: Partner
Phone: 323-951-4600
IMDB: *www.imdb.com/name/nm0004744*
Assistant: Vincent Gatewood

Janet Jeffries
Title: Development
Phone: 323-951-4600
IMDB: *www.imdb.com/name/nm0420377*

Kevin Brown
Title: Production
Phone: 323-951-4600
IMDB: *www.imdb.com/name/nm0114019*

LEGENDARY PICTURES

4000 Warner Boulevard
Building 76
Burbank, CA 91522

Phone: 818-954-3888
Fax: 818-954-3884

Submission Policy: Does not accept any unsolicited material
Genre: Action, Comedy, Memoir & True Stories, Romance, Thriller, Family, Drama
Company Focus: Feature Films, TV
Year Established: 2005

Thomas Tull
Title: Chairman/CEO
Phone: 818-954-3888
IMDB: *www.imdb.com/name/nm2100078*

Lauren Ruggiero
Title: Director of TV Development
Phone: 818-954-3888
IMDB: *www.imdb.com/name/nm4549739*

Alex Hedlund
Title: Creative Executive
Phone: 818-954-3888
IMDB: *www.imdb.com/name/nm2906163*

LIAISON FILMS

9000 West Sunset Boulevard, #709
West Hollywood, CA 90069
or
44 Rue des Acacias
Paris, France 75017

Phone: 310-210-0766
Fax: 310-248-3755
Email: *contact@liasonfilms.com*

Submission Policy: Does not accept any unsolicited material
Company Focus: Feature Films

Stephane Sperry
Title: President
Email: *stephane.sperry@liasonfilms.com*
IMDB: *www.imdb.com/name/nm0818373*

LIN PICTURES

4000 Warner Boulevard
Building 143
Burbank, CA 91522

Phone: 818-954-6759
Fax: 818-954-2329

Submission Policy: Does not accept any unsolicited material
Company Focus: Feature Films, TV

Dan Lin
Title: Producer/CEO
Phone: 818-954-6759
IMDB: *www.imdb.com/name/nm1469853*

Jon Silk
Title: Vice-President, Production/Development
Phone: 818-954-6759
IMDB: *www.imdb.com/name/nm1698314*

Jennifer Gwartz
Title: Head of Television Development
Phone: 818-954-6759
IMDB: *www.imdb.com/name/nm0350311*
Assistant: Jared Blitz

LIONSGATE

2700 Colorado Avenue, Suite 200
Santa Monica, CA 90404

Phone: 310-449-9200
Fax: 310-255-3870
Email: *general-inquiries@lgf.com*

Submission Policy: Accepts Query Letter from
unproduced, unrepresented writers via email
Company Focus: Feature Films, TV
Year Established: 1997

Jon Feltheimer
Title: Co-Chairman/CEO
Phone: 310-449-9200
Email: *jfeltheimer@lionsgate.com*
IMDB: *www.imdb.com/name/nm1410838*

Matthew Janzen
Title: Director of Development
Phone: 310-449-9200
IMDB: *www.imdb.com/name/nm0418432*

Charisse Nesbit
Title: Director of Development/Consultant
Phone: 310-449-9200
Email: *cnesbit@lionsgate.com*
IMDB: *www.imdb.com/name/nm2697451*

LITTLE ENGINE PRODUCTIONS

500 South Buena Vista Street
Animation Building 3F-6
Burbank, CA 91521

Phone: 818-560-4670
Fax: 818-560-4014

Submission Policy: Accepts Query Letter from
unproduced, unrepresented writers
Company Focus: Feature Films, TV, Reality

Programming (Reality TV, Documentaries,
Special Events, Sporting Events)

Gina Matthews
Title: Partner/Producer
Phone: 818-560-4670
IMDB: *www.imdb.com/name/nm0560033*

Mitchell Gutman
Title: Director of Development
Phone: 818-560-4670
IMDB: *www.imdb.com/name/nm1393767*

Grant Scharbo
Title: Partner/Producer
Phone: 818-560-4670
IMDB: *www.imdb.com/name/nm0770090*

LYNDA OBST PRODUCTIONS

10202 West Washington Boulevard
Astaire Building, Suite 1000
Culver City, CA 90232

Phone: 310-244-6122
Fax: 310-244-0092

Submission Policy: Does not accept any
unsolicited material
Company Focus: Feature Films, TV

Lynda Obst
Title: Vice President of Production
Phone: 310-244-6112
IMDB: *www.imdb.com/name/nm0643553*

Rachel Abarbanell
Title: Vice President of Production
Phone: 310-233-6112
IMDB: *www.imdb.com/name/nm1561964*

MAD CHANCE

4000 Warner Boulevard
Building 81, Room 208
Burbank, CA 91522

Phone: 818-954-3500
Fax: 818-954-3586

Submission Policy: Does not accept any
unsolicited material
Genre: Action, Comedy, Romance, Drama
Company Focus: Feature Films

Andrew Lazar
Title: Producer
Phone: 818-954-3500
IMDB: *www.imdb.com/name/nm0493662*
Assistant: Matthew Ferrante (Covering Assistant)

Alana Mayo
Title: Creative Executive
Phone: 818-954-3500
IMDB: *www.imdb.com/name/nm2641506*

Miri Yoon
Title: Executive
Phone: 818-954-3500
IMDB: *www.imdb.com/name/nm1186661*

MAD HATTER ENTERTAINMENT

9229 Sunset Boulevard, Suite 225
West Hollywood, CA 90069

Phone: 310-860-0441

Submission Policy: Accepts Scripts from unproduced, unrepresented writers
Genre: Action, Comedy, Fantasy, Myth, Science Fiction, Family, Animation, Drama
Company Focus: Feature Films, TV

Michael Connolly
Title: Founder/Manager/Producer
Email: *mike@madhatterentertainment.com*
IMDB: *www.imdb.com/name/nm0175326*

MADRIK MULTIMEDIA

Los Angeles Center Studios
1201 West Fifth Street, Suite F222
Los Angeles, CA 90017

Phone: 213-596-5180
Email: *info@madrik.com*

Submission Policy: Accepts Query Letter from unproduced, unrepresented writers

Chris Adams
Title: Founder
Email: *chris@madrik.com*
IMDB: *www.imdb.com/name/nm1886228*

MALPASO PRODUCTIONS

4000 Warner Boulevard
Building 81
Burbank, CA 91522-0811

Phone: 818-954-3367
Fax: 818-954-4803

Submission Policy: Does not accept any unsolicited material
Genre: Drama
Company Focus: Feature Films
Year Established: 1967

Clint Eastwood
Title: Producer/Actor/Director
Phone: 818-954-3367
IMDB: *www.imdb.com/name/nm0000142*

Robert Lorenz
Title: Partner/Producer
Phone: 818-954-3367
IMDB: *www.imdb.com/name/nm0520749*

Joel Cox
Title: Editor
Phone: 310-205-5812
IMDB: *www.imdb.com/name/nm0185088*

MANDALAY PICTURES

4751 Wilshire Boulevard, 3rd Floor
Los Angeles, CA 90010

Phone: 323-549-4300
Fax: 323-549-9832
Email: *info@mandalay.com*

Submission Policy: Accepts Query Letter from produced or represented writers
Genre: Action, Horror, Romance, Thriller, Family, Drama
Company Focus: Feature Films, TV
Year Established: 1995

Peter Guber
Title: Chairman/CEO
Phone: 323-549-4300
Email: *info@mandalay.com*
IMDB: *www.imdb.com/name/nm0345542*

Adam Stone
Title: Vice-President of Development
Phone: 323-549-4300
Email: *info@mandalay.com*
IMDB: *www.imdb.com/name/nm2625826*
Assistant: Gabriel Chu

Joey De La Rosa
Title: Creative Executive
Phone: 323-549-4300

MANDALAY TELEVISION

4751 Wilshire Boulevard, 3rd Floor
Los Angeles, CA 90010

Phone: 323-549-4300
Fax: 323-549-9832
Email: *info@mandalay.com*

Submission Policy: Does not accept any
unsolicited material
Genre: TV Drama
Company Focus: TV

Paul Schaeffer
Title: Vice Chairman/COO
Phone: 323-549-4300
IMDB: *www.imdb.com/name/nm2325215*

Michelle Hastings
Title: Senior Vice-President Motion Picture
Administration
Phone: 323-549-4300
IMDB: *www.imdb.com/name/nm3295407*

Shelly Riney
Title: Executive Vice-President, Corporate
Operations
Phone: 323-549-4300
IMDB: *www.imdb.com/name/nm2325152*

MANDATE PICTURES

2700 Colorado Avenue, Suite 501
Santa Monica, CA 90404

Phone: 310-360-1441
Fax: 310-360-1447
Email: *info@mandatepictures.com*

Submission Policy: Accepts Query Letter from

unproduced, unrepresented writers via email
Company Focus: Feature Films
Year Established: 2003

Nathan Kahane
Title: President
Phone: 310-255-5700
IMDB: *www.imdb.com/name/nm1144042*

Nicole Brown
Title: Executive Vice-President, Production
Phone: 310-255-5710
Email: *nbrown@mandatepictures.com*
IMDB: *www.imdb.com/name/nm0114352*

Aaron Ensweiler
Title: Creative Executive
Phone: 310-255-5721
Email: *aensweiler@mandatepictures.com*
IMDB: *www.imdb.com/name/nm3943221*

MANDEVILLE FILMS

500 South Buena Vista Street
Animation Building, 2G
Burbank, CA 91521-1783

Phone: 818-560-4077
Fax: 818-842-2937

Submission Policy: Accepts Query Letter from
unproduced, unrepresented writers
Genre: Action, Romance, TV Drama, Family,
Drama
Company Focus: Feature Films, TV
Year Established: 1994

David Hoberman
Title: Partner (With Todd Lieberman)
Phone: 818-560-4077
IMDB: *www.imdb.com/name/nm0387674*
Assistant: Kim Ferandelii

David Manpearl
Title: Vice-President of Development
Phone: 818-560-7237
IMDB: *www.imdb.com/name/nm1818404*
Assistant: Diana Theobold

Laura Cray
Title: Creative Executive
Phone: 818-560-4332
IMDB: *www.imdb.com/name/nm1733050*

MANDY FILMS

9201 Wilshire Boulevard, Suite 206
Beverly Hills, CA 90210

Phone: 310-246-0500
Fax: 310-246-0350

Submission Policy: Accepts Query Letter from unproduced, unrepresented writers
Company Focus: Feature Films, TV

Leonard Goldberg
Title: President
Phone: 310-246-0500
IMDB: *www.imdb.com/name/nm0325252*

Amanda Goldberg
Title: Vice-President of Development/ Production
Phone: 310-246-0500
IMDB: *www.imdb.com/name/nm0325144*

Jaime Toporovich
Title: Executive Assistant
Phone: 310-246-0500
IMDB: *www.imdb.com/name/nm2325311*

MAPLE SHADE FILMS

4000 Warner Boulevard
Building 138, Room 1103
Burbank, CA 91522

Phone: 818-954-3137

Submission Policy: Accepts Query Letter from unproduced, unrepresented writers
Genre: Action, Comedy, Drama
Company Focus: Feature Films

Ed (Edward) McDonnell
Title: President
Phone: 818-954-3137
IMDB: *www.imdb.com/name/nm0568093*

Carolyn Manetti
Title: Vice-President, Production
Phone: 818-954-3137
IMDB: *www.imdb.com/name/nm0542024*

MARC PLATT PRODUCTIONS

100 Universal City Plaza, Bungalow 5163
Universal City, CA 91608

Phone: 818-777-8811
Fax: 818-866-6353

Submission Policy: Accepts Query Letter from unproduced, unrepresented writers
Genre: Action, Romance, TV Drama, Family, Drama
Company Focus: Feature Films, TV

Marc Platt
Title: Producer
Phone: 818-777-1122
Email: *platt@nbcuni.com*
IMDB: *www.imdb.com/name/nm0686887*

Adam Siegel
Title: President
Phone: 818-777-9544
IMDB: *www.imdb.com/name/nm2132113*

Jared LeBoff
Title: Development
Phone: 818-777-9961
IMDB: *www.imdb.com/name/nm1545176*

MARK VICTOR PRODUCTIONS

2931 Wilshire Boulevard, Suite 201
Santa Monica, CA 90403

Phone: 310-828-3339
Fax: 310-828-9588
Email: *info@markvictorproductions.com*

Submission Policy: Accepts Query Letter from unproduced, unrepresented writers via email
Genre: Action, Horror, Thriller, Animation
Company Focus: Feature Films, TV, Reality Programming (Reality TV, Documentaries, Special Events, Sporting Events)

Mark Victor
Title: Producer/Writer
Phone: 310-828-3339
Email: *markvictorproductions@hotmail.com*
IMDB: *www.imdb.com/name/nm0896131*

Sarah Johnson
Title: Director of Development
Phone: 310-828-3339
IMDB: *www.imdb.com/name/nm1154417*

MARK YELLEN PRODUCTION

183 South Orange Drive
Los Angeles, CA 90036

Phone: 323-935-5525
Fax: 323-935-5755

Submission Policy: Accepts Query Letter from unproduced, unrepresented writers via email
Genre: Action, Family
Company Focus: Feature Films, TV, Media (Commercials/Branding/Marketing)
Year Established: 2003

Mark Yellen
Title: Producer
Phone: 323-935-5525
Email: *mark@myfilmconsult.com*
IMDB: *www.imdb.com/name/nm0947390*

MARTIN CHASE PRODUCTIONS

500 South Buena Vista Street
Burbank, CA 91521

Phone: 818-526-4252
Fax: 818-560-5113

Submission Policy: Does not accept any unsolicited material
Genre: Family
Company Focus: Feature Films, TV
Year Established: 2000

Debra Martin Chase
Title: President/Producer
Phone: 818-526-4252
IMDB: *www.imdb.com/name/nm0153744*

Gaylyn Fraiche
Title: Executive Vice-President
Phone: 818-526-4252
IMDB: *www.imdb.com/name/nm2325210*

Josh Stewart
Title: Executive Assistant
Phone: 818-526-4252

MARTY KATZ PRODUCTIONS

22631 Pacific Coast Highway #327
Malibu, CA 90265

Phone: 310-589-1560
Fax: 310-589-1565
Email: *martykatzproductions@earthlink.net*

Submission Policy: Accepts Query Letter from unproduced, unrepresented writers via email
Genre: Action, Comedy, Romance, Drama
Company Focus: Feature Films
Year Established: 1996

Marty Katz
Title: Producer
Phone: 310-589-1560
Email: *martykatzproductions@earthlink.net*
IMDB: *www.imdb.com/name/nm0441794*

Campbell Katz
Title: Vice-President, Productions & Development
Phone: 310-589-1560
Email: *martykatzproductions@earthlink.net*
IMDB: *www.imdb.com/name/nm0441645*

MARVISTA ENTERTAINMENT

12519 Venice Boulevard
Los Angeles, CA 90066

Phone: 310-737-0950
Fax: 310-737-9115
Email: *info@marvista.net*

Submission Policy: Accepts Query Letter from unproduced, unrepresented writers via email
Company Focus: Feature Films, TV

Fernando Szew
Title: CEO
Phone: 310-737-0950
Email: *fszew@marvista.net*
IMDB: *www.imdb.com/name/nm2280496*

Robyn Snyder
Title: Executive Vice-President of Production & Development
Phone: 310-737-0950
Email: *rsnyder@marvista.net*
IMDB: *www.imdb.com/name/nm2237557*

Sharon Bordas
Title: Vice-President of Development &

Production
Phone: 310-737-0950
Email: *sbordas@marvista.net*
IMDB: *www.imdb.com/name/nm2188762*

MASS HYSTERIA ENTERTAINMENT

8899 Beverly Boulevard, Suite 710
Los Angeles, CA 90048

Phone: 310-285-7800
Fax: 310-285-7801
Email: *info@masshysteriafilms.com*

Submission Policy: Accepts Query Letter from unproduced, unrepresented writers via email
Company Focus: Feature Films, TV

Daniel Grodnik
Title: President
Phone: 310-285-7800
Email: *grodzilla@earthlink.net*
IMDB: *www.imdb.com/name/nm0342841*

Brent V. Friedman
Title: Senior Vice-President of Product Development & Marketing
Phone: 310-285-7800
IMDB: *www.imdb.com/name/nm0295165*

Pat Proft
Title: Senior Vice-President of Comedy
Phone: 310-285-7800
IMDB: *www.imdb.com/name/nm0698493*

MATADOR PICTURES

20 Gloucester Place
London W1U 8HA
United Kingdom

Phone: +44 (0) 20 7009-9640
Fax: +44 (0) 20 7009-9641
Email: *admin@matadorpictures.com*

Submission Policy: Accepts Query Letter from unproduced, unrepresented writers via email
Genre: Action, Comedy, Romance, Drama
Company Focus: Feature Films
Year Established: 1999

Nigel Thomas
Title: Producer
Phone: +44 (0) 20-7009-9640
IMDB: *www.imdb.com/name/nm0859302*

Lucia Lopez
Title: Development Producer
Phone: +44 (0) 20-7009-9640
IMDB: *www.imdb.com/name/nm2389416*

Orlando Cubit
Title: Development Executive
Phone: +44 (0) 20-7009-9640
IMDB: *www.imdb.com/name/nm4919747*

MAXIMUM FILMS & MANAGEMENT

33 West 17th Street, 11th Floor
New York, NY 10011

Phone: 212-414-4801
Fax: 212-414-4803
Email: *lauren@maximumfilmsny.com*

Submission Policy: Does not accept any unsolicited material
Company Focus: Feature Films, TV, Theater

Marcy Drogin
Title: Producer/Manager
Phone: 212-414-4801
IMDB: *www.imdb.com/name/nm1216320*

Lauren O'Connor
Title: Creative Executive
Phone: 212-414-4801

MAYA ENTERTAINMENT GROUP

1201 West Fifth Street, Suite T210
Los Angeles, CA 90017

Phone: 213-542-4420
Fax: 213-534-3846
Email: *info@maya-entertainment.com*

Submission Policy: Accepts Query Letter from unproduced, unrepresented writers via email
Genre: Comedy, TV Drama, Drama
Company Focus: Feature Films, TV, Reality Programming (Reality TV, Documentaries, Special Events, Sporting Events)
Year Established: 2008

Moctesuma Esparza
Title: CEO/Chairman/Producer
Phone: 213-542-4420
IMDB: *www.imdb.com/name/nm0260800*

Sandra Avila
Title: Development Executive
Phone: 213-542-4420
IMDB: *www.imdb.com/name/nm2087699*

Christina Hirigoyen
Title: Development Executive
Phone: 213-542-4420
IMDB: *www.imdb.com/name/nm3491113*

MAYHEM PICTURES

725 Arizona Avenue, Suite 402
Santa Monica, CA 90401

Phone: 310-393-5005
Fax: 310-393-5017

Submission Policy: Does not accept any
unsolicited material
Genre: Comedy, Memoir & True Stories, Family
Company Focus: Feature Films, TV, Reality
Programming (Reality TV, Documentaries,
Special Events, Sporting Events)
Year Established: 2003

Mark Ciardi
Title: Producer
Phone: 310-393-5005
Email: *mark@mayhempictures.com*
IMDB: *www.imdb.com/name/nm0161891*

Brad Butler
Title: Creative Executive
Phone: 310-393-5005
Email: *brad@mayhempictures.com*
IMDB: *www.imdb.com/name/nm2744089*

Victor H. Constantino
Title: Sr. Vice-President of Production &
Development
Phone: 310-393-5005
Email: *victor@mayhempictures.com*
IMDB: *www.imdb.com/name/nm2028391*

MBST ENTERTAINMENT

345 North Maple Drive, Suite 200
Beverly Hills, CA 90210

Phone: 310-385-1820
Fax: 310-385-1834

Submission Policy: Accepts Query Letter from
unproduced, unrepresented writers
Genre: Action, Comedy, Romance, Drama
Company Focus: Feature Films, TV, Theater
Year Established: 2005

Larry Brezner
Title: Partner
Phone: 310-385-1820
IMDB: *www.imdb.com/name/nm0108368*

Jonathan Brandstein
Title: Partner
Phone: 310-385-1820
IMDB: *www.imdb.com/name/nm0104844*

David Steinberg
Title: Partner
Phone: 310-385-1820
IMDB: *www.imdb.com/name/nm2314804*

MEDIA 8 ENTERTAINMENT

15260 Ventura Boulevard, Suite 710
Sherman Oaks, CA 91403

Phone: 818-826-8000
Fax: 818-325-8020
Email: *info@media8ent.com*

Submission Policy: Does not accept any
unsolicited material
Genre: Action, Comedy, Romance, Drama
Company Focus: Feature Films, TV
Year Established: 1993

Stewart Hall
Title: President
Phone: 818-826-8000
Email: *info@media8ent.com*
IMDB: *www.imdb.com/name/nm1279593*

Devin Cutler
Title: CFO and Board Member
Phone: 818-826-8000
Email: *devinc@media8ent.com*
IMDB: *www.imdb.com/name/nm1884733*

Randy Dannenberg
Title: Development, Acquisitions and Media
Phone: 818-826-8000
Email: *randyd@media8ent.com*
IMDB: *www.imdb.com/name/nm1006811*

MEDIA TALENT GROUP

9200 Sunset Boulevard, Suite 500
West Hollywood, CA 90069

Phone: 310-275-7900
Fax: 310-275-7910

Submission Policy: Accepts Query Letter from
unproduced, unrepresented writers
Company Focus: Feature Films, TV
Year Established: 2009

Geyer Kosinski
Title: Chairman/CEO
Phone: 310-275-7900
IMDB: *www.imdb.com/name/nm0467083*

Chris Davey
Title: Producer/Manager
Phone: 310-275-7900
IMDB: *www.imdb.com/name/nm1312702*

MEL STUART PRODUCTIONS, INC.

204 South Beverly Drive, Suite 109
Beverly Hills, CA 90210

Phone: 310-550-5872
Fax: 310-550-5895
Email: *info@melstuartproductions.com*

Submission Policy: Accepts Query Letter from
unproduced, unrepresented writers via email
Company Focus: Feature Films, TV, Reality
Programming (Reality TV, Documentaries,
Special Events, Sporting Events)

Mel Stuart
Title: President
Phone: 310-550-5872
Email: *info@melstuartproductions.com*
IMDB: *www.imdb.com/name/nm0835799*

MELEE ENTERTAINMENT

144 South Beverly Drive, Suite 402
Beverly Hills, CA 90212

Phone: 310-248-3931
Fax: 310-248-3921
Email: *acquisitions@melee.com*

Submission Policy: Does not accept any
unsolicited material
Company Focus: Feature Films
Year Established: 2003

Bryan Turner
Title: CEO
Phone: 310-248-3931
IMDB: *www.imdb.com/name/nm0877440*

Scott Aronson
Title: COO
Phone: 310-248-3931
IMDB: *www.imdb.com/name/nm1529615*

Brittany Williams
Title: Creative Executive
Phone: 310-248-3931
IMDB: *www.imdb.com/name/nm2950356*

MERCHANT IVORY PRODUCTIONS

US Office:
PO Box 338
New York, NY 10276

United Kingdom Office:
372 Old Street, Office 150
London EC1V 9LT
United Kingdom

Phone: 212-582-8049
Fax: 212-706-8340
Email: *contact@merchantivory.com*

Submission Policy: Accepts Query Letter from
unproduced, unrepresented writers via email
Genre: Drama
Company Focus: Feature Films, Reality
Programming (Reality TV, Documentaries,
Special Events, Sporting Events)
Year Established: 1961

James Ivory
Title: President/Director
Phone: 212-582-8049
Email: *contact@merchantivory.com*
IMDB: *www.imdb.com/name/nm0412465*

Neil Jesuele
Title: Director of Development (NY)
Phone: 212-582-8049
Email: *njesuele@merchantivory.com*
IMDB: *www.imdb.com/name/nm3134373*

Paul Bradley
Title: Producer
Phone: +44 207-657-3988 (fax)
Email: *paul@merchantivory.co.uk*
IMDB: *www.imdb.com/name/nm0103364*

MICHAEL DE LUCA PRODUCTIONS

10202 West Washington Boulevard
Astaire Building, Suite 3028
Culver City, CA 90232

Phone: 310-244-4990
Fax: 310-244-0449

Submission Policy: Does not accept any
unsolicited material
Genre: Action, Comedy, Thriller, Drama
Company Focus: Feature Films

Michael De Luca
Title: Producer
Phone: 310-244-4990
IMDB: *www.imdb.com/name/nm0006894*
Assistant: Kristen Detwiler

Josh Bratman
Title: Development Executive
Phone: 310-244-4916
IMDB: *www.imdb.com/name/nm2302300*
Assistant: Sandy Yep

Alissa Phillips
Title: Development
Phone: 310-244-4918
IMDB: *www.imdb.com/name/nm1913014*
Assistant: Bill Karesh

MICHAEL GRAIS PRODUCTIONS

321 South Beverly Drive, Suite M
Beverly Hills, CA 90210

Phone: 323-857-4510
Fax: 323-319-4002

Submission Policy: Accepts Query Letter from
unproduced, unrepresented writers via email
Genre: Horror, Thriller
Company Focus: Feature Films, TV

Michael Grais
Title: Producer/Writer
Phone: 323-857-4510
Email: *michaelgrais@yahoo.com*
IMDB: *www.imdb.com/name/nm0334457*

MICHAEL TAYLOR PRODUCTIONS

2370 Bowmont Drive
Beverly Hills, CA 90210

Phone: 213-821-3113
Fax: 213-740-3395
Email: *taycoprod@aol.com*

Submission Policy: Accepts Query Letter from
unproduced, unrepresented writers via email
Company Focus: Feature Films, TV, Reality
Programming (Reality TV, Documentaries,
Special Events, Sporting Events)

Michael Taylor
Title: Producer
Phone: 213-821-3113
IMDB: *www.imdb.com/name/nm0852888*
Assistant: Yolanda Rodriguez

MIDD KID PRODUCTIONS

10202 West Washington Boulevard
Fred Astaire Building, Suite 2010
Culver City, CA 90232

Phone: 310-244-2688
Fax: 310-244-2603

Submission Policy: Accepts Query Letter from
unproduced, unrepresented writers
Genre: Crime, Detective, TV Drama
Company Focus: TV

Shawn Ryan
Title: Principal
Phone: 310-244-2688
IMDB: *www.imdb.com/name/nm0752841*
Assistant: Kent Rotherham

Marney Hochman
Title: President of Development
Phone: 310-244-2688
IMDB: *www.imdb.com/name/nm2701117*
Assistant: Kent Rotherham

MIDNIGHT SUN PICTURES

10960 Wilshire Boulevard, Suite 700
Los Angeles, CA 90024

Phone: 310-902-0431
Fax: 310-450-4988

Submission Policy: Accepts Query Letter from
produced or represented writers
Genre: Comedy, Horror, Romance, Drama
Company Focus: Feature Films, TV

Renny Harlin
Title: Producer/Director
Phone: 310-902-0431
IMDB: *www.imdb.com/name/nm0001317*

Nikki Stanghetti
Title: Co-Producer
Phone: 310-902-0431
Email: *nikki@midnightsunproductions.com*
IMDB: *www.imdb.com/name/nm2325595*

MIKE LOBELL PRODUCTIONS

9477 Lloydcrest Drive
Beverly Hills, CA 90210

Phone: 323-822-2910
Fax: 310-205-2767

Submission Policy: Accepts Query Letter from
unproduced, unrepresented writers
Genre: Action, Comedy, Romance, Drama
Company Focus: Feature Films
Year Established: 1973

Mike Lobell
Title: Producer
Phone: 323-822-2910
IMDB: *www.imdb.com/name/nm0516465*
Assistant: Janet Chiarabaglio

MILLAR/GOUGH INK

500 South Buena Vista Street
Animation Building 1E16
Burbank, CA 91521

Phone: 818-560-4260
Fax: 818-560-4216

Submission Policy: Accepts Query Letter from
unproduced, unrepresented writers
Genre: Action, Science Fiction, TV Drama,
Family, Drama
Company Focus: Feature Films, TV

Miles Millar
Title: Principal
Phone: 818-560-4260
IMDB: *www.imdb.com/name/nm0587692*
Assistant: Mal Stares

Alfred Gough
Title: Principal
Phone: 818-560-4260
IMDB: *www.imdb.com/name/nm0332184*
Assistant: Mal Stares

Matthew Okumura
Title: Executive
Phone: 818-560-4260
IMDB: *www.imdb.com/name/nm1390963*

MILLENNIUM FILMS

6423 Wilshire Boulevard
Los Angeles, CA 90048

Phone: 310-388-6900
Fax: 310-388-6901
Email: *info@millenniumfilms.com*

Submission Policy: Accepts Query Letter from
unproduced, unrepresented writers via email
Genre: Action, Comedy, Detective, Fantasy,
Memoir & True Stories, Science Fiction,
Thriller, Drama
Company Focus: Feature Films
Year Established: 1992 (under Nu Image, Inc.)

Avi Lerner
Title: Co-Founder
IMDB: *www.imdb.com/name/nm0503592*

Trevor Short
Title: Co-Founder
IMDB: *www.imdb.com/name/nm0795121*

Boaz Davidson
Title: Head of Development and Creative Affairs
IMDB: *www.imdb.com/name/nm0203246*

MIMRAN SCHUR PICTURES

2400 Broadway, Suite 550
Santa Monica, CA 90404

Phone: 310-526-5410
Fax: 310-526-5405
Email: *info@mimranschurpictures.com*

Submission Policy: Accepts Query Letter from produced or represented writers
Genre: Drama
Company Focus: Feature Films
Year Established: 2009

Jordan Schur
Title: Co-Chairman/CEO
Phone: 310-526-5410
IMDB: *www.imdb.com/name/nm2028525*

David Mimran
Title: Co-Chairman
Phone: 310-526-5410
IMDB: *www.imdb.com/name/nm3450764*
Assistant: Caroline Haubold

Lauren Pettit
Title: Creative Executive
Phone: 310-526-5410
IMDB: *www.imdb.com/name/nm2335692*

MIRADA

4235 Redwood Avenue
Los Angeles, CA 90066

Phone: 424-216-7470

Submission Policy: Does not accept any unsolicited material
Genre: Fantasy, Myth, Animation, Drama
Company Focus: Feature Films, TV, Theater
Year Established: 2010

Guillermo del Toro
IMDB: *www.imdb.com/name/nm0868219*

Guillermo Navarro
IMDB: *www.imdb.com/name/nm0622897*

Javier Jimenez
IMDB: *www.imdb.com/name/nm3901643*

MIRANDA ENTERTAINMENT

7337 Pacific View Drive
Los Angeles, CA 90068

Phone: 323-874-3600
Fax: 323-851-5350

Submission Policy: Does not accept any unsolicited material
Genre: Comedy, Horror, Thriller
Company Focus: Feature Films, TV

Carsten Lorenz
Title: Producer
Phone: 323-874-3600
Email: *clorenz1@aol.com*
IMDB: *www.imdb.com/name/nm0520696*

MISHER FILMS

12233 Olympic Boulevard, Suite 354
Los Angeles, CA 90064

Phone: 310-405-7999
Fax: 310-405-7991

Submission Policy: Does not accept any unsolicited material
Genre: Action, Crime, Drama
Company Focus: Feature Films, TV

Kevin Misher
Title: Producer/Owner
Phone: 310-405-7999
Email: *kevin.misher@misherfilms.com*
IMDB: *www.imdb.com/name/nm0592746*
Assistant: Sarah Ezrin

Swanna MacNair
Title: Feature Development/Director
Phone: 310-405-7999
Email: *swanna.macnair@misherfilms.com*
IMDB: *www.imdb.com/name/nm1207182*

Leigh Janiak
Title: Creative Executive
Phone: 310-405-7999
Email: *leigh.janiak@misherfilms.com*
IMDB: *www.imdb.com/name/nm4074404*

MOJO FILMS

500 South Buena Vista Street
Animation Building, Suite 1D 13
Burbank, CA 91521

Phone: 818-560-8370
Fax: 818-560-5045

Submission Policy: Accepts Query Letter from unproduced, unrepresented writers
Company Focus: Feature Films, TV
Year Established: 2007

Gary Fleder
Title: President
Phone: 818-560-8370
IMDB: *www.imdb.com/name/nm0001219*
Assistant: Pamy Sue Anton

Mary-Beth Basile
Title: Vice-President, Production & Development
Phone: 818-560-8370
IMDB: *www.imdb.com/name/nm1039389*
Assistant: Jay Ashenfelter

MOMENTUM ENTERTAINMENT GROUP

8687 Melrose Avenue
8th Floor
Los Angeles, CA 90069

Submission Policy: Accepts Query Letter from unproduced, unrepresented writers via email
Genre: Action, Comedy, Crime, Detective, Fantasy, Horror, Memoir & True Stories, Myth, Romance, Science Fiction, Thriller, TV Drama, TV Sitcom, Family, Animation, Drama, Socio-cultural, Reality
Company Focus: TV, Media (Commercials/Branding/Marketing)

Nick Hamm
Title: Head of Scripted Development
Email: *nick.hamm@megww.com*
IMDB: *www.imdb.com/name/nm0358327*

MONSTERFOOT PRODUCTIONS

3450 Cahuenga Boulevard West
Loft 105
Los Angeles, CA 90068

Phone: 323-850-6116
Fax: 323-378-5232

Submission Policy: Accepts Query Letter from unproduced, unrepresented writers
Company Focus: Feature Films, TV, Reality Programming (Reality TV, Documentaries, Special Events, Sporting Events)

Ahmet Zappa
Title: CEO
Phone: 323-850-6116
IMDB: *www.imdb.com/name/nm0953257*

Andrew Kimble
Title: Creative Executive
Phone: 323-850-6116
IMDB: *www.imdb.com/name/nm1130966*

Devon Schiff
Title: Executive
Phone: 323-850-6116
IMDB: *www.imdb.com/name/nm3825595*

MONTAGE ENTERTAINMENT

2118 Wilshire Boulevard, Suite 297
Santa Monica, CA 90403

Phone: 310-966-0222
Fax: 310-966-0223
Email: *david@montageentertainment.com*

Submission Policy: Accepts Query Letter from unproduced, unrepresented writers via email
Company Focus: Feature Films, TV

David Peters
Title: Producer
Phone: 310-966-0222
Email: *david@montageentertainment.com*
IMDB: *www.imdb.com/name/nm0007070*

Bill Ewart
Title: Producer
Phone: 310-966-0222
Email: *bill@montageentertainment.com*
IMDB: *www.imdb.com/name/nm0263867*

MONTONE/YORN (UNNAMED YORN PRODUCTION COMPANY)

2000 Avenue of the Stars
3rd Floor North Tower
Los Angeles, CA 90067

Submission Policy: Accepts Query Letter from unproduced, unrepresented writers
Genre: Action, Comedy, Fantasy, Family
Year Established: 2008

Rick Yorn
Title: Principal
IMDB: *www.imdb.com/name/nm0948833*

MOONSTONE ENTERTAINMENT

PO Box 7400
Studio City, CA 91614

Phone: 818-985-3003
Fax: 818-985-3009
Email: *submissions@moonstonefilms.com*

Submission Policy: Accepts Query Letter from unproduced, unrepresented writers via email
Company Focus: Feature Films
Year Established: 1992

Shahar Stroh
Title: Director, Development & Acquisitions
Phone: 818-985-3003
IMDB: *www.imdb.com/name/nm2325576*

MORGAN CREEK PRODUCTIONS

10351 Santa Monica Boulevard, Suite 200
Los Angeles, CA 90025

Phone: 310-432-4848
Fax: 310-432-4844

Submission Policy: Accepts Query Letter from unproduced, unrepresented writers
Company Focus: Feature Films
Year Established: 1988

Ryan Jones
Title: Director of Development
Phone: 310-432-4848
IMDB: *www.imdb.com/name/nm2325121*

Larry Katz
Title: Senior Vice-President Development
Phone: 310-432-4848
IMDB: *www.imdb.com/name/nm0441765*

Jordan Okun
Title: Creative Executive
Phone: 310-432-4848
IMDB: *www.imdb.com/name/nm1442312*

MORNINGSTAR ENTERTAINMENT

350 North Glenoaks Boulevard, Suite 300
Burbank, CA 91502

Phone: 818-559-7255
Fax: 818-559-7251

Submission Policy: Accepts Query Letter from unproduced, unrepresented writers via email
Company Focus: TV, Reality Programming (Reality TV, Documentaries, Special Events, Sporting Events)
Year Established: 1980

Christian Robinson
Title: Director, Development
Phone: 818-559-7255
IMDB: *www.imdb.com/name/nm2384297*

MOSAIC/MOSAIC MEDIA GROUP

9200 West Sunset Boulevard
10th Floor
Los Angeles, CA 90069

Phone: 310-786-4900
Fax: 310-786-8984

Submission Policy: Accepts Query Letter from unproduced, unrepresented writers
Genre: Action, Comedy, Myth, TV Drama, TV Sitcom, Family
Company Focus: Feature Films, TV

Jimmy Miller
Title: CEO/Chairman/Producer
Phone: 310-786-4900
Email: *acarr@mosaicla.com*
IMDB: *www.imdb.com/name/nm0588612*
Assistant: Alyx Carr

David Householter
Title: President, Production
Phone: 310-786-4900
Email: *dhouseholter@mosaicla.com*
IMDB: *www.imdb.com/name/nm0396720*
Assistant: Brendan Clougherty

Mike Falbo
Title: Vice-President Production & Development
Phone: 310-786-4900
Email: *mfalbo@mosaicla.com*
IMDB: *www.imdb.com/name/nm3824648*
Assistant: Mark Acomb

MOSHAG PRODUCTIONS

c/o Mark Mower
1531 Wellesley Avenue
Los Angeles, CA 90025

Phone: 310-820-6760
Fax: 310-820-6960
Email: *moshag@aol.com*

Submission Policy: Accepts Query Letter from unproduced, unrepresented writers via email
Company Focus: Feature Films, TV

Mark Mower
Title: Producer
Phone: 310-820-6760
IMDB: *www.imdb.com/name/nm0610272*

MR. MUDD

137 North Larchmont Boulevard, #113
Los Angeles, CA 9004

Phone: 323-932-5656
Fax: 323-932-5666

Submission Policy: Does not accept any unsolicited material
Genre: Comedy, Romance, Family, Drama, Socio-cultural
Company Focus: Feature Films
Year Established: 1998

John Malkovich
Title: Producer/Director
IMDB: *www.imdb.com/name/nm0000518*

Lianne Halfon
Title: Producer
IMDB: *www.imdb.com/name/nm0355147*

Russell Smith
Title: Producer
IMDB: *www.imdb.com/name/nm0809833*

MYRIAD PICTURES

3015 Main Street, Suite 400
Santa Monica, CA 90405

Phone: 310-279-4000
Fax: 310-279-4001
Email: *info@myriadpictures.com*
IMDB: *www.imdb.com/company/co0033226*

Submission Policy: Does not accept any unsolicited material
Genre: Comedy, Fantasy, Horror, Memoir & True Stories, Romance, Drama, Socio-cultural
Company Focus: Feature Films
Year Established: 1998

Kirk D'Amico
Title: CEO
IMDB: *www.imdb.com/name/nm0195136*

Ari Haas
Title: Director, Production & Acquisitions
IMDB: *www.imdb.com/name/nm0351907*

Juliana Dacunha
Title: Office Assistant
Email: *myriadasst@gmail.com*

NALA FILMS

2016 Broadway Place
Santa Monica, CA 90404

Phone: 310-264-2555
Email: *info@nalafilms.com*

Submission Policy: Does not accept any unsolicited material
Genre: Thriller, Drama, Socio-cultural
Company Focus: Feature Films, TV

Emilio Diez Barroso
Title: CEO
IMDB: *www.imdb.com/name/nm1950898*

Rudy Scalese
Title: Vice-President of Development &
Production
IMDB: *www.imdb.com/name/nm0768800*

Blair Richman
Title: Creative Executive
IMDB: *www.imdb.com/name/nm3923771*

NECROPIA ENTERTAINMENT

9171 Wilshire Boulevard, Suite 300
Beverly Hills, CA 9021

Phone: 323-865-0547

Submission Policy: Does not accept any
unsolicited material
Genre: Action, Fantasy, Horror, Myth, Science
Fiction
Company Focus: Feature Films

Guillermo de Toro
Title: Director
IMDB: *www.imdb.com/name/nm0868219*

NEW ARTISTS ALLIANCE

16633 Ventura Boulevard, #1440
Encino, CA 91436
Email: *info@newartistsalliance.com*

Submission Policy: Accepts Query Letter from
unproduced, unrepresented writers via email
Genre: Action, Horror, Thriller, Drama
Company Focus: Feature Films
Year Established: 2003

Gabe Cowan
Title: Founder/Producer
Email: *gabe@naafilms.com*
IMDB: *www.imdb.com/name/nm1410462*

John Suits
Title: Founder/Producer
Email: *john@naafilms.com*
IMDB: *www.imdb.com/name/nm2986811*

NEW CRIME PRODUCTIONS

1041 North Formosa Avenue
Formosa Building, Room 219
West Hollywood, CA 90016

Phone: 323-850-2525
Email: *newcrime@aol.com*
IMDB: *www.imdb.com/company/co0079035*

Submission Policy: Accepts Query Letter from
unproduced, unrepresented writers via email
Genre: Comedy, Romance, Thriller, Drama
Company Focus: Feature Films

John Cusack
Title: Executive
IMDB: *www.imdb.com/name/nm0000131*

Grace Loh
Title: Executive
Assistant: Judy Heinzen
IMDB: *www.imdb.com/name/nm0517808*

NEW SCHOOL MEDIA

9229 Sunset Boulevard, Suite 301
West Hollywood, CA 90069

Phone: 310-858-2989
Fax: 310-858 1841

Submission Policy: Accepts Query Letter from
unproduced, unrepresented writers
Company Focus: Feature Films

Brian Levy
Title: Manager/CEO
IMDB: *www.imdb.com/name/nm2546392*

NEW WAVE ENTERTAINMENT

2660 West Olive Avenue
Burbank, CA 91505

Phone: 818-295-5000
Fax: 818-295-5002

Submission Policy: Does not accept any
unsolicited material
Genre: Action, Comedy, Crime, Detective,
Fantasy, Horror, Memoir & True Stories, Myth,
Romance, Science Fiction, Thriller, TV Drama,
TV Sitcom, Family, Animation, Drama, Socio-
cultural, Reality
Company Focus: Feature Films, TV, Post-
Production (Editing, Special Effects), Reality
Programming (Reality TV, Documentaries,
Special Events, Sporting Events), Media
(Commercials/Branding/Marketing)

Gary Lister
Title: Senior Vice-President Creative Director
Email: *glister@nwe.com*
IMDB: *www.imdb.com/name/nm3266191*

Lisa Blond
Title: Senior Vice-President Creative Content
Email: *lblond@nwe.com*
IMDB: *www.imdb.com/name/nm1135380*

Mary Snyder
Title: Creative Director
Email: *msnyder@nwe.com*
IMDB: *www.imdb.com/name/nm1716089*

NICK WECHSLER PRODUCTIONS

1437 7th Street, Suite 250
Santa Monica, CA 90401

Phone: 310-309-5759
Fax: 310-309-5716
Email: *info@nwprods.com*

Submission Policy: Does not accept any
unsolicited material
Genre: Action, Comedy, Crime, Fantasy,
Horror, Science Fiction, Thriller, TV Drama,
TV Sitcom, Family, Animation, Drama,
Socio-cultural
Company Focus: Feature Films, TV
Year Established: 2005

Nick Wechsler
Title: Producer/Chairman
Email: *nick@nwprods.com*
IMDB: *www.imdb.com/name/nm0917059*

Elizabeth "Lizzy" Bradford
Title: Director of Development
Email: *lizzy@nwprods.com*
IMDB: *www.imdb.com/name/nm4504768*

Felicity Aldridge
Title: Creative Executive
Email: *felicity@nwprods.com*
IMDB: *www.imdb.com/name/nm4504820*

NIGHT & DAY PICTURES

5225 Wilshire Boulevard, Suite 524
Los Angeles, CA 90036

Phone: 323-930-2212
Email: *info@nightanddaypictures.com*
IMDB: *www.imdb.com/company/co0253348*

Submission Policy: Accepts Query Letter from
unproduced, unrepresented writers via email
Company Focus: Feature Films

Rachel Berk
Title: Creative Executive
IMDB: *www.imdb.com/company/co0157684*

Michael Roiff
Title: President
IMDB: *www.imdb.com/name/nm1988698*

NINJA'S RUNNIN' WILD PRODUCTIONS

7024 Melrose Ave, Suite 420
Los Angeles, CA 90038

Phone: 323-937-6100

Submission Policy: Accepts Scripts from
produced or represented writers
Company Focus: Feature Films

Zac Effron
Title: Actor/Producer
IMDB: *www.imdb.com/name/nm1374980*

Jason Barrett
Title: Producer
IMDB: *www.imdb.com/name/nm2249074*

NUYORICAN PRODUCTIONS

1100 Glendon Ave, Suite 920
Los Angeles, CA 90024

Phone: 310-943-6600
Fax: 310-943-6609

Submission Policy: Does not accept any
unsolicited material
Genre: Action, Comedy, Memoir & True
Stories, Drama, Socio-cultural
Company Focus: Feature Films, TV, Reality
Programming (Reality TV, Documentaries,
Special Events, Sporting Events), Media
(Commercials/Branding/Marketing)

Jennifer Lopez
Title: Founder-Entertainer-Producer
IMDB: *www.imdb.com/name/nm0000182*

Brian Schornak
Title: Executive Film & TV
Email: *bsasst@jlopezent.com*
IMDB: *www.imdb.com/name/nm1935985*

Simon Fields
Title: Producer—Vice-President of
Development
Email: *sfasst@jlopezent.com*
IMDB: *www.imdb.com/name/nm0276353*

O.N.C.

11150 Santa Monica Boulevard, Suite 450
Los Angeles, CA 90025

Phone: 310-477-0670
Fax: 310-477-7710

Submission Policy: Does not accept any
unsolicited material
Genre: Action, Comedy, Crime, Romance,
Thriller, Family
Company Focus: Feature Films

Michael G. Nathanson
Title: Producer
Email: *michaelnathanson@oncentertainment.*
com
IMDB: *www.imdb.com/name/nm0622296*
Assistant: Robyn Altman

O'TAYE PRODUCTIONS

c/o Walt Disney Studios
500 South Buena Vista Street
Burbank, CA 91521

Phone: 818-560-6677
Fax: 818-560-6688

Submission Policy: Accepts Query Letter from
unproduced, unrepresented writers
Company Focus: TV

Taye Diggs
Title: Executive/partner
IMDB: *www.imdb.com/name/nm0004875*

Jennifer Bozell
Title: Head of Development

ODD LOT ENTERTAINMENT

9601 Jefferson Boulevard, Suite A
Culver City, CA 90232

Phone: 310-652-0999
Fax: 310-652-0718
Email: *info@oddlotent.com*

Submission Policy: Does not accept any
unsolicited material
Genre: Drama
Company Focus: Feature Films

Gigi Pritzker
Title: CEO
IMDB: *www.imdb.com/name/nm0698133*

Linda McDonough
Title: Exec Vice-President, Production and
Development
IMDB: *www.imdb.com/name/nm1261078*

Stacy Keppler
Title: Creative Executive

OFFSPRING ENTERTAINMENT

8755 Colgate Avenue
Los Angeles, CA 90048

Phone: 310-247-0019
Fax: 310-550-6908

Submission Policy: Does not accept any
unsolicited material
Genre: Comedy, Family, Drama
Company Focus: Feature Films

Adam Shankman
Title: Executive
IMDB: *www.imdb.com/name/nm0788202*

Jennifer Gibgot
Title: Executive
IMDB: *www.imdb.com/name/nm0316774*

OLMOS PRODUCTIONS INC.

500 South Buena Vista Street
Old Animation Building, Suite 1G
Burbank, CA 91521

Phone: 818-560-8651
Fax: 818-560-8655
Email: *olmosonline@yahoo.com*

Submission Policy: Accepts Query Letter from unproduced, unrepresented writers via email
Genre: Comedy, Family, Drama
Company Focus: Feature Films, TV, Reality Programming (Reality TV, Documentaries, Special Events, Sporting Events), Media (Commercials/Branding/Marketing)
Year Established: 1980

Edward James Olmos

Title: President
IMDB: *www.imdb.com/name/nm0001579*

OLYMPUS PICTURES

2901 Ocean Park Boulevard, Suite 217
Santa Monica, CA 90405

Phone: 310-452-3335
Fax: 310-452-0108
Email: *getinfo@olympuspics.com*

Submission Policy: Accepts Query Letter from unproduced, unrepresented writers via email
Company Focus: Feature Films
Year Established: 2007

Leslie Urdang

Title: President, Producer
IMDB: *www.imdb.com/name/nm0881811*

Mandy Beckner

Title: Creative Executive
Email: *rrdecter@olympuspics.com*

OMBRA FILMS

12444 Ventura Boulevard, Suite 103
Studio City, CA 91604

Phone: 818-509-0552
Email: *info@ombrafilms.com*

Submission Policy: Accepts Query Letter from unproduced, unrepresented writers via email
Genre: Fantasy, Horror, Thriller
Company Focus: Feature Films, TV
Year Established: 2011

Jaume Collet Serra

Title: Producer
IMDB: *www.imdb.com/name/nm1429471*

Juan Sola

Title: Producer
IMDB: *www.imdb.com/name/nm4928159*

ONE RACE FILMS

9100 Wilshire Boulevard
East Tower, Suite 535
Beverly Hills, CA 90212

Phone: 310-401-6880
Fax: 310-401-6890
Email: *info@oneracefilms.com*

Submission Policy: Accepts Query Letter from unproduced, unrepresented writers via email
Genre: Action, Crime, Science Fiction, Thriller, TV Drama
Company Focus: Feature Films, TV
Year Established: 1995

Vin Diesel

Title: Actor/Writer/Prodcer
IMDB: *www.imdb.com/name/nm0004874*

Samantha Vincent

Title: Producer/Partner
Email: *samantha@oneracefilms.com*
IMDB: *www.imdb.com/name/nm2176972*

Thyrale Thai

Title: Marketing and New Media
Email: *thyrale@oneracefilms.com*
IMDB: *www.imdb.com/name/nm1394166*

OOPS DOUGHNUTS PRODUCTIONS

500 South Buena Vista Street
Old Animation Building, Room 2F8
Burbank, CA 91521

Phone: 818-460-7777
IMDB: *www.imdb.com/company/co0248742*

Submission Policy: Accepts Query Letter from unproduced, unrepresented writers
Company Focus: Feature Films, TV, Media (Commercials/Branding/Marketing)

Andy Fickman

Title: Director/Producer
IMDB: *www.imdb.com/name/nm0275698*
Assistant: Whitney Engstrom

Betsy Sullenger
IMDB: *www.imdb.com/name/nm0998095*

OPEN CITY FILMS

155 Water Street
Brooklyn, NY 11201

Phone: 212-255-0500
Email: *oc@opencityfilms.com*

Submission Policy: Accepts Query Letter from unproduced, unrepresented writers via email
Company Focus: Feature Films, Reality Programming (Reality TV, Documentaries, Special Events, Sporting Events)

Jason Kilot
Title: co-president, founder
IMDB: *www.imdb.com/name/nm0459852*

Joana Vicente
Title: Co-President, Founder

ORIGINAL FILM

11466 San Vicente Boulevard
Los Angeles, CA 90049

Phone: 310-575-6950

Submission Policy: Accepts Query Letter from unproduced, unrepresented writers
Genre: Action, Comedy, Drama
Company Focus: Feature Films

Toby Ascher
Title: Producer
IMDB: *www.imdb.com/name/nm4457111*

Jeni Mulein
Title: Creative Executive
IMDB: *www.imdb.com/name/nm2630667*

OUT OF THE BLUE...ENTERTAINMENT

c/o Sony Pictures Entertainment
10202 West Washington Boulevard
Astaire Building, Suite 1200
Culver City, CA 90232-3195

Phone: 310-244-7811
Fax: 310-244-1539
Email: *info@outoftheblueent.com*

Submission Policy: Accepts Query Letter from unproduced, unrepresented writers via email
Company Focus: Feature Films, TV

Sidney Ganis
Title: Founder/Executive
IMDB: *www.imdb.com/name/nm0304398*

Marta Gene Camps
Title: Creative Executive
IMDB: *www.imdb.com/name/nm2585482*

Toby Conroy
Title: Creative Executive
IMDB: *www.imdb.com/name/nm1926762*

OUTERBANKS ENTERTAINMENT

1149 North Gower Street, #101
Los Angeles, CA 90038

Phone: 323-785-2221
Fax: 323-785-3926

Submission Policy: Accepts Query Letter from unproduced, unrepresented writers via email
Company Focus: Feature Films, TV

Kevin Williamson
Title: President
Phone: 323-785-2221
IMDB: *www.imdb.com/name/nm0932078*
Assistant: Danny Tolli

Alexis Bayoud
Title: Creative Executive
Phone: 323-785-2221
IMDB: *www.imdb.com/name/nm1941670*

OVERBROOK ENTERTAINMENT

450 North Roxbury Drive
4th Floor
Beverly Hills, CA 90210

Phone: 310-432-2400
Fax: 310-432-2401

Submission Policy: Accepts Query Letter from unproduced, unrepresented writers
Company Focus: Feature Films, TV
Year Established: 1998

Will Smith
Title: Producer/Partner, Actor
Phone: 310-432-2400
IMDB: *www.imdb.com/name/nm0000226*

Danielle Reardon
Title: Creative Executive
Phone: 310-432-2400
IMDB: *www.imdb.com/name/nm1129051*

Gary Glushon
Title: Film Executive
Phone: 310-432-2400
IMDB: *www.imdb.com/name/nm2237223*

OVERNIGHT PRODUCTIONS

15 Mercer Street, Suite 4
New York, NY 10013

Phone: 212-625-0530

Submission Policy: Does not accept any unsolicited material
Company Focus: Feature Films
Year Established: 2008

Rick Schwartz
Title: Chairman/CEO
Phone: 212-625-0530
IMDB: *www.imdb.com/name/nm0777408*

Clara Kim
Title: Head of Development and Production
Phone: 212-625-0530
IMDB: *www.imdb.com/name/nm3247964*

OZLA PICTURES, INC.

1800 Camino Palmero Street
Los Angeles, CA 90046

Phone: 323-876-0180
Fax: 323-876-0189
Email: *ozla@ozla.com*

Submission Policy: Does not accept any unsolicited material
Company Focus: Feature Films, TV
Year Established: 1992

Taka Ichise
Title: Producer
Phone: 323-876-0180
IMDB: *www.imdb.com/name/nm0406772*
Assistant: Chiaki Yanagimoto

Erin Eggers
Title: Development Vice-President
Phone: 323-876-0180
IMDB: *www.imdb.com/name/nm0250929*

Matt Portes
Title: Story Editor
Phone: 323-876-0180

PACIFIC STANDARD

100 Universal City Plaza
Los Angeles, CA 91608

Phone: 818-777-1000

IMDB: *www.imdb.com/company/co0373561*

Submission Policy: Does not accept any unsolicited material
Company Focus: Feature Films
Year Established: 2012

Reese Witherspoon
Title: Actor/Producer/Partner
IMDB: *www.imdb.com/name/nm0000702*

Bruna Papandrea
Title: Producer/Partner
IMDB: *www.imdb.com/name/nm0660295*

PALERMO PRODUCTIONS

c/o Twentieth Century Fox
10201 West Pico Boulevard
Building 52, Room 103
Los Angeles, CA 90064

Phone: 310-369-1900

Submission Policy: Accepts Query Letter from unproduced, unrepresented writers
Company Focus: Feature Films, TV

John Palermo
Title: Producer
Phone: 310-369-1911
IMDB: *www.imdb.com/name/nm0657561*
Assistant: Mike Belyea

Allan Mandelbaum
Title: Executive
Phone: 310-369-5681

PALOMAR PICTURES

PO Box 491986
Los Angeles, CA 90049

Phone: 310-440-3494

Submission Policy: Does not accept any
unsolicited material
Company Focus: Feature Films, TV
Year Established: 1992

Joni Sighvatsson
Title: CEO/Producer
Phone: 310-440-3494
IMDB: *www.imdb.com/name/nm0797451*

Aditya Ezhuthachan
Title: Head of Development
Phone: 310-440-3494
IMDB: *www.imdb.com/name/nm2149074*

PANAY FILMS

500 South Buena Vista
Old Animation Building, Room 3c-6
Burbank, CA 91521

Phone: 818-560-4265

Submission Policy: Accepts Query Letter from
unproduced, unrepresented writers
Company Focus: Feature Films
Year Established: 2001

Andrew Panay
Title: Producer
Phone: 818-560-4265
IMDB: *www.imdb.com/name/nm0659123*
Assistant: Max Kramer

Adam Blum
Title: Development Executive
Phone: 818-560-4265
IMDB: *www.imdb.com/name/nm3597471*

PANDEMONIUM

9777 Wilshire Boulevard, Suite 700
Beverly Hills, CA 90212

Phone: 310-550-9900
Fax: 310-550-9910

Submission Policy: Accepts Query Letter from
unproduced, unrepresented writers via email
Company Focus: Feature Films

Bill Mechanic
Title: President/CEO
Phone: 310-550-9900
IMDB: *www.imdb.com/name/nm0575312*
Assistant: David Freedman

Suzanne Warren
Title: Vice-President Production
Phone: 310-550-9900
IMDB: *www.imdb.com/name/nm0913049*

PANTHER FILMS

1888 Century Park East
14th Floor
Los Angeles, CA 90067

Phone: 424-202-6630
Fax: 310-887-1001

Submission Policy: Does not accept any
unsolicited material
Company Focus: Feature Films

Brad Epstein
Title: Producer/Owner
Phone: 424-202-6630
IMDB: *www.imdb.com/name/nm0258431*

Lindsay Culpepper
Phone: 424-202-6630
IMDB: *www.imdb.com/name/nm0258431*

PAPA JOE ENTERTAINMENT

14804 Greenleaf Street
Sherman Oaks, CA 91403

Phone: 818-788-7608
Fax: 818-788-7612
Email: *info@papjoefilms.com*

Submission Policy: Accepts Query Letter from
unproduced, unrepresented writers via email
Company Focus: Feature Films, TV

Joe Simpson
Title: CEO
Phone: 818-788-7608
IMDB: *www.imdb.com/name/nm1471425*
Assistant: Heath Pliler

Erin Alexander
Title: Vice-President Development &
Production
Phone: 818-788-7608
IMDB: *www.imdb.com/name/nm0018408*
Assistant: Amelia Garrison

PARADIGM STUDIO

2701 2nd Avenue North
Seattle, WA 98109

Phone: 206-282-2161
Fax: 206-283-6433
Email: *info@paradigmstudio.com*

Submission Policy: Accepts Query Letter from
unproduced, unrepresented writers via email
Company Focus: Feature Films, TV

John Comerford
Title: President
Phone: 206-282-2161
IMDB: *www.imdb.com/name/nm0173766*

B Dahlia
Title: Manager
Phone: 206-282-2161
IMDB: *www.imdb.com/name/nm1148338*

PARALLEL MEDIA

301 North Canon Dr, Suite 223
Beverly Hills, CA 90210

Phone: 310-858-3003
Fax: 310-858-3034
Email: *info@parallelmediallc.com*

Submission Policy: Does not accept any
unsolicited material
Company Focus: Feature Films
Year Established: 2006

Armen Mahdessian
Title: Head of Development
Phone: 310-858-3003
IMDB: *www.imdb.com/name/nm3177001*

Tim O'Hair
Title: Head of Production
Phone: 310-858-3003
IMDB: *www.imdb.com/name/nm1943824*

PARAMOUNT FILM GROUP

5555 Melrose Avenue
Los Angeles, CA 90038

Phone: 323-956-5000

Submission Policy: Does not accept any
unsolicited material
Company Focus: Feature Films

Marc Evans
Title: President of Production
IMDB: *www.imdb.com/name/nm0263010*

Ashley Brucks
Title: Vice-President Creative Affairs
IMDB: *www.imdb.com/name/nm2087318*

Allison Small
Title: Creative Executive
IMDB: *www.imdb.com/name/nm1861333*

PARIAH

9744 Wilshire Boulevard, Suite 205
Beverly Hills, CA 90212-2612

Phone: 310-461-3460
Fax: 310-246-9622

Submission Policy: Does not accept any
unsolicited material
Company Focus: Feature Films, TV

Gavin Polone
Title: Owner
Phone: 310-461-3460
IMDB: *www.imdb.com/name/nm0689780*
Assistant: Stephen Iwanyk

Kathy Landsberg
Title: Vice-President Physical Production
Phone: 310-461-3460
IMDB: *www.imdb.com/name/nm0485130*
Assistant: Ali Gordon-Goldstein

Lauren Pfeiffer
Title: Director of Development
Phone: 310-461-3460

PARKER ENTERTAINMENT GROUP

8581 Santa Monica Boulevard #261
West Hollywood, CA 90069

Phone: 323-400-6622
Fax: 323-400-6655
Email: *info@parkerentgroup.com*

Submission Policy: Accepts Scripts from
produced or represented writers
Company Focus: Feature Films
Year Established: 2008

Christopher Parker
Email: *cparker@parkerentgroup.com*
IMDB: *www.imdb.com/name/nm2034521*

PARKES/MACDONALD PRODUCTIONS

1663 Euclid Street
Santa Monica, CA 90404

Phone: 310-581-5990

Submission Policy: Accepts Query Letter from
unproduced, unrepresented writers
Company Focus: Feature Films, TV
Year Established: 2007

Walter Parkes
Title: Producer
Phone: 310-581-5990
IMDB: *www.imdb.com/name/nm0662748*

Laurie MacDonald
Title: Producer
Phone: 310-581-5990
IMDB: *www.imdb.com/name/nm0531827*

Leigh Kittay
Title: Creative Executive
IMDB: *www.imdb.com/name/nm3074753*

PARKWAY PRODUCTIONS

7095 Hollywood Boulevard, Suite 1009
Hollywood, CA 90028

Phone: 323-874-6207
Email: *parkwayprods@aol.com*

Submission Policy: Accepts Query Letter from
unproduced, unrepresented writers via email
Company Focus: Feature Films, TV

Penny Marshall
Title: Director/Producer
Phone: 323-874-6207
IMDB: *www.imdb.com/name/nm0001508*
Assistant: Terry Trahan

Kelly Calligan
Title: Executive Assistant
Phone: 323-874-6207
IMDB: *www.imdb.com/name/nm3350778*

PARTICIPANT MEDIA

331 Foothill Road
3rd Floor
Beverly Hills, CA 90210

Phone: 310-550-5100
Fax: 310-550-5106
Email: *info@participantmedia.com*

Submission Policy: Does not accept any
unsolicited material
Company Focus: Feature Films, TV, Reality
Programming (Reality TV, Documentaries,
Special Events, Sporting Events)
Year Established: 2004

Jonathan King
Title: Executive Vice President of Production
Phone: 310-550-5100
IMDB: *www.imdb.com/name/nm2622896*

Erik Andreasen
Title: Senior Director of Development,
Narrative Films
Phone: 310-550-5100
IMDB: *www.imdb.com/name/nm1849675*

Angel Lopez
Title: Creative Executive
Phone: 310-550-5100

PATHE PICTURES

6 Ramillies Street
4th Floor
London W1F 7TY
United Kingdom

Phone: +44 207-462-4429
Fax: +44 207-631-3568
Email: *reception.desk@pathe-uk.com*

Submission Policy: Accepts Query Letter from unproduced, unrepresented writers via email
Company Focus: Feature Films, Reality Programming (Reality TV, Documentaries, Special Events, Sporting Events)

Mike Runagall
Title: Senior Vice-President International Sales
Phone: +44 207-462-4429
IMDB: *www.imdb.com/name/nm2553445*

PATRIOT PICTURES

PO Box 46100
West Hollywood, CA 90046

Phone: 323-874-8850
Fax: 323-874-8851
Email: *info@patriotpictures.com*

Submission Policy: Accepts Query Letter from unproduced, unrepresented writers via email
Company Focus: Feature Films, TV, Reality Programming (Reality TV, Documentaries, Special Events, Sporting Events)

Michael Mendelsohn
Title: Chairman/CEO
Phone: 323-874-8850
IMDB: *www.imdb.com/name/nm0578861*

PEACE ARCH ENTERTAINMENT GROUP INC.

4640 Admiralty Way, Suite 710
Marina del Rey, CA 90292

Phone: 310-776-7200
Fax: 310-823-7147
Email: *info@peacearch.com*

Submission Policy: Does not accept any unsolicited material
Company Focus: Feature Films, TV
Year Established: 1986

Sudhanshu Saria
Title: Vice-President, Development
Phone: 310-776-7200
IMDB: *www.imdb.com/name/nm2738818*

PEACE BY PEACE PRODUCTIONS

c/o Michael Katcher/CAA
2000 Avenue of the Stars
Los Angeles, CA 90067

Phone: 323-552-1097
Email: *peacebypeace1@mac.com*

Submission Policy: Accepts Query Letter from unproduced, unrepresented writers via email
Company Focus: Feature Films, TV

Alyssa Milano
Title: Producer
Phone: 323-552-1097
IMDB: *www.imdb.com/name/nm0000192*
Assistant: Kelly Kall

PEGGY RAJSKI PRODUCTIONS

2 Washington Square Village, 141
New York, NY 10012

Phone: 646-998-5955

Submission Policy: Does not accept any unsolicited material
Company Focus: Feature Films, Reality Programming (Reality TV, Documentaries, Special Events, Sporting Events)

Peggy Rajski
Title: Producer
Phone: 646-998-5955
Email: *rajskip@aol.com*
IMDB: *www.imdb.com/name/nm0707475*

PERFECT STORM ENTERTAINMENT

1850 Industrial Street, Penthouse
Los Angeles, CA 90021

Phone: 323-546-8886

Submission Policy: Does not accept any unsolicited material
Company Focus: Feature Films

Justin Lin
Title: Director
IMDB: *www.imdb.com/name/nm0510912*

Troy Craig Poon
Title: President
IMDB: *www.imdb.com/name/nm1359290*

PERMUT PRESENTATIONS

1801 Avenue Of The Stars, Suite 505
Los Angeles, CA 90067

Phone: 310-248-2792
Fax: 310-248-2797

Submission Policy: Accepts Query Letter from unproduced, unrepresented writers
Company Focus: Feature Films, TV

David Permut
Title: Producer/President
Phone: 310-248-2792
IMDB: *www.imdb.com/name/nm0674303*

Steven Longi
Title: Vice-President Production
Phone: 310-248-2792
IMDB: *www.imdb.com/name/nm0519347*

Chris Mangano
Title: Development Executive
Phone: 310-248-2792
IMDB: *www.imdb.com/name/nm2032016*

PHOENIX PICTURES

10203 Santa Monica Boulevard, Suite 400
Los Angeles, CA 90067

Phone: 424-298-2788
Fax: 424-298-2588
Email: *dnugent@phoenixpictures.com*

Submission Policy: Accepts Query Letter from unproduced, unrepresented writers via email
Company Focus: Feature Films, TV

Edward McGurn
Title: Vice-President Production
Phone: 424-298-2788
IMDB: *www.imdb.com/name/nm0570342*

Douglas McKay
Title: Vice-President Production
Phone: 424-298-2788
IMDB: *www.imdb.com/name/nm1305822*

Ali Toukan
Title: Creative Executive
Phone: 424-298-2788
IMDB: *www.imdb.com/name/nm4371255*

PILLER/SEGAN/SHEPHERD

7025 Santa Monica Boulevard
Hollywood, CA 90038

Phone: 323-817-1100
Fax: 323-817-1131

Submission Policy: Accepts Query Letter from unproduced, unrepresented writers
Company Focus: Feature Films, TV
Year Established: 2010

Shawn Piller
Title: Producer/Principal
Phone: 323-817-1100
IMDB: *www.imdb.com/name/nm0683525*

Lloyd Segan
Title: Producer/Principal
Phone: 323-817-1100
IMDB: *www.imdb.com/name/nm0781912*

Scott Shepherd
Title: Producer/Principal
Phone: 323-817-1100
IMDB: *www.imdb.com/name/nm0791863*

PINK SLIP PICTURES

4921 San Rafael Avenue
Los Angeles, CA 90042

Phone: 213-483-7100
Fax: 213-483-7200

Submission Policy: Does not accept any unsolicited material
Company Focus: Feature Films, TV

Karen Firestone
Title: Producer
Phone: 213-483-7100
IMDB: *www.imdb.com/name/nm0278652*

Max Wong
Title: Producer
Phone: 213-483-7100
IMDB: *www.imdb.com/name/nm0939246*

PLAN B ENTERTAINMENT

9150 Wilshire Boulevard, Suite 350
Beverly Hills, CA 90210

Phone: 310-275-6135
Fax: 310-275-5234

Submission Policy: Does not accept any unsolicited material
Genre: Action, Fantasy, Myth, Animation, Drama, Socio-cultural
Company Focus: Feature Films, TV
Year Established: 2004

Brad Pitt
Title: Principal/Actor
Phone: 310-275-6135
IMDB: *www.imdb.com/name/nm0000093*

Sarah Esberg
Title: Creative Executive
Phone: 310-275-6135
IMDB: *www.imdb.com/name/nm1209665*

PLATFORM ENTERTAINMENT

128 Sierra Street
El Segundo, CA 90425

Phone: 310-322-3737
Fax: 310-322-3729

Submission Policy: Accepts Query Letter from unproduced, unrepresented writers
Company Focus: Feature Films
Year Established: 1998

Daniel Levin
Title: Producer
Phone: 310-322-3737
IMDB: *www.imdb.com/name/nm0505575*

Larry Gabriel
Title: Producer
Phone: 310-322-3737
IMDB: *www.imdb.com/name/nm0300181*

Scott Sorrentino
Title: Producer
Phone: 310-322-3737
IMDB: *www.imdb.com/name/nm1391744*

PLATINUM DUNES

631 Colorado Avenue
Santa Monica, CA 90401

Phone: 310-319-6565
Fax: 310-319-6570

Submission Policy: Does not accept any unsolicited material
Company Focus: Feature Films, TV
Year Established: 2001

Michael Bay
Title: Partner
Phone: 310-319-6565
IMDB: *www.imdb.com/name/nm0000881*

Sean Cummings
Title: Assistant
Phone: 310-319-6565
IMDB: *www.imdb.com/name/nm3594167*

Allison Garfield
Title: Assistant
Phone: 310-319-6565
IMDB: *www.imdb.com/name/nm2946588*

PLAYTONE PRODUCTIONS

PO Box 7340
Santa Monica, CA 90406

Phone: 310-394-5700
Fax: 310-394-4466

Submission Policy: Accepts Query Letter from unproduced, unrepresented writers
Company Focus: Feature Films, TV
Year Established: 1996

Tom Hanks
Title: Partner
Phone: 310-394-5700
IMDB: *www.imdb.com/name/nm0000158*

Miura Kite
Title: Head of Development
Phone: 310-394-5700
IMDB: *www.imdb.com/name/nm0003982*

Julie Lawrence
Title: Creative Executive
Phone: 310-394-5700

POLYMORPHIC PICTURES

4000 Warner Boulevard
Building 81, Suite 212
Burbank, CA 91522

Phone: 818-954-3822

Submission Policy: Does not accept any unsolicited material
Company Focus: Feature Films
Year Established: 2010

Polly Johnsen
Title: Producer/Principal
Phone: 818-954-3822
IMDB: *www.imdb.com/name/nm1480881*

Christy Ezzell
Title: Creative Assistant

PORTERGELLER ENTERTAINMENT

6352 De Longpre Avenue
Los Angeles, CA 90028

Phone: 323-822-4400
Fax: 323-822-7270
Email: *info@portergeller.com*

Submission Policy: Does not accept any unsolicited material
Company Focus: Feature Films, TV

Aaron Geller
Title: Producer
Phone: 323-822-4400
IMDB: *www.imdb.com/name/nm1510467*

Darryl Porter
Title: Producer
Phone: 323-822-4400
IMDB: *www.imdb.com/name/nm0692080*

Michael Tyree
Title: Producer
Phone: 323-822-4400
IMDB: *www.imdb.com/name/nm2699784*

POW! ENTERTAINMENT

9440 Santa Monica Boulevard, Suite 620
Beverly Hills, CA 90210

Phone: 310-275-9933
Fax: 310-285-9955
Email: *info@powentertainment.com*

Submission Policy: Accepts Query Letter from unproduced, unrepresented writers via email
Company Focus: Feature Films, TV
Year Established: 2001

Stan Lee
Title: Chief Creative Officer
Phone: 310-275-9933
IMDB: *www.imdb.com/name/nm0498278*
Assistant: Mike Kelly

Ron Hawk
Title: Chief Executive Assistant
Phone: 310-275-9933
IMDB: *www.imdb.com/name/nm4078012*

POWER UP

419 North Larchmont Boulevard #283
Los Angeles, CA 90004

Phone: 323-463-3154
Fax: 323-467-6249
Email: *info@powerupfilms.org*

Submission Policy: Accepts Query Letter from unproduced, unrepresented writers via email
Company Focus: Feature Films, TV
Year Established: 2000

Stacy Codikow
Title: Producer/Writer
Phone: 323-463-3154
IMDB: *www.imdb.com/name/nm0168499*

Lisa Thrasher
Title: President, Film Production & Distribution
Phone: 323-463-3154
IMDB: *www.imdb.com/name/nm1511212*

PRACTICAL PICTURES

2211 Corinth Avenue, Suite 303
Los Angeles, CA 90064

Phone: 310-405-7777
Fax: 310-405-7771

Submission Policy: Does not accept any unsolicited material

Jason Koffeman
Title: Creative Executive
IMDB: *www.imdb.com/name/nm1788896*

PREFERRED CONTENT

6363 Wilshire Boulevard, Suite 350
Los Angeles, CA 90048

Phone: 323-782-9193
Email: *info@preferredcontent.net*

Submission Policy: Does not accept any unsolicited material
Genre: Action
Company Focus: Feature Films

Ross M. Dinerstein
Title: Partner/Producer
IMDB: *www.imdb.com/name/nm1895871*

Kevin Iwashina
Title: Partner/Producer
IMDB: *www.imdb.com/name/nm2250990*

Trace Sheehan
Title: Head of Development
IMDB: *www.imdb.com/name/nm2618717*

PRETTY MATCHES PRODUCTIONS

1100 Avenue of the Americas
G26, Suite 32
New York, NY 10036

Phone: 212-512-5755
Fax: 212-512-5716
IMDB: *www.imdb.com/company/co0173730*

Submission Policy: Accepts Query Letter from unproduced, unrepresented writers
Genre: Comedy, Romance, Socio-cultural
Company Focus: Feature Films, TV, Reality Programming (Reality TV, Documentaries, Special Events, Sporting Events)

Sarah Jessica Parker
Title: President
IMDB: *www.imdb.com/name/nm0000572*

Alison Benson
Title: Producer
Assistant: Matt Nathanson
IMDB: *www.imdb.com/name/nm3929030*

Benjamin Stark
Title: Director, Development

PRETTY PICTURES

100 Universal City Plaza
Building 2352-A, 3rd Floor
Universal City, CA 91608

Phone: 818-733-0926
Fax: 818-866-0847

Submission Policy: Does not accept any unsolicited material
Genre: Comedy, Memoir & True Stories, Romance, Thriller, TV Drama, Drama
Company Focus: Feature Films, TV

Gail Mutrux
Title: Producer

Tore Schmidt
Title: Creative Executive

PRINCIPATO-YOUNG ENTERTAINMENT

9465 Wilshire Boulevard, Suite 900
Beverly Hills, CA 90212

Phone: 310-274-4474
Fax: 310-274-4108

Submission Policy: Accepts Query Letter from unproduced, unrepresented writers
Genre: Comedy, TV Sitcom
Company Focus: Feature Films, TV

Peter Principato
Title: President
Phone: 310-274-4130
Assistant: Max Suchov

Susan Solomon
Title: Manager
Phone: 310-274-4408

Tucker Voorhees
Title: Manager
Phone: 310-432-5992

PROSPECT PARK

2049 Century Park East #2550
Century City, CA 90067

Phone: 310-746-4900
Fax: 310-746-4890
IMDB: *www.imdb.com/company/co0276484*

Submission Policy: Accepts Query Letter from unproduced, unrepresented writers via email
Genre: TV Drama, Reality
Company Focus: Feature Films, TV, Reality Programming (Reality TV, Documentaries,

Special Events, Sporting Events)

Paul Frank
Title: Executive Producer/Head, TV
IMDB: *www.imdb.com/name/nm1899773*

Jeff Kwatinetz
Title: Executive Producer
IMDB: *www.imdb.com/name/nm0477153*

Laurie Ferneau
Title: Director, Development, TV
IMDB: *www.imdb.com/name/nm1017980*

PROTOZOA

104 North 7th Street
Brooklyn, NY 11211

Phone: 718-388-5280
Fax: 718-388-5425

Submission Policy: Does not accept any
unsolicited material
Genre: Action, Fantasy, Horror, Science Fiction,
Thriller
Company Focus: Feature Films

Darren Aronofsky
Title: Director/Producer/Writer/CEO
IMDB: *www.imdb.com/name/nm0004716*

Ali Mendes
Title: Director Of Development
Email: *ali@protozoa.com*
IMDB: *www.imdb.com/name/nm4070559*

PURE GRASS FILMS LTD.

1st Floor, 16 Manette Street
London, W1D 4AR
Email: *info@puregrassfilms.com*

Submission Policy: Accepts Query Letter from
unproduced, unrepresented writers via email
Genre: Action, Horror, Memoir & True Stories,
Science Fiction, Thriller, Drama
Company Focus: Feature Films, Post-
Production (Editing, Special Effects)

Ben Grass
Title: CEO/Producer
IMDB: *www.imdb.com/name/nm2447240*

QED INTERNATIONAL

1800 North Highland Ave, 5th Floor
Los Angeles, CA 90028

Phone: 323-785-7900
Fax: 323-785-7901
Email: *info@qedintl.com*

Submission Policy: Accepts Scripts from
unproduced, unrepresented writers
Genre: Action, Comedy, Crime, Fantasy,
Horror, Myth, Romance, Thriller, Drama
Company Focus: Feature Films
Year Established: 2005

Bill Block
Title: Founder/CEO
IMDB: *www.imdb.com/name/nm1088848*

QUADRANT PICTURES

9229 Sunset Boulevard, Suite 225
West Hollywood, CA 90069

Phone: 424-244-1860
Email: *assistant@quadrantpictures.com*

Submission Policy: Accepts Query Letter from
unproduced, unrepresented writers via email
Genre: Action, Horror, Science Fiction, Thriller,
TV Drama, Family, Drama
Company Focus: Feature Films, TV
Year Established: 2011

Doug Davison
Title: President/Producer
IMDB: *www.imdb.com/name/nm0205713*

Jon Morra
Title: Development Executive
Email: *jmora@quadrantpictures.com*
IMDB: *www.imdb.com/name/nm4180253*

RADAR PICTURES

10900 Wilshire Boulevard, Suite 1400
Los Angeles, CA 90024

Phone: 310-208-8525
Fax: 310-208-1764
Email: *info@radarpictures.com*
IMDB: *www.imdb.com/company/co0023815*

Submission Policy: Does not accept any

unsolicited material
Genre: Action, Drama
Company Focus: Feature Films

Ted Field
Title: Chairman
IMDB: *www.imdb.com/name/nm0276059*

Thomas E. Van Dell
Title: Partner/Producer
IMDB: *www.imdb.com/name/nm0886033*

RAINBOW FILM COMPANY/RAINBOW RELEASING

1301 Montanta Avenue, Suite A
Santa Monica, CA 90403

Phone: 310-271-0202
Fax: 310-271-2753
Email: *therainbowfilmco@aol.com*

Submission Policy: Accepts Query Letter from unproduced, unrepresented writers via email
Genre: Comedy, Memoir & True Stories, Romance, Drama
Company Focus: Feature Films

Henry Jaglom
Title: President

Sharon Lester Kohn
Title: Vice-President, Distribution

Lauren Beck
Title: Development

RAINMAKER ENTERTAINMENT

500-2025 West Broadway
Vancouver, BC
Canada
V6J 1Z6

Phone: 604-714-2600
Fax: 604-714-2641
IMDB: *www.imdb.com/company/co0298750*

Submission Policy: Does not accept any unsolicited material
Genre: Fantasy, Family, Animation
Company Focus: Feature Films, TV

Catherine Winder
Title: President—Executive Producer
IMDB: *www.imdb.com/name/nm0934671*

Kim Dent Wilder
Title: Senior Vice-President of Productions and Operations
IMDB: *www.imdb.com/name/nm0219785*

Kimberly Dennison
Title: Director of Development
IMDB: *www.imdb.com/name/nm2541873*

RAINMAKER FILMS INC.

4212 San Felipe St 399
Houston, TX 77027

Phone: 832-287-9372
Email: *rainmaker.inc@gmail.com*

Submission Policy: Accepts Query Letter from unproduced, unrepresented writers via email
Genre: Science Fiction
Company Focus: Feature Films

Grant Gurthie
Title: President—Executive Producer
IMDB: *www.imdb.com/name/nm0349262*

RAINSTORM ENTERTAINMENT, INC.

345 North Maple Dr, Suite 105
Beverly Hills, CA 90210

Phone: 818-269-3300
Fax: 310-496-0223

Submission Policy: Accepts Query Letter from unproduced, unrepresented writers via email
Company Focus: Feature Films, TV, Reality Programming (Reality TV, Documentaries, Special Events, Sporting Events)

Gregg Daniel
Title: Creative Affairs/Producer
Phone: 818-269-3300
Email: *gregg@rainstormentertainment.com*
IMDB: *www.imdb.com/name/nm0199639*

Liz Gross
Title: Development Executive
Phone: 818-269-3300

Alec Rossel
Title: Development Executive
Phone: 818-269-3300
IMDB: *www.imdb.com/name/nm1952377*

RALPH WINTER PRODUCTIONS

10201 West Pico Boulevard Building
Los Angeles, CA 90035

Phone: 310-369-4723
Fax: 310-969-0727

Submission Policy: Does not accept any
unsolicited material
Genre: Action, Comedy
Company Focus: Feature Films

Ralph Winter
Title: Founder/Producer
IMDB: *www.imdb.com/name/nm0003515*

Susana R. Zepeda
Title: President
Email: *susana.zepeda@fox.com*
IMDB: *www.imdb.com/name/nm0954978*

RANDOM HOUSE FILMS

1745 Broadway
New York, NY 10019

Phone: 212-782-9000

Submission Policy: Accepts Query Letter from
unproduced, unrepresented writers
Company Focus: Feature Films
Year Established: 2007

Valerie Cates
Title: Executive Story Editor
Phone: 212-782-9000
IMDB: *www.imdb.com/name/nm1161200*

Brady Emerson
Title: Story Editor
Phone: 212-782-9000
IMDB: *www.imdb.com/name/nm3031708*

Christina Malach
Title: Story Editor
Phone: 212-782-9000
IMDB: *www.imdb.com/name/nm4090138*

RAT ENTERTAINMENT

100 Universal City Plz
Bungalow 5196
Universal City, CA 91608

Phone: 818-733-4603
Fax: 818-733-4612

Submission Policy: Accepts Query Letter from
unproduced, unrepresented writers
Company Focus: Feature Films, TV, Reality
Programming (Reality TV, Documentaries,
Special Events, Sporting Events)

Bret Ratner
Title: Director/Producer/Chairman
Phone: 818-733-4603
IMDB: *www.imdb.com/name/nm0711840*
Assistant: Anita Chang

John Cheng
Title: Head of Feature Development
Phone: 818-733-4603
IMDB: *www.imdb.com/name/nm1766738*
Assistant: Agustine Calderon

RCR PICTURES

8840 Wilshire Boulevard
Beverly Hills, CA 90211

Phone: 310-358-3234
Fax: 310-358-3109

Submission Policy: Accepts Query Letter from
unproduced, unrepresented writers
Genre: Crime, Romance, Science Fiction,
Drama
Company Focus: Feature Films

Robin Schorr
Title: Producer
IMDB: *www.imdb.com/name/nm0774908*

Noah Weinstein
Title: Creative Executive
IMDB: *www.imdb.com/name/nm3634512*

RECORDED PICTURE COMPANY

24 Hanway Street
London W1T 1UH
United Kingdom

Phone: +44 20-7636-2251
Fax: +44 20-7636-2261
Email: *rpc@recordedpicture.com*

Submission Policy: Accepts Scripts from produced or represented writers
Company Focus: Feature Films

Jeremy Thomas
Title: Producer/Chairman
Phone: +44 20 7636 2251
IMDB: *www.imdb.com/name/nm0859016*
Assistant: Karin Padgham

Alainee Kent
Title: Senior Development Executive
Phone: +44 20 7636 2251
IMDB: *www.imdb.com/name/nm1599134*

RED CROWN PRODUCTIONS

630 5th Ave, Suite 2505
New York, NY 10111

Phone: 212-355-9200
Fax: 212-719-7029
Email: *info@redcrownproductions.com*

Submission Policy: Does not accept any unsolicited material
Genre: Comedy, Drama
Company Focus: Feature Films
Year Established: 2010

Daniel Crown
Title: Founder/Producer
Phone: 212-355-9200
Email: *info@redcrownproductions.com*
IMDB: *www.imdb.com/name/nm3259054*

Riva Marker
Title: Head of Production & Development
Email: *riva@redcrownproductions.com*
IMDB: *www.imdb.com/name/nm1889450*

Alish Erman
Title: Creative Executive
Email: *alish@redcrownproductions.com*
IMDB: *www.imdb.com/name/nm2289542*

RED GIANT MEDIA

535 5th Avenue, 5th Floor
New York, NY 10017

Phone: 212-989-7200
Fax: 212-937-3505
Email: *info@redgiantmedia.com*

Submission Policy: Does not accept any unsolicited material
Genre: Science Fiction
Company Focus: Feature Films
Year Established: 2008

Kevin Fox
Title: Executive Producer/Writer

Isen Robbins
Title: Producer

Aimee Schoof
Title: Producer

RED GRANITE PICTURES

9255 Sunset Boulevard, Suite 710
Los Angeles, CA 90069

Phone: 310-703-5800
Fax: 310-246-3849
IMDB: *www.imdb.com/company/co0325207*

Submission Policy: Does not accept any unsolicited material
Genre: Drama
Company Focus: Feature Films

Riza Aziz
Title: CEO
IMDB: *www.imdb.com/name/nm4265383*

Joe Gatta
Title: President of Production
IMDB: *www.imdb.com/name/nm2211910*

RED HOUR FILMS

629 North La Brea Avenue
Los Angeles, CA 90036

Phone: 323-602-5000
Fax: 323-602 5001

Submission Policy: Does not accept any unsolicited material
Genre: Action, Comedy, Fantasy, Science Fiction, Family
Company Focus: Feature Films, TV

Ben Stiller
Title: Writer/Director/Producer
IMDB: *www.imdb.com/name/nm0001774*

Conor Welch
Title: Director of Development
Email: *conor@redhourfilms.com*
IMDB: *www.imdb.com/name/nm3137428*

Robin Mabrito
Title: Story Editor
Email: *robin@redhourfilms.com*
IMDB: *www.imdb.com/name/nm3142663*

RED OM FILMS, INC.

3000 Olympic Boulevard
Building 3, Suite 2330
Santa Monica, CA 90404

Phone: 310-594-3467

Submission Policy: Does not accept any
unsolicited material
Genre: Action, Comedy, Family, Drama
Company Focus: Feature Films, TV

Julia Roberts
Title: Actress/Producer
IMDB: *www.imdb.com/name/nm0000210*

Lisa Roberts Gillian
Title: Producer
IMDB: *www.imdb.com/name/nm0731359*

Philip Rose
Title: Producer
IMDB: *www.imdb.com/name/nm0741615*

RED WAGON ENTERTAINMENT

10202 West Washington Boulevard
Hepburn Building West
Culver City, CA 90232-3195

Phone: 310-244-4466
Fax: 310-244-1480

Submission Policy: Does not accept any
unsolicited material
Genre: Fantasy, Horror, Animation, Drama
Company Focus: Feature Films, TV

Douglas Wick
Title: Producer
IMDB: *www.imdb.com/name/nm0926824*

Lucy Fisher
Title: Producer
IMDB: *www.imdb.com/name/nm0279651*

Rachel Shane
Title: Executive Vice-President
IMDB: *www.imdb.com/name/nm1247594*

REGENCY ENTERPRISES

10201 West Pico Boulevard
Building 12
Los Angeles, CA 90035

Phone: 310-369-8300
Fax: 310-969-0470
Email: *info@newregency.com*
IMDB: *www.imdb.com/company/co0021592*

Submission Policy: Accepts Query Letter from
unproduced, unrepresented writers via email
Company Focus: Feature Films

Carla Hacken
Title: President of Production
IMDB: *www.imdb.com/name/nm0352402*

Michelle Kroes
Title: Director, Feature & Literary Development
IMDB: *www.imdb.com/name/nm3129676*

Ryan Horrigan
Title: Director of Development
IMDB: *www.imdb.com/name/nm1673839*

REGENT ENTERTAINMENT

10940 Wilshire Boulevard, Suite 1600
Los Angeles, CA 90024

Phone: 310-806-4290
Email: *info@regententertainment.com*
IMDB: *www.imdb.com/company/co0045895*

Submission Policy: Accepts Query Letter from
unproduced, unrepresented writers via email
Genre: Action, Horror, Science Fiction, Drama
Company Focus: Feature Films, TV

David Millbern
Title: Director of Development
Phone: 310-806-4290
IMDB: *www.imdb.com/name/nm0587778*

Roxana Vatan
IMDB: *www.imdb.com/name/nm2985872*

REHAB ENTERTAINMENT

1416 North La Brea Avenue
Hollywood, CA 90028

Phone: 323-645-6444
Fax: 323-645-6445
Email: *info@rehabent.com*

Submission Policy: Accepts Query Letter from unproduced, unrepresented writers via email
Company Focus: Feature Films

John Hyde
Title: President

Brett Coker
Title: Production Executive

REINER/GREISMAN

335 North Maple Drive, Suite 135
Beverly Hills, CA 90210

Phone: 310-285-2300
Fax: 310-285-2345

Submission Policy: Accepts Query Letter from unproduced, unrepresented writers
Genre: Comedy, Drama
Company Focus: Feature Films

Rob Reiner
Title: Director/Producer
Phone: 310-285-2328
IMDB: *www.imdb.com/name/nm0001661*
Assistant: Pam Jones

Alan Greisman
Title: Producer
Phone: 310-205-2766

Pam Jones
Title: Assistant to Rob Reiner
Phone: 310-285-2352

RELATIVITY MEDIA, LLC

9242 Beverly Boulevard, Suite 300
Beverly Hills, CA 90210

Phone: 310-724-7700
Fax: 310-724-7701

Submission Policy: Accepts Query Letter from produced or represented writers
Company Focus: Feature Films, TV, Reality Programming (Reality TV, Documentaries, Special Events, Sporting Events), Media (Commercials/Branding/Marketing)

Jonathan Karsh
Title: Sr. Vice-President, Creative Affairs

Julie Link
Title: Sr. Vice-President, Development

REMEMBER DREAMING, LLC

8252 1/2 Santa Monica Boulevard, Suite B
West Hollywood, CA 90046

Phone: 323-654-3333

Submission Policy: Accepts Query Letter from unproduced, unrepresented writers
Company Focus: Feature Films, Reality Programming (Reality TV, Documentaries, Special Events, Sporting Events)

Stan Spry
Title: President

Courtney Brin
Title: Director, Production & Development
Email: *courtney@freefall-films.com*

RENAISSANCE PICTURES

315 South Beverly Drive, Suite 216
Beverly Hills, CA 90210

Phone: 310-785-3900
Fax: 310-785-9176

Submission Policy: Accepts Query Letter from unproduced, unrepresented writers
Genre: Action, Fantasy, Horror, Drama
Company Focus: Feature Films, TV

Sam Raimi
Title: Director/Executive Producer

J.R. Young
Title: Producer, Creative Executive

RENEE MISSEL PRODUCTIONS

2376 Adrian Street, Suite A
Newbury Park, CA 91320

Phone: 310-463-0638
Fax: 805-669-4511
Email: *filmtao@aol.com*

Submission Policy: Accepts Query Letter from unproduced, unrepresented writers via email
Company Focus: Feature Films
Year Established: 1983

Renee Missel
Title: Producer

Bridget Stone
Title: Story Editor

RENEE VALENTE PRODUCTIONS

13547 Ventura Boulevard, #195
Sherman Oaks, CA 91423

Phone: 310-472-5342
Email: *valenteprod@aol.com*

Submission Policy: Accepts Query Letter from unproduced, unrepresented writers via email
Company Focus: Feature Films, TV

Renee Valente
Title: Executive Producer

RENEGADE ANIMATION, INC.

111 East Broadway, Suite 208
Glendale, CA 91205

Phone: 818-551-2351
Fax: 818-551-2350
Email: *contactus@renegadeanimation.com*

Submission Policy: Accepts Query Letter from unproduced, unrepresented writers via email
Company Focus: TV

Ashley Postlewaite
Title: Vice-President/Executive Producer

Darrell Van Citters
Title: President/Director

RENFIELD PRODUCTIONS

c/o The Lot
1041 North Formosa Avenue
Writer's Building, Suite 321
West Hollywood, CA 90046

Phone: 323-850-3905
Fax: 323-850-3907
Email: *development@renfieldproductions.com*

Submission Policy: Accepts Query Letter from unproduced, unrepresented writers via email
Genre: Action, Comedy, Horror, Family, Animation, Drama, Socio-cultural
Company Focus: TV, Reality Programming (Reality TV, Documentaries, Special Events, Sporting Events)

Joe Dante
Title: Director/Producer

T.L. Kittle
Title: Director, Development

Mark Alan
Title: Development Executive

REVEILLE, LLC/SHINE INTERNATIONAL

1741 Ivar Avenue
Los Angeles, CA 90028

Phone: 323-790-8000
Fax: 323-790-8399

Submission Policy: Does not accept any unsolicited material
Company Focus: TV, Reality Programming (Reality TV, Documentaries, Special Events, Sporting Events)

Carolyn Bernstein
Title: Executive Vice-President, Scripted TV

Todd Cohen
Title: Vice-President, Domestic Scripted TV

Rob Cohen
Title: Vice-President Creative Affairs

REVELATIONS ENTERTAINMENT

1221 Second Street
4th Floor
Santa Monica, CA 90401

Phone: 310-394-3131
Fax: 310-394-3133
Email: *info@revelationsent.com*

Submission Policy: Does not accept any unsolicited material
Genre: Action, Detective, Family, Drama
Company Focus: Feature Films, TV

Morgan Freeman
Title: President/Actor/Producer

Lori McCreary
Title: CEO/Producer
Assistant: Mitch del Valle

Tracy Mercer
Title: Vice-President, Development

RHINO FILMS

10501 Wilshire Boulevard, Suite 814
Los Angeles, CA 90024

Phone: 310-441-6557
Fax: 310-441-6584
Email: *contact@rhinofilms.com*

Submission Policy: Accepts Query Letter from unproduced, unrepresented writers via email
Company Focus: Feature Films

Stephen Nemeth
Title: CEO
Email: *stephennemeth@rhinofilms.com*
IMDB: *www.imdb.com/name/nm0625932*

Betsy Stahl
Email: *betsystahl@rhinofilms.com*
IMDB: *www.imdb.com/name/nm0821439*

RICE & BEANS PRODUCTIONS

30 North Raymond, Suite 605
Pasadena, CA 91103

Phone: 626-792-9171
Fax: 626-792-9171
Email: *vin88@pacbell.net*

Submission Policy: Accepts Query Letter from unproduced, unrepresented writers via email
Genre: Comedy, TV Drama, TV Sitcom
Company Focus: Feature Films, TV

Vince Cheung
Title: Writer/Producer

Ben Montanio
Title: Writer/Producer

RICHE PRODUCTIONS

9336 West Washington Boulevard
Above Stage 3 West, Room 305
Culver City, CA 90232

Phone: 310-202-4850

Submission Policy: Accepts Query Letter from unproduced, unrepresented writers
Genre: Action, Family
Company Focus: Feature Films, TV

Alan Riche
Title: Partner
Assistant: Adrienne Novelly

Peter Riche
Title: Partner

RIVER ROAD ENTERTAINMENT

2000 Avenue of the Stars, Suite 620-N
Los Angeles, CA 90067

Phone: 213-253-4610
Fax: 310-843-9551

Submission Policy: Does not accept any unsolicited material
Genre: Comedy, Memoir & True Stories, Drama
Company Focus: Feature Films, Reality Programming (Reality TV, Documentaries, Special Events, Sporting Events)

Sarah Hammer
Title: Head, Creative Affairs

ROBERT CORT PRODUCTIONS

1041 North Formosa Avenue
Administration Building, Suite 196
West Hollywood, CA 90046

Phone: 323-850-2644
Fax: 323-850-2634

Submission Policy: Accepts Query Letter from

unproduced, unrepresented writers
Genre: Comedy, Drama
Company Focus: Feature Films, TV

Robert Cort
Title: Producer
Assistant: Maritza Berta

Eric Hetzel
Title: Vice-President, Production

ROBERT GREENWALD PRODUCTIONS

10510 Culver Boulevard
Culver City, CA 90232-3400

Phone: 310-204-0404
Fax: 310-204-0174
Email: *info@rgpinc.com*

Submission Policy: Does not accept any
unsolicited material
Genre: Comedy, Memoir & True Stories,
Drama
Company Focus: Feature Films, TV

Robert Greenwald
Title: Producer/Director
Assistant: Rachel Presby

Philip Kleinbart
Title: Producer/Executive Vice-President

ROBERT LAWRENCE PRODUCTIONS

201 Ocean Avenue
803B
Santa Monica, CA 90402

Phone: 310-471-4793

Submission Policy: Accepts Query Letter from
unproduced, unrepresented writers
Genre: Action, Comedy, Drama
Company Focus: Feature Films

Robert Lawrence
Title: President
Assistant: Nathan Pettijohn

ROBERT SIMONDS COMPANY

10202 Washington Boulevard
Stage 6, 7th Floor
Culver City, CA 90232

Phone: 310-244-5222
Fax: 310-244-0348

Submission Policy: Does not accept any
unsolicited material
Genre: Action, Comedy, Thriller, Family
Company Focus: Feature Films
Year Established: 2012

Robert Simonds
Title: CEO
Email: *rasst@rscfilms.com*
IMDB: *www.imdb.com/name/nm0800465*
Assistant: Jennifer Jiang

ROBERTS/DAVID FILMS, INC.

1717 West Magnolia Boulevard, Suite 105
Burbank, CA 91506

Phone: 818-539-0033

Submission Policy: Does not accept any
unsolicited material
Genre: Comedy
Company Focus: Feature Films, TV, Reality
Programming (Reality TV, Documentaries,
Special Events, Sporting Events)

Mark Roberts
Title: Partner
Email: *mark@robertsdavid.com*

Lorena David
Title: Partner
Email: *lorena@robertsdavid.com*

Max Velez
Title: Director, Development
Email: *max@robertsdavid.com*

ROCKLIN/FAUST

10390 Santa Monica Boulevard, Suite 200
Los Angeles, CA 90025

Phone: 310-789-3066
Fax: 310-789-3060

Submission Policy: Does not accept any
unsolicited material
Genre: Comedy, Animation, Drama
Company Focus: Feature Films, TV, Reality
Programming (Reality TV, Documentaries,
Special Events, Sporting Events)

Nicole Rocklin
Title: Producer

Blye Faust
Title: Producer

ROOM 101, INC.

5055 Wilshire Boulevard, Suite #300
Los Angeles 90036

Phone: 323-930-1101

Submission Policy: Accepts Query Letter from
unproduced, unrepresented writers
Genre: Crime, Horror, Drama
Company Focus: Feature Films, TV

Steven Schneider
Title: Producer
Assistant: Kailey Marsh

ROOM 9 ENTERTAINMENT

9229 Sunset Boulevard, Suite 505
West Hollywood, CA 90069

Phone: 310-651-2001
Fax: 310-651-2010
Email: *info@room9entertainment.com*

Submission Policy: Does not accept any
unsolicited material
Genre: Memoir & True Stories, Drama
Company Focus: Feature Films, TV

David Sacks
Title: CEO

Michael Newman
Title: Partner, Co-President

Daniel Brunt
Title: Partner, Co-President

ROSA ENTERTAINMENT

7288 Sunset Boulevard, Suite 208
Los Angeles, CA 90046

Phone: 310-470-3506
Fax: 310-470-3509
Email: *info@rosaentertainment.com*

Submission Policy: Does not accept any
unsolicited material
Genre: Comedy, Drama
Company Focus: Feature Films, TV

Sidney Sherman
Title: Producer
Email: *sidney@rosaentertainment.com*
IMDB: *www.imdb.com/name/nm0792587*

ROSEROCK FILMS

4000 Warner Boulevard
Building 81
Burbank, CA 91522

Phone: 818-954-7528

Submission Policy: Does not accept any
unsolicited material
Company Focus: Feature Films

Hunt Lowry
Title: Producer

Patricia Reed
Title: Director of Development
Phone: 818-954-7673

Stacy Cohen
Title: Producer
Phone: 818-954-7438

ROTH FILMS

2900 West Olympic Boulevard
Santa Monica, CA 90404

Phone: 310-255-7000

Submission Policy: Accepts Query Letter from
unproduced, unrepresented writers
Company Focus: Feature Films

Joe Roth
Title: Producer
Assistant: Jayme Carr

Palak Patel
Title: President, Production
IMDB: *www.imdb.com/name/nm2026983*
Assistant: Jenna Wright

ROUGH HOUSE

1722 Whitley Avenue
Hollywood, CA 90028

Phone: 323-469-3161

Submission Policy: Accepts Scripts from produced or represented writers
Genre: Romance, Drama
Company Focus: Feature Films

David Gordon Green
Title: Director/Writer/Producer
IMDB: *www.imdb.com/name/nm0337773*

ROUTE ONE FILMS

1041 North Formosa Avenue
Santa Monica East #200
West Hollywood, CA 90046

Phone: 323-850-3855
Fax: 323-850-3866

Submission Policy: Does not accept any unsolicited material
Company Focus: Feature Films

Jay Stern
Title: Founder/Partner/Producer
IMDB: *www.imdb.com/name/nm0827731*

Russell Levine
Title: Founder/Partner/Producer
IMDB: *www.imdb.com/name/nm4149902*

Chip Diggins
Title: Founder/Partner/Producer
IMDB: *www.imdb.com/name/nm0226505*

S PICTURES, INC.

2036 Norwalk Avenue
Los Angeles, CA 90041

Phone: 310-866-7977
Fax: 818-995-1677

Submission Policy: Does not accept any unsolicited material
Genre: Comedy, Memoir & True Stories, Science Fiction
Company Focus: Feature Films, TV, Reality Programming (Reality TV, Documentaries, Special Events, Sporting Events)

Chuck Simon
Title: President/Producer
Phone: 818-995-1585
Email: *chuck@Spictures.TV*

Brean Cunningham
Title: Director, Acquisitions

SAFRAN COMPANY

8748 Holloway Drive
West Hollywood, CA 90069

Phone: 310-278-8234

Submission Policy: Does not accept any unsolicited material
Genre: Comedy, Family
Company Focus: Feature Films, TV
Year Established: 2006

Peter Safran
Title: Manager/Producer
IMDB: *www.imdb.com/name/nm0755911*

Tom Drumm
Title: Manager
IMDB: *www.imdb.com/name/nm1619641*

Jack St. Martin
Title: Creative Executive
IMDB: *www.imdb.com/name/nm3015480*

SALTIRE ENTERTAINMENT

6352 De Longpre Avenue
Los Angeles, CA 90028

IMDB: *www.imdb.com/company/co0104114*

Submission Policy: Does not accept any unsolicited material
Genre: Myth, Science Fiction, Drama
Company Focus: Feature Films

Stuart Pollok
Title: Producer
IMDB: *www.imdb.com/name/nm0689415*

SALTY FEATURES

682 Avenue of the Americas, Suite 3
New York, NY 10010

Phone: 212-924-1601
Fax: 212-924-2306
Email: *info@saltyfeatures.com*

Submission Policy: Accepts Query Letter from unproduced, unrepresented writers via email
Company Focus: Feature Films, Reality Programming (Reality TV, Documentaries, Special Events, Sporting Events)

Yael Melamede
Title: Producer

Eva Kolodner
Title: Co-Founder, Producer

SAMUELSON PRODUCTIONS LIMITED

10401 Wyton Drive
Los Angeles, CA 90024-2527

Phone: 310-208-1000
Fax: 323-315-5188
Email: *info@samuelson.la*

Submission Policy: Does not accept any unsolicited material
Genre: Action, Comedy, Drama
Company Focus: Feature Films, TV

Peter Samuelson
Title: Owner
Assistant: Brian Casey
IMDB: *www.imdb.com/name/nm0006873*

Saryl Hirsch
Title: Controller
IMDB: *www.imdb.com/name/nm1950244*

Marc Samuelson
IMDB: *www.imdb.com/name/nm0760555*

Renato Celani
IMDB: *www.imdb.com/name/nm1954607*

Josie Law
IMDB: *www.imdb.com/name/nm1656468*

SANDER/MOSES PRODUCTIONS, INC.

c/o Disney
500 South Buena Vista Street
Animation Building 1 E 13
Burbank, CA 91521-1657

Phone: 818-560-4500
Fax: 818-860-6284
Email: *info@sandermoses.com*

Submission Policy: Accepts Query Letter from unproduced, unrepresented writers via email
Genre: Memoir & True Stories, Drama, Socio-cultural
Company Focus: Feature Films, TV, Reality Programming (Reality TV, Documentaries, Special Events, Sporting Events), Media (Commercials/Branding/Marketing)

Ian Sander
Title: Executive Producer/Writer/Director
Assistant: Mimi Sanouvong

Kim Moses
Title: Executive Producer/Writer/Director
Assistant: Amanda Toye

SCOTT FREE PRODUCTIONS

634 North La Peer Drive
Los Angeles, CA 90069

Phone: 310-659-1577
Fax: 310-659-1377

Submission Policy: Does not accept any unsolicited material
Genre: Action, Crime, Detective, Memoir & True Stories, Thriller, TV Drama, Animation, Drama
Company Focus: Feature Films, TV, Reality Programming (Reality TV, Documentaries, Special Events, Sporting Events)

Ridley Scott
Title: Co-Chairman
IMDB: *www.imdb.com/name/nm0000631*
Assistant: Nancy Ryan

David Zucker
Title: President, TV
IMDB: *www.imdb.com/name/nm0001878*
Assistant: Mark Pfeffer

Maresa Pullman
Title: Director, Film Development

SCOTT RUDIN PRODUCTIONS

120 West 45th Street
10th Floor
New York, NY 10036

Phone: 212-704-4600

Submission Policy: Accepts Query Letter from unproduced, unrepresented writers
Company Focus: Feature Films
Year Established: 1993

Scott Rudin
Title: Producer
Phone: 212-704-4600
IMDB: *www.imdb.com/name/nm0748784*

Eli Bush
Title: Executive
Phone: 212-704-4600
Email: *eli@scottrudinprod.com*
IMDB: *www.imdb.com/name/nm4791912*

Julie Oh
Title: Executive
Phone: 212-704-4600
IMDB: *www.imdb.com/name/nm4791935*

SCOTT SANDERS PRODUCTIONS

500 South Buena Vista Drive
Animation Building 3C-1
Burbank, CA 91521

Phone: 818-560-6350
Fax: 818-560-3541

Submission Policy: Accepts Query Letter from unproduced, unrepresented writers
Company Focus: Feature Films, TV

Scott Sanders
Title: President, CEO
Assistant: Jaime Quiroz

Bryan Kalfus
Title: Creative Executive, Film

SE8 GROUP

9560 Cedarbrook Drive
Beverly Hills, CA 90210

Phone: 310-285-6090
Fax: 310-285-6097

Submission Policy: Accepts Query Letter from unproduced, unrepresented writers
Genre: Thriller, Drama
Company Focus: Feature Films

Gary Oldman
Title: Actor/Producer
IMDB: *www.imdb.com/name/nm0000198*

Douglas Urbanski
Title: Producer
IMDB: *www.imdb.com/name/nm0881703*

SECOND AND 10TH INC.

51 MacDougal Street, Suite 383
New York, NY 10012

Phone: 347-882-4493

Submission Policy: Does not accept any unsolicited material
Genre: Drama
Company Focus: Feature Films

Anne Carey
Title: Producer

Shani Geva
Title: Creative Executive

SEE FILM INC./LAGO FILM GMBH

6399 Wilshire Boulevard, Suite 1002
Los Angeles, CA 90048

Phone: 310-653-7826
Email: *lago@lagofilm.com*

Submission Policy: Does not accept any unsolicited material
Genre: Comedy, Horror, Drama
Company Focus: Feature Films

Marco Mehlitz
Title: Producer

Luane Sandrin Gauer
Title: Project Manager

SEISMIC PICTURES

8899 Beverly Boulevard, Suite 810
Los Angeles, CA 90048

Phone: 213-245-1180
Email: *info@seismicpictures.com*

Submission Policy: Does not accept any unsolicited material
Genre: Comedy, Memoir & True Stories, Drama, Socio-cultural
Company Focus: Feature Films, Reality Programming (Reality TV, Documentaries, Special Events, Sporting Events)

Robert Schwartz
Title: Producer/President

SENART FILMS

555 West 25th Street, 4th Floor
New York, NY 10001

Phone: 212-406-9610
Fax: 212-406-9581
Email: *info@senartfilms.com*

Submission Policy: Does not accept any unsolicited material
Genre: Memoir & True Stories, Drama
Company Focus: Feature Films, Reality Programming (Reality TV, Documentaries, Special Events, Sporting Events)

Robert May
Title: Producer

Lauren Timmons
Title: Story Editor/Producer

SERAPHIM FILMS

c/o Sheryl Petersen/APA
405 South Beverly Drive
Beverly Hills, CA 90212

Phone: 310-888-4200 or 310-246-0050
Email: *assistant@seraphimfilms.com*

Submission Policy: Accepts Query Letter from unproduced, unrepresented writers via email
Genre: Fantasy, Horror, Animation, Drama
Company Focus: Feature Films

Clive Barker
Title: President

Joe Daley
Title: Executive Vice-President, Production

Anthony DiBlasi
Title: Writer/Director

SERENDIPITY POINT FILMS

9 Price Street
Toronto, ON M4W 1Z1
Canada

Phone: 416-960-0300
Fax: 416-960-8656

Submission Policy: Does not accept any unsolicited material
Genre: Action, Comedy, Thriller, Drama
Company Focus: Feature Films, TV

Robert Lantos
Title: Producer
Assistant: Cherri Campbell

Wendy Saffer
Title: Head, Publicity & Marketing

SERENDIPITY PRODUCTIONS, INC.

15260 Ventura Boulevard, Suite 1040
Sherman Oaks, CA 91403

Phone: 818-789-3035
Fax: 818-235-0150
Email: *serendipityprod@earthlink.net*

Submission Policy: Does not accept any unsolicited material
Genre: Horror, Memoir & True Stories, Drama
Company Focus: Feature Films, TV

Daniel Heffner
Title: Producer/Principal

Ketura Kestin
Title: *keturak@gmail.com*

SEVEN ARTS PICTURES

8439 Sunset Boulevard 4th Floor
Los Angeles, CA 90069

Phone: 323-372-3080
Fax: 323-372-3088
Email: *info@7artspictures.com*

Submission Policy: Does not accept any unsolicited material
Genre: Comedy, Science Fiction, Thriller,

Drama
Company Focus: Feature Films

Peter Hoffman
Title: CEO
Assistant: Linda Silverthorn

Susan Hoffman
Title: Producer

Caroline Couret Delegue
Title: Director, Development & Marketing

SHADOWCATCHER ENTERTAINMENT

4701 SW Admiral Way
Box 32
Seattle, WA 98116

Phone: 206-328-6266
Fax: 206-447-1462
Email: *kate@shadowcatcherent.com*

Submission Policy: Accepts Query Letter from unproduced, unrepresented writers via email
Genre: Comedy, Memoir & True Stories, TV Sitcom, Animation, Drama
Company Focus: Feature Films, TV, Reality Programming (Reality TV, Documentaries, Special Events, Sporting Events), Theater

David Skinner
Title: Executive Producer
Assistant: Kate Wickstrom

Tom Gorai
Title: Producer

Robin Gurland
Title: Producer

SHAUN CASSIDY PRODUCTIONS

500 South Buena Vista Street, Old Animation Building
Burbank, CA 91521-1844

Phone: 818-560-6320

Submission Policy: Accepts Query Letter from unproduced, unrepresented writers
Genre: TV Drama, TV Sitcom
Company Focus: TV

Shaun Cassidy
Title: Producer/Writer
Assistant: Dan Williams

SHEEP NOIR FILMS

438 West 17th Avenue
Vancouver, BC V5Y 2A2
Fax: 604-762-8933
Email: *info@sheepnoir.com*

Submission Policy: Does not accept any unsolicited material
Genre: Drama
Company Focus: Feature Films, TV

Wendy Hyman
Title: Producer
IMDB: *www.imdb.com/name/nm0405207*

Nathaniel Geary
Title: Writer/Director
IMDB: *www.imdb.com/name/nm0311303*

Marc Stephenson
Title: Producer
Phone: 604-762-8933
Email: *marc@sheepnoir.com*

SHOE MONEY PRODUCTIONS

10202 West Washington Boulevard
Poitier Building, Suite 3100
Culver City, CA 90232

Phone: 310-244-6188
Email: *shoemoneyproductions@mac.com*

Submission Policy: Accepts Query Letter from unproduced, unrepresented writers via email
Genre: TV Drama, Drama
Company Focus: Feature Films, TV

Thomas Schlamme
Title: Executive Producer/Director
Assistant: Elisabeth Cormier

Julie De Joie
Title: Executive, Production

SHONDALAND

4151 Prospect Avenue
Los Feliz Tower, 5th Floor
Los Angeles, CA 90027

Phone: 323-671-3370

Submission Policy: Does not accept any unsolicited material
Genre: TV Drama, TV Sitcom
Company Focus: Feature Films, TV

Shonda Rhimes
Title: Writer/Producer

Betsy Beers
Title: Producer

Rachel Eggebeen
Title: Development Executive

SHORELINE ENTERTAINMENT, INC.

1875 Century Park East, Suite 600
Los Angeles, CA 90067

Phone: 310-551-2060
Fax: 310-201-0729
Email: *info@shorelineentertainment.com*

Submission Policy: Does not accept any unsolicited material
Genre: Horror, Science Fiction, Thriller, Drama
Company Focus: Feature Films, Reality Programming (Reality TV, Documentaries, Special Events, Sporting Events)

Morris Ruskin
Title: CEO/Producer
Assistant: Timothy Tahir

Sam Eigen
Title: Executive Vice-President
Assistant: Erin Schroeder

Brandon Paine
Title: Director, Acquisitions

SID & MARTY KROFFT PICTURES CORP.

c/o CBS Studio Center
4024 Radford Avenue
Building 5, Suite 102
Studio City, CA 91604

Phone: 818-655-5314
Fax: 818-655-8235

Submission Policy: Accepts Query Letter from unproduced, unrepresented writers via email
Genre: TV Sitcom, Family, Animation
Company Focus: Feature Films, TV

Marty Krofft
Title: President
Email: *marty@krofftpictures.com*
Assistant: Christine Bedolla

Sid Krofft
Title: Executive Vice-President
Assistant: Bill Tracy

Michael Stokes
Title: Vice-President, Production & Development

SIDNEY KIMMEL ENTERTAINMENT

9460 Wilshire Boulevard
5th Floor
Beverly Hills, CA 90212

Phone: 310-777-8818
Fax: 310-777-8892
Email: *reception@skefilms.com*

Submission Policy: Does not accept any unsolicited material
Genre: Comedy, Detective, Thriller, Drama, Socio-cultural
Company Focus: Feature Films

Sidney Kimmel
Title: Chairman/CEO

Matt Berenson
Title: President, Production

Mark Mikutowicz
Title: Vice-President of Development

SIGNATURE PICTURES

8285 West Sunset Boulevard, Suite 7
West Hollywood, CA 90046

Phone: 323-848-9005
Fax: 323-848-9305
Email: *james@signaturepictures.com*

Submission Policy: Does not accept any unsolicited material
Genre: Action, Memoir & True Stories,

Romance, Thriller, Drama
Company Focus: Feature Films

Moshe Diamant
Title: Producer

Illana Diamant
Title: Producer

James Portolese
Title: Production Executive

SIKELIA PRODUCTIONS

110 West 57th Street
5th Floor
New York, NY 10019

Phone: 212-906-8800
Fax: 212-906-8891

Submission Policy: Does not accept any
unsolicited material
Company Focus: Feature Films

Martin Scorsese
Title: Director/Producer
IMDB: *www.imdb.com/name/nm0000217*

Emma Tillinger Koskoff
Title: President of Production
IMDB: *www.imdb.com/name/nm0863374*

SILLY ROBIN PRODUCTIONS

c/o Paradigm Talent Agency
360 North Crescent Drive, North Building
Beverly Hills, CA 90210

Phone: 310-288-8000
Fax: 310-275-6180

Submission Policy: Accepts Query Letter from
unproduced, unrepresented writers via email
Genre: TV Drama, TV Sitcom, Drama
Company Focus: Feature Films, TV, Theater

Alan Zweibel
Title: Writer/Producer/Director

Sarit Catz
Title: Director, Development

SILVER DREAM PRODUCTIONS

3452 East Foothill Boulevard, Suite 620
Pasadena, CA 91107

Phone: 626-799-3880
Fax: 626-799-5363
Email: *luoyan@silverdreamprods.com*

Submission Policy: Accepts Query Letter from
unproduced, unrepresented writers via email
Genre: Myth, Drama, Socio-cultural
Company Focus: Feature Films

Luo Yan
Title: Actress/Producer
Assistant: Diana Chiu

SILVER NITRATE

12268 Ventura Boulevard
Studio City, CA 91604

Phone: 818-762-9559
Fax: 818-762-9177

Submission Policy: Does not accept any
unsolicited material
Genre: Comedy, Science Fiction, Animation,
Drama
Company Focus: Feature Films

Ash Shah
Title: Producer

SILVER PICTURES

4000 Warner Boulevard
Building 90
Burbank, CA 91522

Phone: 818-954-4490
Fax: 818-954-3237

Submission Policy: Accepts Query Letter from
unproduced, unrepresented writers
Genre: Action, Science Fiction, Thriller, Family,
Animation, Drama
Company Focus: Feature Films, TV, Reality
Programming (Reality TV, Documentaries,
Special Events, Sporting Events)

Joel Silver
Title: Chairman

Alex Heineman
Title: Sr. Vice-President, Production

Sean Finegan
Title: Creative Executive

SILVERS/KOSTER PRODUCTIONS, LLC

353 South Reeves Drive, Penthouse
Beverly Hills, CA 90212

Phone: 310-991-4736
Fax: 310-284-5797
Email: *skfilmco@aol.com*

Submission Policy: Accepts Query Letter from
unproduced, unrepresented writers via email
Company Focus: Feature Films, TV, Reality
Programming (Reality TV, Documentaries,
Special Events, Sporting Events), Media
(Commercials/Branding/Marketing)

Tracy Silvers
Title: Chairman

Iren Koster
Title: President

Karen Corcoran
Title: Vice-President, Development

SIMON WEST PRODUCTIONS

3450 Cahuenga Boulevard West
Building 510
Los Angeles, CA 90068

Phone: 323-845-0821
Fax: 323-845-4582

Submission Policy: Accepts Query Letter from
unproduced, unrepresented writers
Genre: Action, Science Fiction, Drama
Company Focus: Feature Films, TV

Simon West
Title: Director/Producer

Jib Polhemus
Title: President, Production

SINGE CELL PICTURES

1016 North Palm Avenue
West Hollywood, CA 90069

Phone: 310-360-7600
Fax: 310-360-7011

Submission Policy: Accepts Query Letter from
unproduced, unrepresented writers
Genre: Comedy, Drama
Company Focus: Feature Films, TV

Michael Stipe
Title: Producer

Sandy Stern
Title: Producer

David Rothley
Title: Development

SINOVOI ENTERTAINMENT

1317 North San Fernando Boulevard, Suite 395
Burbank, CA 91504

Phone: 818-562-6404
Fax: 818-567-0104
Email: *maxwell@sinovoientertainment.com*

Submission Policy: Accepts Query Letter from
unproduced, unrepresented writers via email
Genre: Comedy, Horror, Drama, Socio-cultural
Company Focus: Feature Films

Maxwell Sinovoi
Title: Producer

SKETCH FILMS

Submission Policy: Does not accept any
unsolicited material
Genre: Action, Fantasy, Horror, Myth, Science
Fiction
Company Focus: Feature Films

Len Wiseman
Title: Producer/Director/Writer
IMDB: *www.imdb.com/name/nm0936482*

David Bernardi
Title: President
Email: *d.bernardi@sbcglobal.net*
IMDB: *www.imdb.com/name/nm2050171*

SKY NETWORKS

9220 Sunset Boulevard, Suite 230
West Hollywood, CA 90069

Phone: 310-860-2740
Fax: 310-860-2471

Submission Policy: Accepts Query Letter from unproduced, unrepresented writers
Genre: Action, Science Fiction, Socio-cultural
Company Focus: TV

Rebecca Segal
Title: Sr. Vice-President

Jason Lacob
Title: Programming Executive

SKYDANCE PRODUCTIONS

5555 Melrose Avenue
Dean Martin Building
Hollywood, CA 90038

Phone: 323-956-9900
Fax: 323-956-9901
Email: info@skydance.com

Submission Policy: Accepts Scripts from produced or represented writers
Genre: Action, Comedy, Fantasy, Myth, Science Fiction, Thriller, Family, Drama
Company Focus: Feature Films, TV

David Ellison
Title: President
IMDB: www.imdb.com/name/nm1911103

Dana Goldberg
Title: President of Production
IMDB: www.imdb.com/name/nm1602154

Matthew Milam
Title: Vice-President Production
IMDB: www.imdb.com/name/nm1297784

SKYLARK ENTERTAINMENT, INC.

12405 Venice Boulevard, Suite 237
Los Angeles, CA 90066

Phone: 310-390-2659

Submission Policy: Does not accept any unsolicited material
Genre: Comedy, Memoir & True Stories, Drama
Company Focus: Feature Films, TV

Jacobus Rose
Title: President/Producer

SKYLINE PICTURES, LLC

5555 Melrose Ave, Bob Hope Building 102-108
Los Angeles, CA 90038

Phone: 323-956-4440
Fax: 323-862-4020
Email: info@skylinepix.com

Submission Policy: Does not accept any unsolicited material
Genre: Memoir & True Stories, TV Drama, Drama, Socio-cultural
Company Focus: Feature Films, TV

Dror Soref
Title: Producer/Director

Michelle Seward
Title: Executive Producer

Noga Ashkenazi
Title: Director, Development

SMART ENTERTAINMENT

9595 Wilshire Boulevard, Suite 900
Beverly Hills, CA 90212

Phone: 310-205-6090
Fax: 310-205-6093
Email: assistant@smartentertainment.com

Submission Policy: Accepts Query Letter from unproduced, unrepresented writers via email
Genre: Comedy, Horror, Thriller, TV Sitcom
Company Focus: Feature Films, TV, Reality Programming (Reality TV, Documentaries, Special Events, Sporting Events)

John Jacobs
Title: President
Assistant: James Krane

Zac Unterman
Title: Director, Development

SMASH MEDIA, INC.

1208 Georgina Avenue
Santa Monica, CA 90402

Phone: 310-395-0058
Fax: 310-395-8850
Email: *info@smashmediafilms.com*

Submission Policy: Accepts Query Letter from unproduced, unrepresented writers via email
Genre: Comedy, Science Fiction, TV Drama, Drama
Company Focus: Feature Films, TV

Harry Winer
Title: President
Email: *harry.winer@smashmediafilms.com*

Shelley Hack
Title: Vice-President, Development
Email: *shelley.hack@smashmediafilms.com*

Susan Winer
Title: Vice-President, Business Affairs
Email: *susan.winer@smashmediafilms.com*

SMOKEHOUSE PICTURES

12001 Ventura Pl., Suite 200
Studio City, CA 91604

Phone: 818-432-0330
Fax: 818-432-0337
IMDB: *www.imdb.com/company/co0184096*

Submission Policy: Does not accept any unsolicited material
Genre: Comedy, Thriller, Drama
Company Focus: Feature Films

George Clooney
Title: Partner
IMDB: *www.imdb.com/name/nm0000123*

Grant Heslov
Title: Partner
IMDB: *www.imdb.com/name/nm0381416*
Assistant: Tara Oslin

Katie Murphy
Title: Creative Executive
IMDB: *www.imdb.com/name/nm3682023*

SNEAK PREVIEW ENTERTAINMENT

6705 Sunset Boulevard
2nd Floor
Hollywood, CA 90028

Phone: 323-962-0295
Fax: 323-962-0372
Email: *indiefilm@sneakpreviewentertain.com*

Submission Policy: Accepts Query Letter from unproduced, unrepresented writers via email
Company Focus: Feature Films
Year Established: 1991

Steven J. Wolfe
Title: Chairman/CEO/Producer
Phone: 323-962-0295
Email: *sjwolfe@sneakpreviewentertain.com*
IMDB: *www.imdb.com/name/nm0938145*

Chris Hazzard
Title: Director of Development
Phone: 323-962-0295
Email: *ch@sneakpe.com*
IMDB: *www.imdb.com/name/nm3302502*

SOBINI FILMS

10203 Santa Monica Boulevard
Los Angeles, CA 90067

Phone: 310-432-6900
Fax: 310-432-6939
IMDB: *www.imdb.com/company/co0086773*

Submission Policy: Does not accept any unsolicited material
Genre: Comedy, Thriller, Family, Drama, Socio-cultural
Company Focus: Feature Films

Mark Amin
Title: Producer/Chairman
IMDB: *www.imdb.com/name/nm0024909*

David Higgin
Title: President/Producer
IMDB: *www.imdb.com/name/nm0383371*

Cami Winikoff
Title: President
IMDB: *www.imdb.com/name/nm0935121*

SOCIAL CAPITAL FILMS

1617 Brodway, Mezzanine Suite
Santa Monica, CA 90404

Phone: 310-401-6100
Fax: 310-401-6289
Email: *info@socialcapitalfilms.com*

Submission Policy: Does not accept any unsolicited material
Genre: Comedy, Horror, Science Fiction, Thriller, Family, Drama
Company Focus: Feature Films, TV, Reality Programming (Reality TV, Documentaries, Special Events, Sporting Events)

Martin Shore
Title: Chairman/Producer

Christopher Tuffin
Title: Producer
Assistant: Lindsey Denison

SOLIPSIST FILMS

8350 Wilshire Boulevard, Suite 200
Beverly Hills, CA 90211

Phone: 323-939-1068
Fax: 866-862-4411
Email: *info@solipsistfilms.com*

Submission Policy: Accepts Query Letter from unproduced, unrepresented writers via email
Genre: Detective, Fantasy, Memoir & True Stories, Thriller, Drama
Company Focus: Feature Films, Reality Programming (Reality TV, Documentaries, Special Events, Sporting Events)

Stephen L'Heureux
Title: Managing Director

Steven Haddad
Title: Creative Executive

Amber Wellfleet
Title: Creative Executive

SPYGLASS ENTERTAINMENT

245 North Beverly Drive
Beverly Hills, CA 90024

Phone: 310-443-5800
Fax: 310-443-5912

Submission Policy: Does not accept any unsolicited material
Genre: Action, Comedy, Horror, Memoir & True Stories, Thriller, Family, Drama
Company Focus: Feature Films

Gary Barber
Title: Co-Chairman/Founder

Rebekah Rudd
Title: Executive Vice-President, Post Production

Cassidy Lange
Title: Vice-President, Production

ST. AMOS PRODUCTIONS

3480 Barham Boulevard, Suite 108
Los Angeles, CA 90068

Phone: 323-850-9872
Email: *st.amosproductions@earthlink.net*

Submission Policy: Accepts Query Letter from unproduced, unrepresented writers via email
Genre: Comedy, Memoir & True Stories, TV Drama, TV Sitcom
Company Focus: Feature Films, TV, Reality Programming (Reality TV, Documentaries, Special Events, Sporting Events)

John Stamos
Title: Producer/Actor

Marc Alexander
Title: Producer/Writer/Development

STARRY NIGHT ENTERTAINMENT

1414 Avenue of the Americas, 12th Floor
New York, NY 10019

Phone: 212-717-2750
Fax: 212-794-6150
Email: *info@starrynightentertainment.com*

Submission Policy: Accepts Query Letter from unproduced, unrepresented writers via email
Genre: Comedy, Drama
Company Focus: Feature Films, TV, Reality Programming (Reality TV, Documentaries, Special Events, Sporting Events), Media (Commercials/Branding/Marketing), Theater

Craig Saavedra
Title: Partner (LA)
Email: *cs@starrynightentertainment.com*

Michael Shulman
Title: Partner (NY)
Email: *ms@starrynightentertainment.com*

Ryan Meekins
Title: Creative Executive (LA)

STATE STREET PICTURES

8075 West 3rd Street, Suite 306
Los Angeles, CA
90048

Phone: 323-556-2240
Fax: 323-556-2242

Submission Policy: Does not accept any
unsolicited material
Genre: Comedy, Drama
Company Focus: Feature Films, TV

Robert Teitel
Title: Producer
Assistant: Michael Flavin

George Tillman, Jr.
Title: Director
Assistant: Jason Veley

STEAMROLLER PRODUCTIONS, INC.

100 Universal City Plaza #7151
Universal City, CA 91608

Phone: 818-733-4622
Fax: 818-733-4608
Email: *steamrollerprod@aol.com*

Submission Policy: Accepts Query Letter from
unproduced, unrepresented writers via email
Genre: Action, Crime, Detective, Thriller
Company Focus: Feature Films, TV, Reality
Programming (Reality TV, Documentaries,
Special Events, Sporting Events)

Steven Seagal
Title: CEO/Director/Writer/Producer/Actor
Assistant: Tracy Irvine

Binh Dang
Title: Production Executive

STEFANIE EPSTEIN PRODUCTIONS

427 North Canon Drive, Suite 214
Beverly Hills, CA 90210

Phone: 310-385-0300
Fax: 310-385-0302

Phone: 310-385-0300
Fax: 310-385-0302
Email: *billseprods@aol.com*

Submission Policy: Accepts Query Letter from
unproduced, unrepresented writers via email
Genre: Comedy, TV Drama, Drama
Company Focus: Feature Films, TV

Stefanie Epstein
Title: Producer

Bill Gienapp
Title: Creative Executive

STEVEN BOCHCO PRODUCTIONS

3000 Olympic Boulevard, Suite 1310
Santa Monica, CA 90404

Phone: 310-566-6900

Submission Policy: Accepts Query Letter from
unproduced, unrepresented writers
Genre: Crime, Detective, Drama
Company Focus: TV

Steven Bochco
Title: Chairman/CEO

Craig Shenkler
Title: CFO/Vice-President, Finance

STOKELY CHAFFIN PRODUCTIONS

1456 Sunset Plaza Drive
Los Angeles, CA 90069

Phone: 310-657-4559
Email: *davidreed@chaffinproductions.com*

Submission Policy: Accepts Query Letter from
unproduced, unrepresented writers via email
Genre: Action, Comedy, Horror, Memoir &
True Stories, Thriller
Company Focus: Feature Films, TV

Stokely Chaffin
Title: Producer

David Reed
Title: Development Assistant

STONE & COMPANY ENTERTAINMENT

c/o Hollywood Center Studios
1040 North Las Palmas Avenue
Building 1
Los Angeles, CA 90038

Phone: 323-960-2599
Fax: 323-960-2437
Email: *info@stonetv.com*

Submission Policy: Accepts Query Letter from unproduced, unrepresented writers via email
Genre: Reality
Company Focus: Reality Programming (Reality TV, Documentaries, Special Events, Sporting Events)

Scott Stone
Title: Principal

Kevin Bloom
Title: Vice-President, Production

David Weintraub
Title: Vice-President, Series Development

STONEBROOK ENTERTAINMENT

10061 Riverside Drive, Suite 813
Toluca Lake, CA 91602

Phone: 818-766-8797

Submission Policy: Accepts Query Letter from unproduced, unrepresented writers via email
Company Focus: Feature Films, TV

Danny Roth
Title: Producer
Email: *danny@stonebrookent.com*

STOREFRONT PICTURES

1112 Montana Avenue
Santa Monica, CA 90403

Phone: 310-459-4235

Submission Policy: Accepts Query Letter from unproduced, unrepresented writers via email
Genre: Comedy, Fantasy, Romance, Family,

Drama
Company Focus: Feature Films

Susan Cartsonis
Title: Producer
Assistant: Betty Davolo

Roz Weisberg
Title: Vice-President/Producer

STORY AND FILM

2934 1/2 Beverly Glen Circle, Suite 195
Los Angeles, CA 90077

Phone: 310-480-8833
Email: *info@storyandfilm.com*

Submission Policy: Accepts Query Letter from unproduced, unrepresented writers via email

STORYLINE ENTERTAINMENT

8335 Sunset Boulevard, Suite 207
West Hollywood, CA 90069

Phone: 323-337-9045
Fax: 323-210-7263
Email: *info@storyline-entertainment.com*

Submission Policy: Does not accept any unsolicited material
Genre: Comedy, Memoir & True Stories, Romance, Drama, Reality
Company Focus: Feature Films, TV, Theater

Craig Zadan
Title: Executive Producer
Phone: 323-337-9045
Email: *craig@storyline-entertainment.com*

Neil Meron
Title: Executive Producer
Phone: 323-337-9046
Email: *neil@storyline-entertainment.com*

Mark Nicholson
Title: Head, Development
Phone: 323-337-9047
Email: *mark@storyline-entertainment.com*

STRIKE ENTERTAINMENT

3000 West Olympic Boulevard
Building 5, Suite 1250
Santa Monica, CA 90404

Phone: 310-315-0550
Fax: 310-315-0560

Submission Policy: Accepts Query Letter from unproduced, unrepresented writers via email
Genre: Action, Comedy, Horror, Science Fiction, Thriller, Drama
Company Focus: Feature Films

Marc Abraham
Title: Producer
Assistant: Jamie Zakowski

Tom Bliss
Title: Producer
Assistant: Mark Barclay

Eric Newman
Title: Producer
Assistant: Jesse Moore

STUDIO CANAL

9250 Wilshire Boulevard, Suite 210
Beverly Hills, CA 90212

Phone: 310-247-0994

Submission Policy: Does not accept any unsolicited material
Genre: Comedy, Crime, Fantasy, Horror, Memoir & True Stories, Romance, Thriller, Drama
Company Focus: Feature Films, Reality Programming (Reality TV, Documentaries, Special Events, Sporting Events)

Ron Halpern
Title: Executive Vice-President, Int'l Production & Special Projects

SUNLIGHT PRODUCTIONS

854-A Fifth Street
Santa Monica, CA 90403

Phone: 310-899-1522
Email: *mail@sunlightproductions.com*

Submission Policy: Does not accept any unsolicited material
Genre: Comedy, Memoir & True Stories, Drama
Company Focus: Feature Films, TV

Mike Binder
Title: Writer/Director/Actor

Jack Binder
Title: Producer/Line Producer/Unit Production Manager

Rachel Zimmerman
Title: Co-Producer

SUNSWEPT ENTERTAINMENT

10201 West Pico Boulevard
Building 45
Los Angeles, CA 90064

Phone: 310-369-0878
Fax: 310-969-0726

Submission Policy: Does not accept any unsolicited material
Genre: Comedy, Fantasy, Romance, Family, Animation
Company Focus: Feature Films

Karen Rosenfelt
Title: President/Producer
Assistant: Caroline MacVicar

Emmy Castlen
Title: Story Editor

SUNTAUR ENTERTAINMENT

1581 North Crescent Heights Boulevard
Los Angeles, CA 90046

Phone: 323-656-3800
Email: *info@suntaurent.com*

Submission Policy: Does not accept any unsolicited material
Genre: Comedy, Fantasy, Memoir & True Stories, Drama, Socio-cultural, Reality
Company Focus: Feature Films, TV, Reality Programming (Reality TV, Documentaries, Special Events, Sporting Events)

Paul Aaron
Title: President/CEO
Assistant: Matt Blessing

Zac Sanford
Title: Vice-President, Development
Assistant: Adam Morris

SUPERFINGER ENTERTAINMENT

c/o Chris Hart/UTA
9560 Wilshire Boulevard
Beverly Hills, CA 90212

Phone: 310-385-6715

Submission Policy: Accepts Query Letter from unproduced, unrepresented writers via email
Genre: Comedy, Animation, Reality
Company Focus: Feature Films, TV, Reality Programming (Reality TV, Documentaries, Special Events, Sporting Events)

Dane Cook
Title: President/Actor/Comedian

SWEET 180

141 West 28th Street #300
NYC, NY 10001

Phone: 212-541-4443
Fax: 212-563-9655

Submission Policy: Does not accept any unsolicited material
Genre: Comedy, Memoir & True Stories, Romance, Drama, Reality
Company Focus: Feature Films, TV

Lillian LaSalle
Title: Prseident/Manager/Producer

Catherine Clausi
Title: Office Manager/Executive Assistant
Assistant: Lindsay Carlson

T&C PICTURES

3122 Santa Monica Boulevard #200
Santa Monica, CA 90404

Phone: 310-828-7801
Fax: 310-828-1581

Submission Policy: Accepts Query Letter from unproduced, unrepresented writers
Genre: Action, Comedy, Fantasy, Memoir & True Stories, Thriller, Drama, Socio-cultural
Company Focus: Feature Films, TV

Arata Matsushima
Title: Producer
IMDB: *www.imdb.com/name/nm2606503*

Bill Borden
Title: Producer
IMDB: *www.imdb.com/name/nm0096115*

Barry Rosenbush
Title: Producer
IMDB: *www.imdb.com/name/nm0742492*

Matthew Temple
Title: Producer
IMDB: *www.imdb.com/name/nm1642850*

TAGLINE PICTURES

9250 Wilshire Boulevard
Ground Floor
Beverly Hills, CA 90212

Phone: 310-595-1515
Fax: 310-595-1505
Email: *info@taglinela.com*

Submission Policy: Does not accept any unsolicited material
Genre: TV Drama, TV Sitcom
Company Focus: Feature Films, TV

Chris Henze
Title: Executive Producer

J.B. Roberts
Title: Executive Producer

Willie Mercer
Title: Executive Producer

TAPESTRY FILMS, INC.

9328 Civic Center Drive, 2nd Floor
Beverly Hills, CA 90210

Phone: 310-275-1191
Fax: 310-275-1266

Submission Policy: Does not accept any

unsolicited material
Genre: Action, Comedy, Romance, Family
Company Focus: Feature Films

Peter Abrams
Title: Producer/Partner
Phone: 310-275-1191
IMDB: *www.imdb.com/name/nm0009222*

Robert Levy
Title: Producer/Partner
Phone: 310-275-1191
IMDB: *www.imdb.com/name/nm0506597*

Michael Schreiber
Title: President
Phone: 310-275-1191
IMDB: *www.imdb.com/name/nm2325100*

TAURUS ENTERTAINMENT COMPANY

5555 Melrose Avenue
Marx Brothers Building, Suite 103/104
Hollywood, CA 90038

Phone: 818-935-5157
Fax: 323-686-5379
Email: *taurusentco@yahoo.com*

Submission Policy: Accepts Query Letter from
unproduced, unrepresented writers via email
Genre: Action, Family, Animation, Drama
Company Focus: Feature Films, TV
Year Established: 1991

James Dudelson
Title: President/CEO
Phone: 818-935-5157
Email: *jgdudelson@yahoo.com*
IMDB: *www.imdb.com/name/nm0240054*

Robert Dudelson
Title: President/COO
Phone: 818-935-5157
Email: *rfdudelson@mac.com*
IMDB: *www.imdb.com/name/nm0240055*

TEAM DOWNEY

1311 Abbot Kinney
Venice, CA 90291

Phone: 310-450-5100

Submission Policy: Does not accept any

unsolicited material
Company Focus: Feature Films
Year Established: 2010

Robert Downey, Jr.
Title: Producer
Phone: 310-450-5100
IMDB: *www.imdb.com/name/nm0000375*

Susan Levin Downey
Title: Producer
Phone: 310-450-5100
IMDB: *www.imdb.com/name/nm1206265*

David Gambino
Title: President of Production
Phone: 310-450-5100
IMDB: *www.imdb.com/name/nm1312724*
Assistant: Sandy Yep

TEAM TODD

2900 West Olympic Boulevard
Santa Monica, CA 91404

Phone: 310-255-7225
Fax: 310-255-7222

Submission Policy: Accepts Scripts from
produced or represented writers
Genre: Myth, Family, Animation
Company Focus: Feature Films

Suzanne Todd
Title: Producer
IMDB: *www.imdb.com/name/nm0865297*

Julianna Hays
Title: Creative Executive
IMDB: *www.imdb.com/name/nm3057670*

TEMPLE HILL PRODUCTIONS

9255 Sunset Boulevard, Suite 801
Los Angeles, CA 90069

Phone: 310-270-4383
Fax: 310-270-4395

Submission Policy: Does not accept any
unsolicited material
Company Focus: Feature Films, TV
Year Established: 2006

Marty Bowen
Title: Partner
Phone: 310-270-4383
IMDB: *www.imdb.com/name/nm2125212*
Assistant: Charlie Morrison

Wyck Godfrey
Title: Partner
Phone: 310-270-4383
IMDB: *www.imdb.com/name/nm0324041*
Assistant: Jaclyn Huntling

Adam Londy
Title: Creative Executive
Phone: 310-270-4383
IMDB: *www.imdb.com/name/nm2173131*

TERRA FIRMA FILMS

468 North Camden Drive, Suite 365T
Beverly Hills, CA 90210

Phone: 310-860-7480
Fax: 310-862-4717
Email: *info@terrafirmafilms.com*

Submission Policy: Accepts Query Letter from unproduced, unrepresented writers via email
Company Focus: Feature Films
Year Established: 2003

Adam Herz
Title: Writer/Producer
Phone: 310-860-7480
Email: *info@terrafirmafilms.com*
IMDB: *www.imdb.com/name/nm0381221*

Gregory Lessans
Title: Co-President
Phone: 310-860-7480
Email: *info@terrafirmafilms.com*
IMDB: *www.imdb.com/name/nm0504298*

Josh Shader
Title: Co-President
Phone: 310-860-7480
Email: *info@terrafirmafilms.com*
IMDB: *www.imdb.com/name/nm1003558*

THE AMERICAN FILM COMPANY

c/o Business Affairs, Inc.
2415 Main Street, 2nd Floor
Santa Monica, CA 90405

Phone: 310-664-1999

Submission Policy: Accepts Query Letter from unproduced, unrepresented writers via email
Genre: Memoir & True Stories
Year Established: 2008

Brian Falk
Title: Producer and Executive
Email: *bfalk@americanfilmco.com*
IMDB: *www.imdb.com/name/nm1803137*

THE BADHAM COMPANY

16830 Ventura Boulevard, Suite 300
Encino, CA, 91436

Fax: 818-981-9163
Email: *development@badhamcompany.com*

Submission Policy: Accepts Scripts from produced or represented writers

John Badham
Title: Director/Producer
IMDB: *www.imdb.com/name/nm0000824*

THE COLLETON COMPANY

20 Fifth Avenue, Suite 13F
New York, NY 10011

Phone: 212-673-0916
Fax: 212-673-1172

Submission Policy: Accepts Scripts from produced or represented writers
Genre: Memoir & True Stories

Sara Colleton
IMDB: *www.imdb.com/name/nm0171780*

THE GOLD COMPANY

499 North Canon Drive, Suite 306
Beverly Hills, CA 90210

Phone: 310-270-4653

Submission Policy: Accepts Query Letter from

unproduced, unrepresented writers
Company Focus: Feature Films

Eric Gold
Title: Chairman/Producer
IMDB: *www.imdb.com/name/nm0324970*

THE GOLDSTEIN COMPANY

1644 Courtney Avenue
Los Angeles, CA 90046

Phone: 310-659-9511

Submission Policy: Accepts Query Letter from unproduced, unrepresented writers via email
Genre: Action, Comedy, Memoir & True Stories, Romance, Thriller
Company Focus: Feature Films, Reality Programming (Reality TV, Documentaries, Special Events, Sporting Events), Media (Commercials/Branding/Marketing)

Gary W. Goldstein
Title: Producer
Email: *gary@garywgoldstein.com*
IMDB: *www.imdb.com/name/nm0326214*

Josh Grossman
Title: Vice-President of Development

THE GOODMAN COMPANY

8491 Sunset Boulevard, Suite 329
Los Angeles, CA 90069

Submission Policy: Accepts Query Letter from unproduced, unrepresented writers
Genre: Comedy, TV Drama, TV Sitcom, Family
Company Focus: Feature Films, TV, Reality Programming (Reality TV, Documentaries, Special Events, Sporting Events)

Ilyssa Goodman
Title: President/Producer
IMDB: *www.imdb.com/name/nm1058415*

THE GOTHAM GROUP

9255 Sunset Boulevard, Suite 515
Los Angeles, CA 90069

Phone: 310-285-0001
Fax: 310-285-0077

Submission Policy: Does not accept any unsolicited material
Genre: Action, Comedy, Fantasy, Science Fiction, TV Drama, TV Sitcom, Family, Animation, Drama
Company Focus: Feature Films, TV, Reality Programming (Reality TV, Documentaries, Special Events, Sporting Events), Media (Commercials/Branding/Marketing)

Ellen Goldsmith-Vein
Title: CEO/Founder
Email: *egv@gotham-group.com*

Julie Kane-Ritsch
Title: Manager/Producer
Email: *jkr@gotham-group.com*
IMDB: *www.imdb.com/name/nm1415970*

Peter McHugh
Title: Manager/Producer
Email: *peter@gotham-group.com*

THE GREENBERG GROUP

2029 South Westgate Avenue
Los Angeles, CA 90025

Phone: 310-807-8140
Fax: 310-887-3943
Email: *info@greenberggroup.net*

Submission Policy: Accepts Query Letter from unproduced, unrepresented writers via email
Company Focus: Feature Films, TV, Reality Programming (Reality TV, Documentaries, Special Events, Sporting Events), Media (Commercials/Branding/Marketing)

Randy Greenberg
Title: CEO, Executive Producer
Email: *randy@greenberggroup.com*
IMDB: *www.imdb.com/name/nm2985843*

THE GROUP ENTERTAINMENT

115 West 29th Street #1102
New York, NY 10001

Phone: 212-868-5233
Fax: 212-504-3082
Email: *info@thegroupentertainment.com*

Submission Policy: Does not accept any

unsolicited material
Company Focus: Feature Films, TV, Reality
Programming (Reality TV, Documentaries,
Special Events, Sporting Events)

Gil Holland
Title: Partner/Producer
IMDB: *www.imdb.com/name/nm0390693*

Rebecca Atwood
Title: Creative Executive
Email: *rebecca@thegroupentertainment.com*

THE HAL LIEBERMAN COMPANY

8522 National Boulevard, Suite 108
Culver City, CA 90232

Phone: 310-202-1929
Email: *asst@thehalliebermancompany.com*

Submission Policy: Accepts Query Letter from
unproduced, unrepresented writers via email
Company Focus: Feature Films

Hal Lieberman
Title: Producer
IMDB: *www.imdb.com/name/nm0509386*

Dan Scheinkman
Title: Development Executive

THE HALCYON COMPANY

8455 Beverly Boulevard
Penthouse Suite
Los Angeles, CA 90048

Phone: 323-650-0222
Email: *info@thehalcyoncompany.com*

Submission Policy: Does not accept any
unsolicited material
Genre: Action, Science Fiction, Thriller
Company Focus: Feature Films
Year Established: 2006

James Middleton
Title: Creative Development and Production
IMDB: *www.imdb.com/name/nm2194360*

THE HATCHERY

2950 North Hollywood Way
3rd Floor
Burbank, CA 91505

Phone: 818-748-4507
Fax: 818-748-4615/Attn: Dan Angel
Email: *dangel@thehatcheryllc.com*

Submission Policy: Does not accept any
unsolicited material
Genre: Comedy, Horror, Science Fiction,
Family
Company Focus: Feature Films, TV

Dan Angel
Title: CCO/Executive Producer
Email: *dangel@thehatcheryllc.com*
IMDB: *www.imdb.com/name/nm0029445*

THE HECHT COMPANY

3607 West Magnolia, Suite L
Burbank, CA 91505

Phone: 310-989-3467
Email: *hechtco@aol.com*

Submission Policy: Accepts Query Letter from
unproduced, unrepresented writers via email
Company Focus: Feature Films, TV, Reality
Programming (Reality TV, Documentaries,
Special Events, Sporting Events)

Duffy Hecht
Title: Producer
IMDB: *www.imdb.com/name/nm0372953*

THE JIM HENSON COMPANY

1416 North La Brea Avenue
Hollywood, CA 90028

Phone: 323-802-1500
Fax: 323-802-1825
Email: *info@henson.com*

Submission Policy: Does not accept any
unsolicited material
Genre: Comedy, Fantasy, Science Fiction, TV
Sitcom, Family, Animation
Company Focus: Feature Films, TV, Post-
Production (Editing, Special Effects), Reality
Programming (Reality TV, Documentaries,

Special Events, Sporting Events), Media (Commercials/Branding/Marketing), Theater

Brian Henson
Title: Chairman

Halle Stanford
Title: Executive Vice-President, Children's TV

Jason Lust
Title: Sr. Vice-President, Feature Films

THE LITTLEFIELD COMPANY

500 South Buena Vista Street
Burbank, CA 91521

Phone: 818-560-2280
Fax: 818-560-3775

Submission Policy: Does not accept any unsolicited material
Genre: TV Drama
Company Focus: TV

Warren Littlefield
Title: Principal
Phone: 818-560-2280
IMDB: *www.imdb.com/name/nm0514716*
Assistant: Patricia Mann

Andrew Bourne
Title: Senior Vice President of Development
Phone: 818-560-2280
IMDB: *www.imdb.com/name/nm2044331*
Assistant: Janelle Young

THE MARK GORDON COMPANY

12200 West Olympic Boulevard, Suite 250
Los Angeles, CA 90064

Phone: 310-943-6401
Fax: 310-943-6402
Email: *kj@mgpics.com*

Submission Policy: Does not accept any unsolicited material
Genre: Action, TV Drama, Drama
Company Focus: Feature Films, TV

Mark Gordon
Title: Principal/Producer
Phone: 310-943-6401
IMDB: *www.imdb.com/name/nm0330428*
Assistant: Lindsey Martin

Bryan Zuriff
Title: Executive Vice-President, Film
Phone: 310-943-6401
IMDB: *www.imdb.com/name/nm3050339*
Assistant: Ivey Harden

Shara Senderoff
Title: Vice-President New Media & Director, Film Development
Phone: 310-943-6401
IMDB: *www.imdb.com/name/nm2994844*

THE MAZUR/KAPLAN COMPANY

3204 Pearl Street
Santa Monica, CA 90405

Phone: 310-450-5838

Submission Policy: Does not accept any unsolicited material
Genre: Comedy, Romance, Family
Company Focus: Feature Films, TV, Reality Programming (Reality TV, Documentaries, Special Events, Sporting Events)
Year Established: 2009

Paula Mazur
Title: Producer
Phone: 310-450-5838
IMDB: *www.imdb.com/name/nm0563394*

Kimi Armstrong Stein
Title: Vice-President of Development
Email: *kimi@mazurkaplan.com*
IMDB: *www.imdb.com/name/nm2148964*

Sarah Carbiener
Title: Office Assistant
Phone: 310-450-5838
Email: *sarah@mazurkaplan.com*
IMDB: *www.imdb.com/name/nm3745774*

THE MONTECITO PICTURE COMPANY

9465 Wilshire Boulevard, Suite 920
Beverly Hills, CA 90212

Phone: 310-247-9880
Fax: 310-247-9498

Submission Policy: Accepts Query Letter from unproduced, unrepresented writers
Company Focus: Feature Films, TV
Year Established: 2000

Ivan Reitman
Title: Producer
Phone: 310-247-9880
IMDB: *www.imdb.com/name/nm0718645*
Assistant: Eric Reich

Alex Plapinger
Title: Vice-President of Development
Phone: 310-247-9880
IMDB: *www.imdb.com/name/nm3292687*

THE PITT GROUP

9465 Wilshire Boulevard, Suite 420
Beverly Hills, CA 90212

Phone: 310-246-4800
Fax: 310-275-9258

Submission Policy: Accepts Query Letter from unproduced, unrepresented writers
Company Focus: Feature Films, TV
Year Established: 2000

Lou Pitt
Title: President
Phone: 310-246-4800
IMDB: *www.imdb.com/name/nm2229316*

Jeremy Conrady
Title: Creative Executive
Phone: 310-246-4800
IMDB: *www.imdb.com/name/nm2620420*

THE RADMIN COMPANY

9201 Wilshire Boulevard, Suite 102
Beverly Hills, CA 90210

Phone: 310-274-9515
Fax: 310-274-0739
Email: *info@radmincompany.com*

Submission Policy: Accepts Query Letter from unproduced, unrepresented writers via email
Genre: Comedy, Romance, Drama
Company Focus: Feature Films

Linne Radmin
Title: Producer

Brandon Klaus
Title: Creative Executive

Ryan Rozar
Title: Story Department

THE SHEPHARD/ROBIN COMPANY

c/o Raleigh Studios
5300 Melrose Avenue, Suite 225E
Los Angeles, CA 90038

Phone: 323-871-4412
Fax: 323-871-4418

Submission Policy: Does not accept any unsolicited material
Genre: TV Drama
Company Focus: TV

Greer Shephard
Title: Executive Producer/Owner
Assistant: Samantha Niemoeller

Michael Robin
Title: Executive Producer/Owner
Assistant: Bryan Raber

THE SHUMAN COMPANY

3815 Hughes Avenue
Fourth Floor
Culver City, CA 90232

Phone: 310-841-4344
Fax: 310-204-3578
Email: *info@shumanco.com*

Submission Policy: Accepts Query Letter from unproduced, unrepresented writers via email
Genre: TV Drama, TV Sitcom
Company Focus: Feature Films, TV

Lawrence Shuman
Title: Producer
IMDB: *www.imdb.com/name/nm2108355*

David Wolthoff
Title: Producer
IMDB: *www.imdb.com/name/nm2303649*

Steven Selikoff
Title: Producer
IMDB: *www.imdb.com/name/nm2992727*

THE STEVE TISCH COMPANY

10202 West Washington Boulevard
Astaire Building, 3rd Floor
Culver City, CA 90232

Phone: 310-244-6612
Fax: 310-204-2713

Submission Policy: Accepts Query Letter from unproduced, unrepresented writers
Genre: Action, Comedy, Thriller, Drama
Company Focus: Feature Films

Steve Tisch
Title: Chairman

Lacy Boughn
Title: Director, Development
Phone: 310-244-6620

THE TANNENBAUM COMPANY

c/o CBS Studios
4024 Radford Avenue, Bungalow 16
Studio City, CA 91604

Phone: 818-655-7181

Submission Policy: Does not accept any unsolicited material
Genre: Comedy, TV Sitcom, Drama, Reality
Company Focus: Feature Films, TV, Reality Programming (Reality TV, Documentaries, Special Events, Sporting Events)

Eric Tannenbaum
Title: Producer

Kim Tannenbaum
Title: Producer

Jason Wang
Title: Creative Affairs

THE WALT DISNEY COMPANY

500 South Buena Vista Street
Burbank, CA 91521

Phone: 818-560-1000

Submission Policy: Does not accept any unsolicited material
Genre: Action, Comedy, Fantasy, Memoir & True Stories, Myth, TV Drama, TV Sitcom, Family, Animation, Drama
Year Established: 1923

Robert Iger
Title: Chairman of the Board, CEO
Phone: 818-560-1000
Email: *bob.iger@disney.com*
IMDB: *www.imdb.com/name/nm2250609*

THE WEINSTEIN COMPANY

375 Greenwich Street
Lbby. A
New York, NY 10013-2376

Phone: 212-941-3800
Email: *info@weinsteinco.com*

Submission Policy: Does not accept any unsolicited material
Genre: Action, Comedy, Memoir & True Stories, Myth, Romance, Thriller, TV Drama, TV Sitcom, Family, Animation, Drama, Socio-cultural
Year Established: 2005

Harvey Weinstein
Title: Co-Chairman
Phone: 212-941-3800
Email: *info@weinsteinco.com*
IMDB: *www.imdb.com/name/nm0005544*

THE WOLPER ORGANIZATION

4000 Warner Boulevard
Building 14, Suite 200
Burbank, CA 91504

Phone: 818-954-1421
Fax: 818-954-1593

Submission Policy: Does not accept any unsolicited material
Company Focus: Feature Films, TV
Year Established: 1987

Mark Wolper
Title: President/Executive Producer
Phone: 818-954-1421
IMDB: *www.imdb.com/name/nm0938679*

Kevin Nicklaus
Title: Vice-President Development
Phone: 818-954-3505
IMDB: *www.imdb.com/name/nm2102454*

Sam Alexander
Title: Director of Development
Phone: 818-954-3465
Email: *Sam.Alexander@wbtvprod.com*
IMDB: *www.imdb.com/name/nm3303012*

THE ZANUCK COMPANY

16 Beverly Park
Beverly Hills, CA 90210

Phone: 310-274-0261
Fax: 310-273-9217

Submission Policy: Does not accept any
unsolicited material
Company Focus: Feature Films, TV
Year Established: 1988

Richard Zanuck
Title: Producer
Phone: 310-274-0261
IMDB: *www.imdb.com/name/nm0005573*
Assistant: Brenda Berriford

Lili Fini Zanuck
Title: Producer/Director
Phone: 310-274-0209
IMDB: *www.imdb.com/name/nm0005572*
Assistant: Aubrie Artiano

Harrison Zanuck
Title: Producer
Phone: 310-274-5929

THOUSAND WORDS

110 South Fairfax Avenue, Suite 370
Los Angeles, CA 90036

Phone: 323-936-4700
Fax: 323-936-4701
Email: *info@thousand-words.com*

Submission Policy: Accepts Query Letter from
unproduced, unrepresented writers via email
Company Focus: Feature Films
Year Established: 2000

Jonah Smith
Title: Co-President
Phone: 323-936-4700
Email: *info@thousand-words.com*
IMDB: *www.imdb.com/name/nm0808819*

Palmer West
Title: Founder, Co-President
Phone: 323-936-4700
Email: *info@thousand-words.com*
IMDB: *www.imdb.com/name/nm0922279*

Michael Van Vliet
Title: Creative Executive
Phone: 323-936-4700
Email: *info@thousand-words.com*
IMDB: *www.imdb.com/name/nm2702900*

THREE STRANGE ANGELS, INC.

9050 West Washington Boulevard
Culver City, CA 90232

Phone: 310-840-8213

Submission Policy: Does not accept any
unsolicited material
Company Focus: Feature Films

Lindsay Doran
Title: President, Producer
Phone: 310-840-8213
IMDB: *www.imdb.com/name/nm0233386*
Assistant: Natasha Khrolenko

THUNDER ROAD PICTURES

c/o Warner Bros
4000 Warner Boulevard
Building 81, Suite 114, Burbank, CA 91522

Phone: 310-573-8885

Submission Policy: Does not accept any
unsolicited material
Company Focus: Feature Films, TV
Year Established: 2003

Basil Iwanyk
Title: Producer
Phone: 310-573-8885
IMDB: *www.imdb.com/name/nm0412588*

Kent Kubena
Title: Sr. Vice-President, Development &

Production/Producer
IMDB: *www.imdb.com/name/nm0473423*

Erica Lee
Title: Creative Executive
IMDB: *www.imdb.com/name/nm3102707*
Assistant: Josh Kahal

TIM BURTON PRODUCTIONS

8033 Sunset Boulevard, Suite 7500
West Hollywood, CA 90046

Phone: 310-300-1670
Fax: 310-300-1671

Submission Policy: Does not accept any
unsolicited material
Company Focus: Feature Films
Year Established: 1989

Tim Burton
Title: Director/Producer
Phone: 310-300-1670
Email: *kory.edwrds@timburton.com*
IMDB: *www.imdb.com/name/nm0000318*
Assistant: Kory Edwards

TOM WELLING PRODUCTIONS

4000 Warner Boulevard
Building 146, Room 201
Burbank, CA 91522

Phone: 818-954-4012

Submission Policy: Does not accept any
unsolicited material
Company Focus: TV
Year Established: 2010

Tom Welling
Title: Principal
Phone: 818-954-4012
IMDB: *www.imdb.com/name/nm0919991*

Amy Suh
Title: Director of Development
Phone: 818-954-4012

TONY JONAS PRODUCTIONS

2934-1/2 Glen Circle, Suite 800
Los Angeles, CA 90077

Phone: 323-804-0970

Submission Policy: Does not accept any
unsolicited material
Company Focus: TV
Year Established: 2000

Tony Jonas
Title: President
IMDB: *www.imdb.com/name/nm0427327*

Darin Wymer
Title: Manager, Development Assistant
Phone: 818-560-8098
IMDB: *www.imdb.com/name/nm1820903*

TOOL OF NORTH AMERICA

2210 Broadway
Santa Monica, CA 90404

Phone: 310-453-9244
Fax: 310-453-4185

Submission Policy: Accepts Query Letter from
unproduced, unrepresented writers via email
Company Focus: Feature Films, TV, Reality
Programming (Reality TV, Documentaries,
Special Events, Sporting Events), Media
(Commercials/Branding/Marketing)

Brian Latt
Title: Managing Director
Email: *brian@toolofna.com*
IMDB: *www.imdb.com/name/nm0490373*

Oliver Fuselier
Title: Executive Producer
Email: *oliver@toolofna.com*
IMDB: *www.imdb.com/name/nm0299336*

Dustin Callif
Email: *dustin@toolofna.com*
IMDB: *www.imdb.com/name/nm2956668*

TORNELL PRODUCTIONS

80 Varick Street, Suite 10C
New York, NY 10013

Phone: 212-625-2530
Fax: 212-625-2532

Submission Policy: Accepts Query Letter from

unproduced, unrepresented writers
Company Focus: Feature Films

Lisa Tornell
Title: Producer
Phone: 212-625-2530
IMDB: *www.imdb.com/name/nm0868178*

TOWER OF BABBLE ENTERTAINMENT

854 North Spaulding Avenue
Los Angeles, CA 90046

Phone: 323-230-6128
Fax: 323-822-0312
Email: *info@towerofb.com*

Submission Policy: Accepts Query Letter from unproduced, unrepresented writers via email
Company Focus: Feature Films, TV

Jeff Wadlow
Title: Writer/Director
Phone: 323-230-6128
Email: *info@towerofb.com*
IMDB: *www.imdb.com/name/nm0905592*

Beau Bauman
Title: Writer/Producer
Phone: 323-230-6128
Email: *info@towerofb.com*
IMDB: *www.imdb.com/name/nm0062149*

TREELINE FILMS

1708 Berkeley Street
Santa Monica, CA 90404-1708

Phone: 310-883-7224

Submission Policy: Does not accept any unsolicited material
Company Focus: Feature Films

James Mangold
Title: Writer/Director/Producer
Phone: 310-883-7224
IMDB: *www.imdb.com/name/nm0003506*

Cathy Konrad
Title: Producer
Phone: 310-883-7224
IMDB: *www.imdb.com/name/nm0465298*

Magnus Moore
Title: Creative Executive
Phone: 310-883-7224

TRIBECA PRODUCTIONS

375 Greenwich Street, 8th Floor
New York, NY 10013

Phone: 212-941-2400
Fax: 212-941-3939
Email: *info@tribecafilm.com*

Submission Policy: Does not accept any unsolicited material
Company Focus: Feature Films, TV
Year Established: 1989

Robert De Niro
Title: Partner
Phone: 212-941-2400
IMDB: *www.imdb.com/name/nm0000134*

Berry Welsh
Title: Director of Development
Phone: 212-941-2400
IMDB: *www.imdb.com/name/nm2654730*

Gigi Graff
Title: Executive Assistant to Jane Rosenthal (Partner)
Phone: 212-941-2400

TRICOAST STUDIOS

11124 West Washington Boulevard
Culver City, CA 90232

Phone: 310-458-7707
Fax: 310-204-2450
Email: *tricoast@tricoast.com*

Submission Policy: Does not accept any unsolicited material
Company Focus: Feature Films, TV

Tory Weisz
Title: Vice-President Development, Producer
Phone: 310-458-7707
IMDB: *www.imdb.com/name/nm3258419*

Gabby Messer
Title: Assistant to CEOs
Phone: 310-458-7707

Phone: 310-458-7707

TRICOR ENTERTAINMENT

1613 Chelsea Road
San Marino, CA 91108

Phone: 626-356-4646
Fax: 626-356-3646
Email: *ExecutiveOffices@TricorEntertainment.com*

Submission Policy: Does not accept any unsolicited material
Company Focus: Feature Films

Craig Darian
Title: Co-Chairman/CEO
Phone: 626-356-4646
IMDB: *www.imdb.com/name/nm1545768*

Jordan Darian
Title: Director, Development
Phone: 626-356-4646

TRILOGY ENTERTAINMENT GROUP

325 Wilshire Boulevard, Suite 203
Santa Monica, CA 90401

Phone: 310-656-9733

Submission Policy: Does not accept any unsolicited material
Company Focus: Feature Films, TV

Pen Densham
Title: Partner
Phone: 310-656-9733
IMDB: *www.imdb.com/name/nm0219720*

Alex Daltas
Title: President, Production
Phone: 310-656-9733
Email: *adaltas@trilogyent.com*
IMDB: *www.imdb.com/name/nm0198226*

Nevin Densham
Title: Creative Executive/Head, Development
Phone: 310-656-9733
Email: *bflam@trilogyent.com*
IMDB: *www.imdb.com/name/nm0219719*
Assistant: Bryan Flam

TROIKA PICTURES

2019 South Westgate Avenue
2nd Floor
Los Angeles, CA 90025

Phone: 310-696-2859
Email: *troikapics@gmail.com*

Submission Policy: Does not accept any unsolicited material
Company Focus: Feature Films

Robert Stein
Title: Co-CEO
Phone: 310-696-2859
IMDB: *www.imdb.com/name/nm3355501*

Michael Helfant
Title: Co-CEO
Phone: 310-696-2859
IMDB: *www.imdb.com/name/nm0375033*

Bradley Gallo
Title: Head of Production & Development
Phone: 310-696-2859
IMDB: *www.imdb.com/name/nm0303010*

TURTLEBACK PRODUCTIONS, INC.

11736 Gwynne Lane
Los Angeles, CA, CA 90077

Phone: 310-440-8587
Fax: 310-440-8903

Submission Policy: Accepts Query Letter from unproduced, unrepresented writers
Company Focus: Feature Films, TV
Year Established: 1988

Howard Meltzer
Title: President/Executive Producer
Phone: 310-440-8587
IMDB: *www.imdb.com/name/nm0578430*

TV LAND

345 Hudson Street
New York, NY 10014

Phone: 212-846-6000
Fax: 212-654-5578
Email: *info@tvland.com*

Submission Policy: Accepts Query Letter from

unproduced, unrepresented writers via email
Genre: TV Drama, TV Sitcom
Year Established: 1996

Larry W. Jones
Title: President
Phone: 212-846-6000
Email: *larry.jones@tvland.com*
IMDB: *www.imdb.com/name/nm1511130*

TV ONE LLC

1010 Wayne Avenue
Silver Spring, MD 20910

Phone: 301-755-0400

Submission Policy: Accepts Query Letter from produced or represented writers
Genre: TV Drama, TV Sitcom
Year Established: 2004

Alfred Liggins
Title: Chairman
Phone: 301-755-0400
Email: *aliggins@tv-one.tv*
IMDB: *www.imdb.com/name/nm3447190*

TV REPAIR

857 Castaic Place
Pacific Palisades, CA 90272

Phone: 310-459-3671
Fax: 310-459-4251
Email: *davidjlatt@earthlink.net*

Submission Policy: Accepts Query Letter from unproduced, unrepresented writers via email
Company Focus: TV

David Latt
Title: Producer/Writer
Phone: 310-459-3671
Email: *davidjlatt@earthlink.net*
IMDB: *www.imdb.com/name/nm0490374*

TWENTIETH CENTURY FOX FILM

10201 West Pico Boulevard
Los Angeles, CA 90035

Phone: 310-277-2211
Fax: 310-203-1558
Email: *foxmovies@fox.com*

Submission Policy: Does not accept any unsolicited material
Genre: Action, Comedy, Crime, Detective, Fantasy, Horror, Memoir & True Stories, Myth, Romance, Thriller, Family, Drama, Socio-cultural
Year Established: 1935

James Gianopulos
Title: Co-Chairman/CEO
Phone: 310-277-2211
Email: *jim.gianopulos@fox.com*
IMDB: *www.imdb.com/name/nm1963549*

TWENTIETH CENTURY FOX TELEVISION

10201 West Pico Boulevard
Building 103, Room 5286
Los Angeles, CA 90035

Phone: 310-369-1000
Fax: 310-369-8726
Email: *info@foxnews.com*

Submission Policy: Does not accept any unsolicited material
Genre: TV Drama, TV Sitcom
Year Established: 1949

Gary Newman
Title: Chairman
Phone: 310-369-1000
Email: *gary.newman@fox.com*
IMDB: *www.imdb.com/name/nm3050096*

TWENTIETH TELEVISION

2121 Avenue of the Stars
17th Floor
Los Angeles, CA 90067

Phone: 310-369-1000
Email: *info@foxnews.com*

Submission Policy: Does not accept any unsolicited material
Genre: TV Drama, TV Sitcom
Year Established: 1992

Greg Meidel
Title: President, Twentieth Television
Phone: 310-369-1000
Email: *meidel@foxnews.com*
IMDB: *www.imdb.com/name/nm2518163*

TWINSTAR ENTERTAINMENT

4041 MacArthur Boulevard, Suite 475
Newport Beach, CA 92660

Phone: 949-474-8600
Email: *info@twinstarentertainment.com*

Submission Policy: Accepts Scripts from unproduced, unrepresented writers
Genre: Comedy, TV Drama, TV Sitcom, Family, Animation
Year Established: 2003

Russell Werdin
Title: CEO
Phone: 949-474-8600
Email: *info@twinstarentertainment.com*
IMDB: *www.imdb.com/name/nm2232609*

TWO TON FILMS

375 Greenwich Street
New York, NY 10013

Phone: 212-941-3863
Email: *info@twotonfilms.com*

Submission Policy: Accepts Query Letter from unproduced, unrepresented writers via email
Genre: Action, TV Drama, TV Sitcom, Family, Drama
Company Focus: Feature Films

Justin Zackham
Title: Partner/Producer/Writer
Phone: 212-941-3863
Email: *info@twotonfilms.com*
IMDB: *www.imdb.com/name/nm0951698*

Clay Pecorin
Title: Partner/Producer
Phone: 212-941-3863
Email: *info@twotonfilms.com*
IMDB: *www.imdb.com/name/nm2668976*

UFLAND PRODUCTIONS

6565 Crescent Park West #101
Los Angeles, CA 90049

Phone: 310-437-0805

Submission Policy: Does not accept any unsolicited material
Genre: Romance, TV Drama, TV Sitcom, Drama, Socio-cultural
Year Established: 1972

Harry J. Ufland
Title: Principal/Producer
Phone: 310-437-0805
IMDB: *www.imdb.com/name/nm0880036*

UNDERGROUND FILMS

447 South Highland Avenue
Los Angeles, CA 90036

Phone: 323-930-2588
Fax: 323-930-2334

Submission Policy: Accepts Query Letter from unproduced, unrepresented writers
Genre: Action, Comedy, Fantasy, Horror, Memoir & True Stories, Myth, Romance, Thriller, TV Drama, TV Sitcom, Family, Animation, Drama
Year Established: 2003

Trevor Engelson
Title: Principal/Producer
Phone: 323-930-2569
Email: *trevor@undergroundfilms.net*
IMDB: *www.imdb.com/name/nm0257333*

UNIFIED PICTURES

19773 Bahama Street
Northridge, CA 91324

Phone: 818-576-1006
Fax: 818-534-3347
Email: *info@unifiedpictures.com*

Submission Policy: Accepts Query Letter from unproduced, unrepresented writers
Genre: Action, Comedy, Crime, Detective, Horror, Thriller, Drama
Company Focus: Feature Films
Year Established: 2004

Keith Kjarval
Title: Founder/Producer
IMDB: *www.imdb.com/name/nm1761309*

Kurt Rauer
Title: Founder/Producer
IMDB: *www.imdb.com/name/nm0970009*

Shaun Clapham
Title: Creative Executive
Email: *sclapham@unifiedpictures.com*
IMDB: *www.imdb.com/name/nm4111097*

UNION ENTERTAINMENT

9255 Sunset Boulevard, Suite 528
West Hollywood, CA 90069

Phone: 310-274-7040
Fax: 310-274-1065
Email: *info@unionent.com*

Submission Policy: Does not accept any
unsolicited material
Genre: Animation
Year Established: 2006

Richard Leibowitz
Title: President
Phone: 310-274-7040
Email: *rich@unionent.com*
IMDB: *www.imdb.com/name/nm2325318*

UNIQUE FEATURES

LA Office:
116 North Robertson Boulevard, Suite 909
Los Angeles, CA 90048
Phone: 310-492-8009

NY Office:
888 7th Avenue, 16th Floor
New York, NY 10106
Phone: 212-649-4980

Submission Policy: Does not accept any
unsolicited material
Company Focus: Feature Films, TV
Year Established: 2008

Mark Kaufman
Title: Head, East Coast Production &
Development
Phone: 212-649-4855
IMDB: *www.imdb.com/name/nm0442212*

Dylan Sellers
Title: Head, West Coast Production &
Development
Phone: 310-492-8009
IMDB: *www.imdb.com/name/nm0783346*

Michael Lynne
Title: Executive—West Coast Branch
Phone: 310-492-8009
IMDB: *www.imdb.com/name/nm1088153*

UNITED ARTISTS

245 North Beverly Drive
Beverly Hills, CA 90210

Phone: 310-449-3000
Fax: 310-586-8358

Submission Policy: Does not accept any
unsolicited material
Genre: Action, Crime, TV Drama, Drama
Company Focus: Feature Films, TV
Year Established: 1919

Tom Cruise
Title: Producer
Phone: 310-449-3000
IMDB: *www.imdb.com/name/nm0000129*

Don Granger
Title: President, Production
Phone: 310-449-3000
IMDB: *www.imdb.com/name/nm1447370*

Elliot Kleinberg
Title: COO
Phone: 310-449-3000
IMDB: *www.imdb.com/name/nm2552087*

UNIVERSAL CABLE PRODUCTIONS

100 Universal City Plaza
Building 1440, 14th Floor
Universal City, CA 91608

Phone: 818-840-4444

Submission Policy: Accepts Query Letter from
unproduced, unrepresented writers
Genre: TV Drama, TV Sitcom
Year Established: 1997

Bonnie Hammer
Title: Chairman, NBCUniversal Cable

Entertainment
Phone: 818-840-4444
IMDB: *www.imdb.com/name/nm1045499*

UNIVERSAL STUDIOS

100 Universal City Plaza
Universal City, CA 91608

Phone: 818-840-4444

Submission Policy: Accepts Query Letter from unproduced, unrepresented writers
Genre: Action, Comedy, Crime, Detective, Fantasy, Horror, Memoir & True Stories, Myth, Romance, Science Fiction, Thriller, Family, Animation, Drama, Socio-cultural
Year Established: 1912

Ron Meyer
Title: President & COO, Universal Studios & NBCUniversal
Phone: 818-840-4444
IMDB: *www.imdb.com/name/nm0005228*

UNIVERSAL TELEVISION (FORMERLY UNIVERSAL MEDIA STUDIOS)

100 Universal City Plaza
Building 1360, 3rd Floor
Universal City, CA 91608

Phone: 818-840-4444

Submission Policy: Accepts Query Letter from unproduced, unrepresented writers
Genre: Action, Comedy, Crime, Detective, Fantasy, Memoir & True Stories, Myth, Romance, Science Fiction, Thriller, TV Drama, TV Sitcom, Family, Animation, Drama, Socio-cultural

Bela Bajaria
Title: Executive Vice-President, Universal Television
Phone: 818-840-4444
IMDB: *www.imdb.com/name/nm0338612*

UNNAMED YORN PRODUCTION COMPANY

2000 Avenue of the Stars
3rd Floor, North Tower
Los Angeles, CA 90067

Phone: 310-775-8600

Submission Policy: Accepts Query Letter from unproduced, unrepresented writers
Year Established: 2008

Rick Yorn
Title: Principal
Phone: 310-775-8600
IMDB: *www.imdb.com/name/nm0948833*

Erik Olsen
Title: Feature Production
Phone: 310-775-8600

Patrick Walmsley
Title: Feature Production
Phone: 310-775-8600
IMDB: *www.imdb.com/name/nm1932113*

UNSTOPPABLE

c/o Independent Talent Agency
76 Oxford Street
London W1D 1BS
United Kingdom
Email: *info@unstoppableentertainmentuk.com*

Submission Policy: Accepts Scripts from unproduced, unrepresented writers
Genre: Action, Comedy, Crime, Romance, Science Fiction, Thriller, Drama
Company Focus: Feature Films
Year Established: 2007

Noel Clarke
Title: Actor/Writer/Producer
Email: *noel@unstoppableentertainmentuk.com*

UNTITLED ENTERTAINMENT

350 South Beverly Drive, Suite 200
Beverly Hills, CA 90212

Phone: 310-601-2100
Fax: 310-601-2344

Submission Policy: Accepts Query Letter from unproduced, unrepresented writers
Genre: Fantasy, Memoir & True Stories, Myth, Romance, TV Drama, TV Sitcom, Drama

Jason Weinberg
Title: Partner
Phone: 310-601-2100
IMDB: *www.imdb.com/name/nm4156256*

UPPITV

c/o CBS Studios
4024 Radford Avenue, Bungalow 9
Studio City, CA 91604

Phone: 818-655-5000

Submission Policy: Does not accept any
unsolicited material
Genre: TV Drama, TV Sitcom

Samuel L. Jackson
Title: Principal
Phone: 818-655-5000
IMDB: *www.imdb.com/name/nm0000168*

USA NETWORK

30 Rockefeller Plaza
21st Floor
New York, NY 10112

Phone: 212-664-4444
Fax: 212-703-8582

Submission Policy: Accepts Query Letter from
unproduced, unrepresented writers via email
Genre: TV Drama, TV Sitcom
Year Established: 1971

Bonnie Hammer
Title: Chairman
Phone: 212-644-4444
IMDB: *www.imdb.com/name/nm1045499*

VALHALLA MOTION PICTURES

3201 Cahuenga Boulevard W
Los Angeles, CA 90068-1301

Phone: 323-850-3030
Email: *vmp@valhallapix.com*

Submission Policy: Does not accept any
unsolicited material
Genre: Action, Fantasy, Horror, Thriller, Drama
Company Focus: Feature Films, TV

Gale Anne Hurd
Title: CEO/Producer
Phone: 323-850-3030
Email: *gah@valhallapix.com*
IMDB: *www.imdb.com/name/nm0005036*

VANDERKLOOT FILM & TELEVISION

750 Ralph McGill Boulevard N.E.
Atlanta, GA 30312

Phone: 404-221-0236
Fax: 404-221-1057
Email: *bv@vanderkloot.com*

Submission Policy: Does not accept any
unsolicited material
Genre: Action, Memoir & True Stories, TV
Drama, TV Sitcom, Family
Year Established: 1976

William VanDerKloot
Title: President/Producer/Director
Phone: 404-221-0236
Email: *william@vanderkloot.com*
IMDB: *www.imdb.com/name/nm0886281*

VANGUARD FILMS/VANGUARD ANIMATION

8703 West Olympic Boulevard
Los Angeles, CA 90035

Phone: 310-888-8020
Fax: 310-362-8685
Email: *contact@vanguardanimation.com*

Submission Policy: Does not accept any
unsolicited material
Genre: Animation
Company Focus: Feature Films
Year Established: 2004

Robert Moreland
Title: President Production & Development
Phone: 310-888-8020
IMDB: *www.imdb.com/name/nm0603668*

John H. Williams
Title: Chairman & CEO
Phone: 310-888-8020
IMDB: *www.imdb.com/name/nm0930964*

VANGUARD PRODUCTIONS

1211 Beatrice Street
Culver City, CA 90230

Phone: 310-306-4910
Fax: 310-306-1978
Email: *info@vanguardproductions.biz*

Submission Policy: Accepts Query Letter from unproduced, unrepresented writers via email
Genre: Action, Memoir & True Stories, TV Drama, TV Sitcom, Family
Year Established: 1986

Terence M. O'Keefe
Title: Founder/Writer/Producer/Director
Phone: 310-306-4910
Email: *terry@vanguardproductions.biz*
IMDB: *www.imdb.com/name/nm0641496*

VANQUISH MOTION PICTURES

10 Universal City Plaza
NBC/Universal Building, 20th Floor
Universal City, CA 91608

Phone: 818-753-2319
Email: *submissions@vanquishmotionpictures.com*

Submission Policy: Accepts Query Letter from unproduced, unrepresented writers via email
Company Focus: Feature Films, TV
Year Established: 2009

Joshua Crawford
Title: Development Executive
Phone: 818-753-2319
Email: *jc@vanquishmotionpictures.com*
IMDB: *www.imdb.com/name/nm4373090*

Neetu Sharma
Title: Creative Executive
Phone: 818-753-2319
Email: *ns@vanquishmotionpictures.com*
IMDB: *www.imdb.com/name/nm3434485*

Ryan Williams
Title: Creative Executive
Phone: 818-753-2319
Email: *rs@vanquishmotionpictures.com*
IMDB: *www.imdb.com/name/nm4426713*

VARSITY PICTURES

1040 North Las Palmas Avenue
Building 2, First Floor
Los Angeles, CA 90038

Phone: 310-601-1960
Fax: 310-601-1961

Submission Policy: Accepts Query Letter from unproduced, unrepresented writers
Company Focus: Feature Films, TV
Year Established: 2007

Meghann Collins
Title: Film Development
Phone: 310-601-1960
IMDB: *www.imdb.com/name/nm1937533*

Shauna Phelan
Title: Television Development
Phone: 310-601-1960
IMDB: *www.imdb.com/name/nm1016912*

Carter Hansen
Title: Creative Executive
Phone: 310-601-1960
IMDB: *www.imdb.com/name/nm3255715*

VELOCITY

c/o Discovery Networks
One Discovery Place
Silver Spring, MD 20910-3354

Phone: 240-662-2000

Submission Policy: Accepts Query Letter from unproduced, unrepresented writers
Year Established: 2011

Robert Scanlon
Title: Sr. Vice-President
Phone: 240-662-2000
IMDB: *www.imdb.com/name/nm2174240*

VELOCITY PICTURES

4132 Woodcliff Road
Sherman Oaks, CA 91403

Phone: 310-804-8554
Fax: 310-496-1329

Submission Policy: Accepts Query Letter from

unproduced, unrepresented writers
Genre: Action, Memoir & True Stories, Romance, Thriller, Drama
Year Established: 2006

Ryan R. Johnson
Title: Co-Founder
Phone: 310-804-8554
Email: *ryanj@prettydangerousfilms.com*
IMDB: *www.imdb.com/name/nm1010198*

Patrick F. Gallagher
Title: Co-Founder
Phone: 310-804-8554
Email: *pfgla@aol.com*
IMDB: *www.imdb.com/name/nm1725050*

VERITE FILMS

2146 Robinson Street
2nd Floor
Regina SK S4T 2P7
Canada

Phone: 306-585-1737
Fax: 306-585-7837
Email: *verite@veritefilms.ca*

Submission Policy: Accepts Query Letter from unproduced, unrepresented writers
Genre: Comedy, TV Drama, TV Sitcom, Family, Drama
Year Established: 2004

Virginia Thompson
Title: Partner/President/Executive Producer
Phone: 306-585-1737
Email: *virginia@veritefilms.ca*
IMDB: *www.imdb.com/name/nm1395111*

VERTEBRA FILMS

1608 Vine Street, Suite 503
Hollywood, CA 90028

Phone: 323-461-0021
Fax: 323-461-0031

Submission Policy: Accepts Query Letter from unproduced, unrepresented writers
Genre: Horror, Thriller
Company Focus: Feature Films
Year Established: 2010

VH1

1515 Broadway
New York, NY 10036

Phone: 212-846-8000
Email: *info@vh1.com*

Submission Policy: Accepts Query Letter from unproduced, unrepresented writers
Genre: Comedy, Memoir & True Stories, Romance, TV Drama, TV Sitcom, Drama
Year Established: 1986

Van Toffler
Title: President, MTVN Music, LOGO & Film
Phone: 212-846-8000
Email: *van.toffler@vh1.com*
IMDB: *www.imdb.com/name/nm0865508*

VIACOM INC.

1515 Broadway
New York, NY 10036

Phone: 212-258-6000

Submission Policy: Does not accept any unsolicited material
Genre: Comedy, Memoir & True Stories, TV Drama, TV Sitcom, Drama, Socio-cultural
Year Established: 1971

Philippe Dauman
Title: President & CEO
Phone: 212-258-6000
Email: *philippe.dauman@viacom.com*
IMDB: *www.imdb.com/name/nm2449184*

VILLAGE ROADSHOW PICTURES

100 North Crescent Drive, Suite 323
Beverly Hills, CA 90210

Phone: 310-385-4300
Fax: 310-385-4301

Submission Policy: Does not accept any unsolicited material
Company Focus: Feature Films
Year Established: 1998

Matt Skiena
Title: Vice President of Production
Phone: 310-385-4300
Email: *mskiena@vrpe.com*
IMDB: *www.imdb.com/name/nm3466832*

Bruce Berman
Title: Chairman/CEO
Phone: 310-385-4300
IMDB: *www.imdb.com/name/nm0075732*
Assistant: Suzy Figueroa

VIN DIBONA PRODUCTIONS

12233 West Olympic Boulevard, Suite 170
Los Angeles, CA 90064

Phone: 310-571-1875

Submission Policy: Accepts Query Letter from unproduced, unrepresented writers
Genre: Comedy, TV Sitcom
Year Established: 1987

Vin DiBona
Title: Chairman
Phone: 310-442-5600
IMDB: *www.imdb.com/name/nm0223688*

VINCENT NEWMAN ENTERTAINMENT

8840 Wilshire Boulevard
3rd Floor
Los Angeles, CA 90211

Phone: 310-358-3050
Fax: 310-358-3289
Email: *general@liveheart-vne.com*

Submission Policy: Accepts Query Letter from unproduced, unrepresented writers via email
Genre: Action, Fantasy, Myth, Thriller, TV Drama, TV Sitcom, Drama
Year Established: 2011

Vincent Newman
Title: Principal
Phone: 310-358-3050
Email: *vincent@liveheart-vne.com*
IMDB: *www.imdb.com/name/nm0628304*
Assistant: John Funk

VIRGIN PRODUCED

315 South Beverly Drive, Suite 506
Beverly Hills, CA 90212

Phone: 310-941-7300
Email: *media@virginproduced.com*

Submission Policy: Does not accept any unsolicited material
Genre: Action, Fantasy, Thriller, TV Drama, TV Sitcom, Animation, Drama
Year Established: 2010

Jason Felts
Title: CEO
Phone: 310-941-7300
Email: *jfelts@virginproduced.com*
IMDB: *www.imdb.com/name/nm1479777*

VOLTAGE PICTURES

662 North Crescent Heights Boulevard
Los Angeles, CA 90048

Phone: 323-464-8351
Fax: 323-464-8362
Email: *office@voltagepictures.com*

Submission Policy: Accepts Scripts from produced or represented writers
Genre: Action, Fantasy, Horror, Memoir & True Stories, Myth, Romance, Science Fiction, Thriller, Drama, Socio-cultural
Company Focus: Feature Films
Year Established: 2005

Nicolas Chartier
Title: Founder/President
Email: *nicolas@voltagepictures.com*
IMDB: *www.imdb.com/name/nm1291566*
Assistant: Kevin Hoiseth

Dean Devlin
Title: Founder/Writer/Producer
IMDB: *www.imdb.com/name/nm0002041*

Nadine de Barros
Title: Vice-President of Sales and Acquisitions
Email: *nadine@voltagepictures.com*
IMDB: *www.imdb.com/name/nm0213323*

VOLTAGE PRODUCTIONS

662 North Crescent Heights Boulevard
Los Angeles, CA 90048

Phone: 323-606-7630
Fax: 323-315-7115

Submission Policy: Accepts Scripts from produced or represented writers
Genre: Action, Fantasy, Memoir & True Stories, Romance, Science Fiction, Animation, Drama
Company Focus: Feature Films
Year Established: 2011

Nicolas Chartier
Email: *nicolas@voltagepictures.com*
IMDB: *www.imdb.com/name/nm1291566*

Craig Flores
Title: President/Partner Voltage Productions
IMDB: *www.imdb.com/name/nm1997836*
Assistant: Edmond Guidry

Zev Foreman
Title: Head of Development
IMDB: *www.imdb.com/name/nm2303301*

VON ZERNECK/SERTNER FILMS

c/o HCVT
11444 West Olympic Boulevard
11th Floor
Los Angeles, CA 90064

Phone: 310-652-3020
Email: *vzs@vzsfilms.com*

Submission Policy: Does not accept any unsolicited material
Genre: Crime, Detective, Memoir & True Stories, Thriller, Drama
Year Established: 1987

Frank Von Zerneck
Title: Partner
Phone: 310-652-3020
Email: *vonzerneck@gmail.com*
IMDB: *www.imdb.com/name/nm0903273*

VOX3 FILMS

315 Bleecker Street #111
New York, NY 10014

Phone: 212-741-0406
Fax: 212-741-0424
Email: *contact@vox3films.com*

Submission Policy: Does not accept any unsolicited material
Genre: Romance, Thriller, TV Drama, Drama, Socio-cultural
Year Established: 2004

Andrew Fierberg
Title: Partner/Founder/Producer
Phone: 212-741-0406
Email: *andrew.fierberg@vox3films.com*
IMDB: *www.imdb.com/name/nm0276404*

Steven Shainberg
Title: Partner
IMDB: *www.imdb.com/name/nm078760*

Christina Weiss Lurie
Title: Partner
IMDB: *www.imdb.com/name/nm1417371*

VULCAN PRODUCTIONS

505 Fifth Ave. S., Suite 900
Seattle WA 98104

Phone: 206-342-2277
Email: *production@vulcan.com*

Submission Policy: Accepts Query Letter from unproduced, unrepresented writers via email
Genre: Action, Memoir & True Stories, Thriller, Socio-cultural
Year Established: 1983

Jody Allen
Title: President
Phone: 206-342-2277
Email: *jody@vulcan.com*
IMDB: *www.imdb.com/name/nm0666580*

WALDEN MEDIA

1888 Century Park East
14th Floor
Los Angeles, CA 90067

Phone: 310-887-1000
Fax: 310-887-1001
Email: *info@walden.com*

Submission Policy: Accepts Query Letter from

unproduced, unrepresented writers via email
Company Focus: Feature Films
Year Established: 2001

Evan Turner
Title: Sr. Vice-President, Development & Production
Phone: 310-887-1000
IMDB: *www.imdb.com/name/nm1602263*

Amanda Morgan Palmer
Title: Sr. Vice-President, Development & Production
Phone: 310-887-1000
IMDB: *www.imdb.com/name/nm2198853*

Eric Tovell
Title: Creative Executive
Email: *etovell@walden.com*
Assistant: Carol Tang *ctang@walden.com*

WALKER/FITZGIBBON TV & FILM PRODUCTION

2399 Mt. Olympus
Los Angeles, CA 90046

Phone: 323-469-6800
Fax: 323-878-0600

Submission Policy: Accepts Query Letter from unproduced, unrepresented writers via email
Genre: Comedy, Memoir & True Stories, TV Drama, Animation, Drama
Year Established: 1996

Mo Fitzgibbon
Title: Principal, Executive Producer/Director
Phone: 323-469-6800
Email: *mo@walkerfitzgibbon.com*
IMDB: *www.imdb.com/name/nm0280422*

WALT BECKER PRODUCTIONS

1680 Vine Street, Suite 1101
Los Angeles, CA 90028

Phone: 323-871-8400
Fax: 323-871-2540

Submission Policy: Does not accept any unsolicited material
Company Focus: TV

Walt Becker
Title: Director/Producer
IMDB: *http://www.imdb.com/name/nm0065608*

WARNER BROS. ANIMATION

411 North Hollywood Way
Burbank, CA 91505

Phone: 818-977-8700
Email: *info@warnerbros.com*

Submission Policy: Does not accept any unsolicited material
Genre: TV Sitcom, Animation
Year Established: 1930

Sam Register
Title: Executive Vice-President, Creative
Phone: 818-977-8700
Email: *sam.register@warnerbros.com*
IMDB: *www.imdb.com/name/nm1882146*

WARNER BROS. ENTERTAINMENT INC.

4000 Warner Boulevard
Burbank, CA 91522-0001

Phone: 818-954-6000
Email: *barry.meyer@warnerbros.com*

Submission Policy: Does not accept any unsolicited material
Genre: Action, Comedy, Crime, Detective, Fantasy, Memoir & True Stories, Myth, Romance, Science Fiction, Thriller, TV Drama, TV Sitcom, Family, Animation, Drama, Socio-cultural
Year Established: 1923

Barry Meyer
Title: Chairman/CEO
Phone: 818-954-6000
Email: *barry.meyer@warnerbros.com*
IMDB: *www.imdb.com/name/nm0583028*

WARNER BROS. HOME ENTERTAINMENT GROUP

4000 Warner Boulevard
Burbank, CA 91522-0001

Phone: 818-954-6000
Email: *info@warnerbros.com*

Submission Policy: Does not accept any unsolicited material
Genre: Action, Comedy, Fantasy, Memoir & True Stories, Myth, Romance, Thriller, Family, Animation, Drama
Year Established: 2005

Kevin Tsujihara

Title: President
Phone: 818-954-6000
Email: *kevin.tsujihara@warnerbros.com*
IMDB: *www.imdb.com/name/nm2493597*

WARNER BROS. PICTURES

4000 Warner Boulevard
Burbank, CA 91522-0001

Phone: 818-954-6000
Email: *info@warnerbros.com*

Submission Policy: Does not accept any unsolicited material
Genre: Action, Comedy, Crime, Detective, Fantasy, Memoir & True Stories, Myth, Romance, Thriller, Family, Animation, Drama
Year Established: 1923

Jeff Robinov

Title: President
Phone: 818-954-6000
Email: *jeff.robinov@warnerbros.com*
IMDB: *www.imdb.com/name/nm0732268*

WARNER BROS. TELEVISION GROUP

4000 Warner Boulevard
Burbank, CA 91522-0001

Phone: 818-954-6000
Email: *info@warnerbros.com*

Submission Policy: Does not accept any unsolicited material
Genre: Action, Comedy, Fantasy, Memoir & True Stories, Myth, Romance, Thriller, TV Drama, TV Sitcom, Family, Animation, Drama
Year Established: 2005

Bruce Rosenblum

Title: President
Phone: 818-954-6000
Email: *bruce.rosenblum@warnerbros.com*
IMDB: *www.imdb.com/name/nm2686463*

WARNER HORIZON TELEVISION

4000 Warner Boulevard
Burbank, CA 91522-0001

Phone: 818-954-6000

Submission Policy: Does not accept any unsolicited material
Genre: Action, Comedy, Fantasy, Memoir & True Stories, Myth, Romance, TV Drama, TV Sitcom, Family, Animation, Drama
Year Established: 1999

Peter Roth

Title: President
Phone: 818-954-6000
Email: *peter.roth@warnerbros.com*
IMDB: *www.imdb.com/name/nm2325137*

WARNER SISTERS PRODUCTIONS

PO Box 50104
Santa Barbara, CA 93150

Phone: 818-766-6952
Email: *info@warnersisters.com*

Submission Policy: Does not accept any unsolicited material
Genre: Memoir & True Stories, Drama
Year Established: 2003

Cass Warner

Title: CEO/President
Phone: 818-766-6952
Email: *info@warnersisters.com*
IMDB: *www.imdb.com/name/nm2064300*

WARREN MILLER ENTERTAINMENT

5720 Flatiron Parkway
Boulder CO 80301

Phone: 303-253-6300
Fax: 303-253-6380
Email: *info@warrenmillertv.com*

Submission Policy: Accepts Query Letter from unproduced, unrepresented writers
Genre: Action, Memoir & True Stories, TV Drama
Year Established: 1952

Jeffrey Moore
Title: Sr. Executive Producer
Phone: 303-253-6300
Email: *jeffm@warrenmiller.com*
IMDB: *www.imdb.com/name/nm2545455*

WARRIOR POETS

407 Broome Street, Suite 7B
New York, NY 10013

Phone: 212-219-7617
Fax: 212-219-2920
Email: *em@warrior-poets.com*

Submission Policy: Does not accept any
unsolicited material
Genre: Memoir & True Stories, TV Drama,
Drama
Year Established: 2005

Morgan Spurlock
Title: President/Producer
Phone: 212-219-7617
IMDB: *www.imdb.com/name/nm1041597*

WAYANS BROTHERS ENTERTAINMENT

8730 West Sunset Boulevard, Suite 290
Los Angeles, CA 90069-2247

Phone: 323-930-6720
Fax: 424-202-3520

Submission Policy: Does not accept any
unsolicited material
Genre: Comedy, TV Sitcom, Family, Animation
Year Established: 1980

Keenan Ivory Wayans
Title: Principal
Phone: 323-930-6720
IMDB: *www.imdb.com/name/nm0005540*

WAYFARE ENTERTAINMENT VENTURES LLC

435 West 19th Street
4th Floor
New York, NY 10011

Phone: 212-989-2200
Email: *info@wayfareentertainment.com*

Submission Policy: Does not accept any
unsolicited material
Genre: Action, Comedy, Fantasy, Memoir &
True Stories, Myth, Romance, Thriller, Family,
Drama, Socio-cultural
Year Established: 2008

Ben Browning
Title: Co-Founder & CEO
Phone: 212-989-2200
Email: *info@wayfareentertainment.com*
IMDB: *www.imdb.com/name/nm1878845*

WE TV

11 Penn Plaza
19th Floor
New York, NY 10001

Phone: 212-324-8500

Submission Policy: Does not accept any
unsolicited material
Genre: Comedy, Memoir & True Stories,
Romance, TV Drama, TV Sitcom, Drama,
Socio-cultural
Year Established: 1997

Edward Caroll
Title: Chief Operating Officer
Phone: 212-324-8500
Email: *ecaroll@amcnetworks.com*

WEED ROAD PICTURES

4000 Warner Boulevard
Building 81, Suite 115
Burbank, CA 91522

Phone: 818-954-3771
Fax: 818-954-3061

Submission Policy: Does not accept any
unsolicited material
Genre: Action, Horror, TV Drama, TV Sitcom,
Animation, Drama
Year Established: 2004

Akiva Goldsman
Title: President/Producer
Phone: 818-954-3771
IMDB: *www.imdb.com/name/nm0326040*

WEINSTOCK PRODUCTIONS

316 North Rossmore Avenue
Los Angeles, CA 90004

Phone: 323-791-1500

Submission Policy: Accepts Query Letter from unproduced, unrepresented writers
Company Focus: Feature Films

Charles Weinstock

Title: Producer
Phone: 323-791-1500
IMDB: *www.imdb.com/name/nm091848*

WEINTRAUB/KUHN PRODUCTIONS

1351 Third Street Promenade, Suite 206
Santa Monica, CA 90401

Phone: 310-458-3300
Fax: 310-458-3302
Email: *fred@fredweintraub.com*

Submission Policy: Does not accept any unsolicited material
Genre: Action, Comedy, Fantasy, Memoir & True Stories, Myth, Romance, Science Fiction, Thriller, TV Drama, TV Sitcom, Family, Drama
Year Established: 1976

Fred Weintraub

Title: President
Phone: 310-458-3300
Email: *fred@fredweintraub.com*
IMDB: *www.imdb.com/name/nm0918518*

WELLER/GROSSMAN PRODUCTIONS

5200 Lankershim Boulevard
5th Floor
North Hollywood, CA 91601

Phone: 818-755-4800
Email: *contact@wellergrossman.com*

Submission Policy: Accepts Scripts from produced or represented writers
Genre: Comedy, Memoir & True Stories, TV Drama, TV Sitcom, Family, Drama, Socio-cultural
Year Established: 1993

Robb Weller

Title: Partner/Executive Producer
Phone: 818-755-4800
Email: *contact@wellergrossman.com*
IMDB: *www.imdb.com/name/nm0919888*

WENDY FINERMAN PRODUCTIONS

144 South Beverly Drive, #304
Beverly Hills, CA 90212

Phone: 310-694-8088
Fax: 310-694-8088

Submission Policy: Accepts Query Letter from unproduced, unrepresented writers via email
Company Focus: Feature Films, TV

Wendy Finerman

Title: Producer
Phone: 310-694-8088
Email: *wfinerman@wendyfinermanproductions. com*
IMDB: *www.imdb.com/name/nm0277704*
Assistant: Belinda Rungsea

Lisa Zupan

Title: Vice-President
Phone: 310-694-8088
IMDB: *www.imdb.com/name/nm0958702*

WHITEWATER FILMS

11264 La Grange Avenue
Los Angeles, CA 90025

Phone: 310-575-5800
Fax: 310-575-5802
Email: *info@whitewaterfilms.com*

Submission Policy: Does not accept any unsolicited material
Company Focus: Feature Films, TV
Year Established: 2008

Nick Morton

Title: Producer
Phone: 310-575-5800
IMDB: *www.imdb.com/name/nm1134288*

Bert Kern

Title: Producer
Phone: 310-575-5800
IMDB: *www.imdb.com/name/nm2817387*

Rick Rosenthal
Title: President/Producer
Phone: 310-575-5800
IMDB: *www.imdb.com/name/nm0742819*

WHYADUCK PRODUCTIONS INC.

4804 Laurel Canyon Boulevard
PMB 502
North Hollywood, CA 91607-3765

Phone: 310-274-6611
Fax: 310-278-6232

Submission Policy: Does not accept any
unsolicited material
Genre: Comedy, TV Drama, TV Sitcom,
Drama, Socio-cultural
Year Established: 1981

Robert B. Weide
Title: Principal
Phone: 310-274-6611
Email: *rbw@duckprods.com*
IMDB: *www.imdb.com/name/nm0004332*

WIDEAWAKE INC.

c/o Jay Baker/CAA
2000 Avenue of the Stars
Los Angeles, CA 90067

Phone: 310-652-9200

Submission Policy: Does not accept any
unsolicited material
Genre: Comedy, Romance, TV Drama, TV
Sitcom, Family, Socio-cultural
Year Established: 2004

Luke Greenfield
Title: Writer/Director/Producer
Phone: 310-652-9200
IMDB: *www.imdb.com/name/nm0339004*

WIGRAM PRODUCTIONS

4000 Warner Boulevard
Building 81, Room 215
Burbank, CA 91522

Phone: 818-954-2412
Fax: 818-954-6538

Submission Policy: Accepts Query Letter from

unproduced, unrepresented writers
Company Focus: Feature Films
Year Established: 2006

Lionel Wigram
Title: Principal/Producer
Phone: 818-954-2412
IMDB: *www.imdb.com/name/nm0927880*

Peter Eskelsen
Title: Vice-President
Phone: 818-954-2412
Email: *peter.eskelsen@wbconsultant.com*
IMDB: *www.imdb.com/name/nm2367411*

Jeffrey Ludwig
Title: Assistant
Phone: 818-954-2412

WILD AT HEART FILMS

868 West Knoll Drive, Suite 9
West Hollywood, CA 90069

Phone: 310-855-1538
Fax: 310-855-0177
Email: *info@wildatheartfilms.us*

Submission Policy: Does not accept any
unsolicited material
Genre: Romance, TV Drama, TV Sitcom,
Family, Animation, Drama
Year Established: 2000

James Egan
Title: CEO/Writer/Producer
Phone: 310-855-1538
Email: *jamesegan@wildatheartfilms.us*
IMDB: *www.imdb.com/name/nm0250680*

WILDBRAIN ENTERTAINMENT INC.

15000 Ventura Boulevard
3rd Floor
Sherman Oaks, CA 91403

Phone: 818-290-7080
Email: *info@wildbrain.com*

Submission Policy: Accepts Query Letter from
produced or represented writers
Genre: Comedy, Fantasy, TV Sitcom, Family,
Animation
Year Established: 1994

Michael Polis
Title: President
Phone: 818-290-7080
Email: *mpolis@wildbrain.com*
IMDB: *www.imdb.com/name/nm1277040*

WILDWOOD ENTERPRISES, INC.

725 Arizona Avenue, Suite 306
Santa Monica, CA 90401

Phone: 310-451-8050

Submission Policy: Does not accept any
unsolicited material
Company Focus: Feature Films

Robert Redford
Title: Owner
Phone: 310-451-8050
IMDB: *www.imdb.com/name/nm0000602*

Bill Holderman
Title: Development Executive
Phone: 310-451-8050
IMDB: *www.imdb.com/name/nm2250139*

Connie Wethington
Title: Development Executive
Phone: 310-395-5112
IMDB: *www.imdb.com/name/nm1872294*

WIND DANCER FILMS

315 South Beverly Drive, Suite 502
Beverly Hills, CA 90212

Phone: 310-601-2720
Fax: 310-601-2725

Submission Policy: Does not accept any
unsolicited material
Company Focus: Feature Films, TV
Year Established: 1989

Matt Williams
Title: Principal
Phone: 310-601-2720
IMDB: *www.imdb.com/name/nm0931285*

David McFadzean
Title: Principal
Phone: 310-601-2720
IMDB: *www.imdb.com/name/nm0568730*

Catherine Redfearn
Title: Creative Executive
Email: *Catherine_Redfearn@winddancer.com*
IMDB: *www.imdb.com/name/nm1976144*

WINGNUT FILMS LTD.

PO Box 15 208
Miramar
Wellington 6003
New Zealand

Phone: +64-4-388-9939
Fax: +64-4-388-9449
Email: *reception@wingnutfilms.co.nz*

Submission Policy: Does not accept any
unsolicited material
Company Focus: Feature Films

Peter Jackson
Title: Director/Producer
Phone: +64-4-388-9939
IMDB: *www.imdb.com/name/nm0001392*

Carolynne Cunningham
Title: Producer
Phone: +64-4-388-9939
IMDB: *www.imdb.com/name/nm0192254*

WINKLER FILMS

211 South Beverly Dr, Suite 200
Beverly Hills, CA 90212

Phone: 310-858-5780
Fax: 310-858-5799

Submission Policy: Accepts Query Letter from
unproduced, unrepresented writers
Company Focus: Feature Films, TV

Irwin Winkler
Title: CEO
Phone: 310-858-5780
IMDB: *www.imdb.com/name/nm0005563*
Assistant: Selina Gomeau

Charles Winkler
Title: Director/Producer
Phone: 310-858-5780
IMDB: *www.imdb.com/name/nm0935203*
Assistant: Jose Ruisanchez

David Winkler
Title: Producer
Phone: 310-858-5780
IMDB: *www.imdb.com/name/nm0935210*

WINSOME PRODUCTIONS

PO Box 2071
Santa Monica, CA 90406

Phone: 310-656-3300
Email: *info@winsomeprods.com*

Submission Policy: Does not accept any
unsolicited material
Genre: TV Drama, TV Sitcom
Year Established: 1989

A.D. Oppenheim
Title: Producer/Writer/Director
Phone: 310-656-3300
Email: *info@winsomeprods.com*
IMDB: *www.imdb.com/name/nm0649148*

WITT-THOMAS-HARRIS PRODUCTIONS

11901 Santa Monica Boulevard, Suite 596
Los Angeles, CA 90025

Phone: 310-472-6004
Fax: 310-476-5015

Submission Policy: Does not accept any
unsolicited material
Company Focus: Feature Films
Year Established: 2010

Paul Junger Witt
Title: Partner
Phone: 310-472-6004
Email: *pwittproductions@aol.com*
IMDB: *www.imdb.com/name/nm0432625*
Assistant: Ellen Benjamin

Susan Harris
Title: Partner
Phone: 310-472-6004
IMDB: *www.imdb.com/name/nm0365358*
Assistant: Ellen Benjamin

Tony Thomas
Title: Partner
Phone: 818-762-7500
IMDB: *www.imdb.com/name/nm0859597*
Assistant: Marlene Fuentes

WOLF FILMS, INC.

100 Universal City Plaza #2252
Universal City, CA 91608-1085

Phone: 818-777-6969
Fax: 818-866-1446

Submission Policy: Does not accept any
unsolicited material
Company Focus: Feature Films, TV

Dick Wolf
Title: CEO
Phone: 818-777-6969

Danielle Gelber
Title: Executive Producer
Phone: 818-777-6969
IMDB: *www.imdb.com/name/nm1891764*

Tony Ganz
Title: Feature Development
Phone: 818-777-6969
IMDB: *www.imdb.com/name/nm0304673*

WOLFMILL ENTERTAINMENT

9027 Larke Ellen Circle
Los Angeles, CA 90035

Phone: 310-559-1622
Fax: 310-559-1623
Email: *info@wolfmill.com*

Submission Policy: Accepts Query Letter from
unproduced, unrepresented writers via email
Company Focus: Feature Films, TV
Year Established: 1997

Marv Wolfman
Title: Partner
Phone: 310-559-1622
Email: *marv@wolfmill.com*
IMDB: *www.imdb.com/name/nm0938379*

Craig Miller
Title: Partner
Phone: 310-559-1622
Email: *craig@wolfmill.com*
IMDB: *www.imdb.com/name/nm0003653*

WOLFROM PRODUCTIONS

2104 Pisani Place
Venice, CA 90291

Phone: 323-253-8185

Submission Policy: Accepts Query Letter from unproduced, unrepresented writers via email
Genre: Romance, Family
Company Focus: Feature Films

Dawn Wolfrom
Title: Producer
Phone: 323-253-8185
Email: *dawnwolfrom@wolfromproductions.com*
IMDB: *www.imdb.com/name/nm0938402*

Dee Pultorak
Title: Creative Executive
Phone: 323-253-8185

WONDERLAND SOUND AND VISION

8739 Sunset Boulevard
West Hollywood, CA 90069

Phone: 310-659-4451
Fax: 310-659-4451

Submission Policy: Does not accept any unsolicited material
Company Focus: Feature Films, TV
Year Established: 2000

McG
Title: President, Operations
Phone: 310-659-4451
IMDB: *www.imdb.com/name/nm0629334*
Assistant: Breean Solberg

Mary Viola
Title: President of Production
Phone: 310-659-4451
IMDB: *www.imdb.com/name/nm0899193*
Assistant: Steven Bello

Steven Bello
Title: Creative Executive
Phone: 310-659-4451
IMDB: *www.imdb.com/name/nm2086605*

WORKING TITLE FILMS

9720 Wilshire Boulevard
4th Floor
Beverly Hills, CA 90212

Phone: 310-777-3100
Fax: 310-777-5243

Submission Policy: Does not accept any unsolicited material
Company Focus: Feature Films, TV
Year Established: 1983

Evan Hayes
Title: Sr. Vice-President, Development
Phone: 310-777-3100
Email: *evan.hayes@workingtitlefilms.com*
IMDB: *www.imdb.com/name/nm0371010*

Amelia Granger
Title: Literary Acquisitions Executive (United Kingdom)
Phone: +44 20 7307 3000
IMDB: *www.imdb.com/name/nm0335028*

Liza Chasin
Title: President, Production (US)
Phone: 310-777-3100
Email: *liza.chasin@workingtitlefilms.com*
IMDB: *www.imdb.com/name/nm0153877*

WORLD FILM SERVICES, INC

150 East 58th Street
29th Floor
New York, NY 10155

Phone: 212-632-3456
Fax: 212-632-3457

Submission Policy: Accepts Query Letter from unproduced, unrepresented writers
Company Focus: Feature Films, TV

John Heyman
Title: CEO
Phone: 212-632-3456
IMDB: *www.imdb.com/name/nm0382274*

Dahlia Heyman
Title: Creative Executive
Phone: 212-632-3456
IMDB: *www.imdb.com/name/nm3101094*

Jessica Stickles
Title: Creative Executive
Phone: 212-632-3456
IMDB: *www.imdb.com/name/nm3101028*

WORLD OF WONDER PRODUCTIONS

6650 Hollywood Boulevard, Suite 400
Hollywood, CA 90028

Phone: 323-603-6300
Fax: 323-603-6301
Email: *wow@worldofwonder.net*

Submission Policy: Does not accept any
unsolicited material
Genre: Action, Comedy, Memoir & True
Stories, TV Drama, TV Sitcom, Socio-cultural
Year Established: 1990

Fenton Bailey
Title: Executive Producer/Co-Director
Phone: 323-603-6300
Email: *wow@worldofwonder.net*
IMDB: *www.imdb.com/name/nm0047259*

WORLDWIDE BIGGIES

545 West 45th Street
5th Floor
New York, NY 10036

Phone: 646-442-1700
Fax: 646-557-0019
Email: *info@wwbiggies.com*

Submission Policy: Does not accept any
unsolicited material
Genre: Action, Comedy, Fantasy, Myth, TV
Drama, TV Sitcom, Family, Animation
Year Established: 2007

Albie Hecht
Title: CEO
Phone: 646-442-1700
Email: *info@wwbiggies.com*
IMDB: *www.imdb.com/name/nm0372935*

WORLDWIDE PANTS INC.

1697 Broadway
New York, NY 10019

Phone: 212-975-5300
Fax: 212-975-4780

Submission Policy: Does not accept any
unsolicited material
Genre: Action, Comedy, TV Drama, TV
Sitcom, Animation, Drama

Rob Burnett
Title: President/CEO
Phone: 212-975-5300
IMDB: *www.imdb.com/name/nm0122427*

WWE STUDIOS

12424 Wilshire Boulevard, Suite 1400
Los Angeles, CA 90025

Phone: 310-481-9370
Email: *talent.marketing@wwe.com*

Submission Policy: Does not accept any
unsolicited material
Genre: Action, Comedy, Crime, Detective, TV
Drama, TV Sitcom, Family, Drama
Year Established: 2002

David Calloway
Title: Vice-President of Production
Phone: 310-481-9370
IMDB: *www.imdb.com/name/nm0130574*

X FILME CREATIVE POOL GMBH

Kurfuerstenstrasse 57
10785 Berlin
Germany

Phone: 49-30-230-833-11
Fax: 49-30-230-833-22
Email: *info@x-filme.de*

Submission Policy: Does not accept any
unsolicited material
Genre: Action, Comedy, Romance, Family,
Drama
Year Established: 1994

Stefan Arndt
Title: Founder/Managing Partner/Producer
Phone: 49-30-230-833-11
Email: *stefan.arndt@x-filme.de*
IMDB: *www.imdb.com/name/nm0036155*

XINGU FILMS LTD.

12 Cleveland Row
St. James
London SW1A 1DH
United Kingdom

Phone: 44-20-7451-0600
Fax: 44-20-7451-0601
Email: *mail@xingufilms.com*

Submission Policy: Does not accept any
unsolicited material
Genre: Action, Comedy, Crime, Detective,
Fantasy, Horror, Memoir & True Stories,
Myth, Romance, Science Fiction, Thriller, TV
Drama, TV Sitcom, Family, Animation, Drama,
Socio-cultural
Year Established: 1993

Trudie Styler
Title: Chairman/Producer/Director
Phone: 44-20-7451-0600
Email: *trudie@xingufilms.com*
IMDB: *www.imdb.com/name/nm0836548*

XIX ENTERTAINMENT

9000 West Sunset Boulevard, Penthouse
West Hollywood, CA 90069

Phone: 310-746-1919
Fax: 310-746-1920
Email: *info@xixentertainment.com*

Submission Policy: Does not accept any
unsolicited material
Genre: Action, Romance, TV Drama, TV
Sitcom, Family
Year Established: 2010

Robert Dodds
Title: CEO
Phone: 310-746-1919
Email: *robert.dodds@xixentertainment.com*
IMDB: *www.imdb.com/name/nm2142323*

XYZ FILMS

4223 Glencoe Ave, Suite B119
Marina del Rey, CA 90292

Phone: 310-956-1550
Fax: 310-827-7690
Email: *info@xyzfilms.com*

Submission Policy: Does not accept any
unsolicited material
Genre: Action, Memoir & True Stories
Company Focus: Feature Films

Nate Bolotin
Title: Partner
Phone: 310-956-1550
Email: *nate@xyzfilms.com*
IMDB: *www.imdb.com/name/nm1924867*

Todd Brown
Title: Partner
Phone: 310-956-1550
Email: *info@xyzfilms.com*
IMDB: *www.imdb.com/name/nm1458075*

Kyle Franke
Title: Head of Development
Phone: 310-359-9099
Email: *kyle@xyzfilms.com*
IMDB: *www.imdb.com/name/nm3733941*

YAHOO!

2400 Broadway
1st Floor
Santa Monica, CA 90404

Phone: 310-907-2700
Fax: 310-907-2701

Submission Policy: Accepts Query Letter from
unproduced, unrepresented writers
Year Established: 1995

Scott Thompson
Title: President/CEO
Phone: 310-907-2700

YFG INTERNATIONAL

10850 Wilshire Boulevard
6th Floor
Los Angeles, CA 90024

Phone: 310-689-1450
Fax: 310-234-8975
Email: *reception@yarifilmgroup.com*

Submission Policy: Does not accept any unsolicited material
Genre: Action, Comedy, Crime, Romance, Thriller, TV Drama, TV Sitcom, Family, Animation, Drama

Bob Yari
Title: President & CEO
Phone: 310-689-1450
Email: *byari@yarifilmgroup.com*
IMDB: *www.imdb.com/name/nm0946441*

YORK SQUARE PRODUCTIONS

17328 Ventura Boulevard, Suite 370
Encino, CA 91316

Phone: 818-789-7372
Email: *assistant@yorksquareproductions.com*

Submission Policy: Accepts Query Letter from unproduced, unrepresented writers via email
Company Focus: Feature Films, TV

Jonathan Mostow
Title: Principal
Phone: 818-789-7372
IMDB: *www.imdb.com/name/nm0609236*
Assistant: Emily Somers

YORKTOWN PRODUCTIONS LTD.

18 Gloucester Lane
4th Floor
Toronto ON M4Y 1L5
Canada

Phone: 416-923-2787
Fax: 416-923-8580

Submission Policy: Does not accept any unsolicited material
Genre: Comedy, Romance, Family, Drama
Year Established: 1986

Norman Jewison
Title: Founder
Phone: 416-923-2787
IMDB: *www.imdb.com/name/nm0422484*

ZACHARY FEUER FILMS

9348 Civic Center Drive, 3rd Floor
Beverly Hills, CA 90210

Phone: 310-729-2110
Fax: 310-820-7535

Submission Policy: Accepts Query Letter from unproduced, unrepresented writers
Genre: Action, Thriller, TV Drama, TV Sitcom, Drama

Zachary Feuer
Title: Producer
Phone: 310-729-2110
IMDB: *www.imdb.com/name/nm0275400*

ZAK PENN'S COMPANY

6240 West Third Street, Suite 421
Los Angeles, CA 90036

Phone: 323-939-1700
Fax: 323-930-2339

Submission Policy: Does not accept any unsolicited material
Company Focus: Feature Films, TV

Zak Penn
Title: Writer/Producer/Director
Phone: 323-939-1700
IMDB: *www.imdb.com/name/nm0672015*
Assistant: Hannah Rosner

Morgan Gross
Title: Editorial Guru
Phone: 323-939-1700
IMDB: *www.imdb.com/name/nm2092616*

ZANUCK INDEPENDENT

1131-1/2 Rexford Drive
Los Angeles, CA 90035

Phone: 310-274-5735
Fax: 310-273-9217

Submission Policy: Accepts Query Letter from unproduced, unrepresented writers
Genre: Comedy, TV Drama, TV Sitcom, Animation, Drama

Dean Zanuck
Title: Producer
Phone: 310-274-5735
IMDB: *www.imdb.com/name/nm0953124*

ZEMECKIS/NEMEROFF FILMS

264 South La Cienega Boulevard, Suite 238
Beverly Hills, CA 90211

Phone: 310-552-3333

Submission Policy: Does not accept any
unsolicited material
Company Focus: Feature Films

Leslie Zemeckis
Title: Producer
Phone: 310-552-3333
IMDB: *www.imdb.com/name/nm0366667*

Terry Nemeroff
Title: Writer/Director/Producer
Phone: 310-552-3333
IMDB: *www.imdb.com/name/nm0625892*

ZENTROPA

Filmbyen 22
Hvidorve 2650
Denmark

Phone: +45-3-678-0055
Fax: +45-3-678-0077
Email: *receptionen@filmbyen.com*

Submission Policy: Accepts Scripts from
unproduced, unrepresented writers
Genre: Action, Thriller
Year Established: 1992

Ib Tardini
Title: Producer
Phone: +45-36-868-792
Email: *ib.tardini@filmbyen.com*

ZEPHYR FILMS, LTD.

33 Percy Street
London W1T 2DF

Phone: +44 207-255-3555
Fax: +44 207-255-3777
Email: *info@zephyrfilms.co.uk*

Submission Policy: Accepts Query Letter from
unproduced, unrepresented writers via email
Company Focus: Feature Films

Chris Curling
Title: Producer
Phone: +44 207-255-3555
IMDB: *www.imdb.com/name/nm0192770*

Phil Robertson
Title: Producer
Phone: +44 207-255-3555
IMDB: *www.imdb.com/name/nm0731990*

Luke Carey
Title: Assistant Producer
Phone: +44 207-255-3555
IMDB: *www.imdb.com/name/nm2294645*

ZETA ENTERTAINMENT (ZANE W. LEVITT PRODUCTIONS)

3422 Rowena Avenue
Los Angeles, CA 90027

Submission Policy: Does not accept any
unsolicited material
Genre: Action, Comedy, Fantasy, TV Drama,
Family, Drama

Zane Levitt
Title: President
Phone: 310-595-0494
Email: *zanewlevitt@gmail.com*
IMDB: *www.imdb.com/name/nm0506254*

ZING PRODUCTIONS, INC.

220 South Van Ness Avenue
Hollywood, CA 90004

Phone: 323-466-9464
Email: *laura@zinghollywood.com*

Submission Policy: Does not accept any
unsolicited material
Company Focus: Feature Films

Rob Loos
Title: President
Phone: 323-466-9464
IMDB: *www.imdb.com/name/nm0519763*

Laura Black
Title: Director Creative of Affairs
Phone: 323-466-9464
Email: *laura@zinghollywood.com*
IMDB: *www.imdb.com/name/nm4549208*

ZODIAK

225 Santa Monica Boulevard, 7th Floor
Santa Monica, CA 90401

Phone: 310-460-4490
Fax: 310-460-4494
Email: *contact@zodiakusa.com*

Submission Policy: Accepts Query Letter from
unproduced, unrepresented writers via email
Genre: Memoir & True Stories, TV Drama, TV
Sitcom, Drama

Grant Mansfield
Title: CEO
Phone: 310-460-4490
Email: *contact@zodiakusa.com*
IMDB: *www.imdb.com/name/nm1420965*

ZUCKER PRODUCTIONS

1250 Sixth Street, Suite 201
Los Angeles, CA 90401

Phone: 310-656-9202
Fax: 310-656-9220

Submission Policy: Accepts Query Letter from
unproduced, unrepresented writers
Genre: Comedy, Romance, TV Sitcom
Year Established: 1972

Jerry Zucker
Title: Producer
Phone: 310-656-9202
IMDB: *www.imdb.com/name/nm0958387*

Janet Zucker
Title: Producer
Phone: 310-656-9202
IMDB: *www.imdb.com/name/nm0958384*

Farrell Ingle
Title: Creative Executive
Phone: 310-656-9202
IMDB: *www.imdb.com/name/nm3377346*

Index by Company Name

Index of Company Websites

Index By Contact Name

Index by Submission Type

ACCEPTS QUERY LETTER FROM PRODUCED OR REPRESENTED WRITERS

@Radical Media—Santa Monica Branch, 24
7ATE9 Enertainment, 29
Atlas Media Corporation, 40
Beth Grossbard Productions, 44
Class 5 Films, 54
Clifford Werber Productions, 54
Constatin Film, 56
Darius Films Incorporated, 63
Gigantic Pictures, 83
Lakeshore Entertainment, 102
Mandalay Pictures, 106
Midnight Sun Pictures, 114
Mimran Schur Pictures, 115
Relativity Media, LLC, 138
TV One LLC, 169
Wildbrain Entertainment Inc., 182

ACCEPTS QUERY LETTER FROM UNPRODUCED, UNREPRESENTED WRITERS

10X10 Entertainment, 24
2-WAY Traffic—A Sony Pictures Entertainment Company, 25
25/7 Productions, 25
2929 Productions, 26
3 Arts Entertainment, Inc., 26
34th St. Films (Tyler Perry's Shingle), 27
72 Productions, 28
81 Pictures, 29
Aardman Animations, 31

Aberration Films, 31
ACT III Productions, 32
Adam Fields Productions, 32
AEI—ATCHITY Entertainment International, Inc., 33
Ahimsa Films, 33
Airmont Pictures, 34
Alex Rose Productions, Inc., 35
Alexander/Enright & Associates, 35
Alianza Films International Ltd., 35
American Work Inc., 36
Anchor Bay Films, 37
Animus Films, 38
Anne Carlucci Productions, 38
Article 19 Films, 40
Barnstorm Films, 42
Barsa Entertainment, 42
Bauer Martinez International, 42
Belladonna Productions, 43
Berlanti Television, 44
Bix Pix Entertainment, 45
Black Sheep Entertainment, 45
Blumhouse Productions, 46
Bobker/Krugar Films, 47
Bona Fide Productions, 47
Boz Productions, 48
Brandman Productions, 48
Burleigh Filmworks, 49
Burnside Entertainment Inc., 49
Chaiken Films, 51
Cinema Ephoch, 53
Cinema Libre Studio, 53
Cinemagic Entertainment, 53
Cineville, 53
Circle of Confusion Productions, 54
Colleen Camp Productions, 55

ACCEPTS QUERY LETTER FROM UNPRODUCED, UNREPRESENTED WRITERS VIA EMAIL

ACCEPTS SCRIPTS FROM PRODUCED OR REPRESENTED WRITERS

American World Pictures, 37
American Zoetrope, 37
An Olive Branch Productions, Inc., 37
Andrew Lauren Productions, 38
Aperture Entertainment, 39
ARS NOVA, 40
Artists Production Group (APG), 40
Asylum Entertainment, 40
Atmosphere Entertainment MM, LLC, 41
Bad Hat Harry, 41
Ballywood Inc., 42
BBC Films, 43
Birch Tree Entertainment Inc., 45
Blacklight Transmedia, 45
Bluegrass Films, 46
Bogner Entertainment, 47
Camelot Entertainment Group, 49
Castle Rock Entertainment, 50
Catapult Films, 50
Celador Films, 50
Centropolis Entertainment, 50
Chartoff Productions, 51
Chernin Entertainment, 51
Cheyenne Enterprises LLC, 51
Chicago Films, 52
Chickflicks, 52
Chotzen/Jenner Productions, 52
Chris/Rose Productions, 52
Chuck Fries, 52
Cindy Cowan Entertainment, Inc., 52
Cine Mosaic, 53
Cloud Eight Films, 55
Code Entertainment, 55
Conundrum Entertainment, 57
Davis Entertainment, 65
Depth of Field, 65
DiNovi Pictures, 66
Dobre Films, 66
Edmonds Entertainment, 68
Fake Empire Features, 74
Fake Empire Television, 74
Flower Films Inc., 76
Fresh & Smoked, 79
Gross-Weston Productions, 89

Grosso Jacobson Communications Corp., 89
Howard Braunstein Films, 93
Hughes Capital Entertainment, 93
Hutch Parker's Entertainment, 93
Industry Entertainment Partners, 96
Kaplan Perone Entertainment, 100
Katalyst Films, 100
Larrikin Entertainment, 103
Mad Hatter Entertainment, 106
Ninja's Runnin' Wild Productions, 120
Olmos Productions Inc., 121
Parker Entertainment Group, 127
QED International, 133
Recorded Picture Company, 135
Rough House, 142
Sander/Moses Productions, Inc., 144
Sid & Marty Krofft Pictures Corp., 148
Skydance Productions, 151
Team Todd, 158
The Badham Company, 159
The Colleton Company, 159
Twinstar Entertainment, 170
Unstoppable, 172
Voltage Pictures, 176
Voltage Productions, 177
Weller/Grossman Productions, 181
Zentropa, 189

DOES NOT ACCEPT ANY UNSOLICITED MATERIAL

@Radical Media—New York Branch, 24
19 Entertainment, LTD., 25
21 LAPS Entertainment, 25
2S Films, 26
360 Pictures, 27
40 Acres & A Mule Filmworks, Inc., 27
495 Productions, 27
4th Row Films, 28
8:38 Productions, 29
A Likely Story, 30
A-LINE Pictures, 30
A-MARK Entertainment, 30